Military Chaplains in Afghanistan, Iraq, and Beyond

About the Peace and Security in the 21st Century Series

Until recently, security was defined mostly in geopolitical terms with the assumption that it could only be achieved through at least the threat of military force. Today, however, people from as different backgrounds as planners in the Pentagon and veteran peace activists think in terms of human or global security, where no one is secure unless everyone is secure in all areas of their lives. This means that it is impossible nowadays to separate issues of war and peace, the environment, sustainability, identity, global health, and the like.

The books in this series aim to make sense of this changing world of peace and security by investigating security issues and peace efforts that involve cooperation at several levels. By looking at how security and peace interrelate at various stages of conflict, the series explores new ideas for a fast-changing world and seeks to redefine and rethink what peace and security mean in the first decades of the new century.

Multidisciplinary in approach and authorship, the books cover a variety of topics, focusing on the overarching theme that students, scholars, practitioners, and policymakers have to find new models and theories to account for, diagnose, and respond to the difficulties of a more complex world. Authors are established scholars and practitioners in their fields of expertise.

In addition, it is hoped that the series will contribute to bringing together authors and readers in concrete, applied projects, and thus help create, under the sponsorship of Alliance for Peacebuilding (AfP), a community of practice.

The series is sponsored by the Alliance for Peacebuilding, http://www.allianceforpeacebuilding.org, and edited by Charles Hauss, government liaison.

Military Chaplains in Afghanistan, Iraq, and Beyond

Advisement and Leader Engagement in Highly Religious Environments

Edited by Eric Patterson

Foreword by
Major General Douglas Carver (ret.)

ROWMAN & LITTLEFIELD
Lanham • Boulder • New York • London

Published by Rowman & Littlefield
A wholly owned subsidary of The Rowman & Littlefield Publishing Group, Inc.
4501 Forbes Boulevard, Suite 200, Lanham, Maryland 20706
www.rowman.com

16 Carlisle Street, London W1D 3BT, United Kingdom

Copyright © 2014 by Rowman & Littlefield

British Library Cataloguing in Publication Information Available

Library of Congress Cataloging-in-Publication Data

Military chaplains in Afghanistan, Iraq, and beyond : advisement and leader
engagement in highly religious environments / edited by Eric Patterson ; foreword
by Major General Douglas Carver (ret.).
     pages cm
  Includes bibliographical references and index.
  ISBN 978-1-4422-3539-7 (cloth : alk. paper) — ISBN 978-1-4422-3540-3 (electronic)
1. Military chaplains—United States—History. 2. War—Religious aspects. 3. Islam
and culture. 4. United States—Armed Forces—Chaplains—History. I. Patterson,
Eric, 1971–, editor of compilation.
  UH23.M46 2014
  355.3'470973—dc23   2014010434

∞™ The paper used in this publication meets the minimum requirements of
American National Standard for Information Sciences—Permanence of Paper
for Printed Library Materials, ANSI/NISO Z39.48-1992.

Printed in the United States of America

This book is dedicated with appreciation to the military chaplains of Western militaries, especially (but not limited to) U.S. chaplains, who provide spiritual support to our men and women in the face of danger, criticism, and threats.

Contents

Foreword

In the fall of 2002 my military unit began to conduct strategic operational planning for various military contingencies in the event that a diplomatic solution failed to resolve the rising tensions with Iraq in the aftermath of the coordinated terrorist attacks in the United States on September 11, 2001. It was obvious that the role of religion and training in religious sensitivity of the cultural environment would play a major role in the invasion of Iraq, a predominantly Muslim country, especially if American forces remained on that foreign soil for a prolonged period time. While preparing to advise senior military leadership on the religious-support mission, I quickly realized the significant effect the indigenous religious environment would have on combat operations, perhaps unlike any other time in recent military history. Like any good staff officer, I sought out every available resource to provide the command with a thorough religious area analysis on the potential theater of operations. I will forever be indebted to Chaplain Eric Keller (a contributor to this volume), who served as the key subject-matter expert in this area from his location at the U.S. Army Chaplain School in Fort Jackson, South Carolina, to my position with the forward-deployed troops. Looking back now in retrospect, and having in our possession over ten years' worth of lessons learned by chaplains and commanders in the area of religious-leader engagement, I can only imagine how much more proficient we would have been in the art of religious-leader liaison and religious advisement, and perhaps how many lives would have been saved, if senior military leaders and chaplains had this book by Dr. Eric Patterson in their hands at the beginning of the global war on terror in Afghanistan and Iraq.

I am truly humbled by Dr. Patterson having offered me the privilege of introducing the reader to this book, which sets out the history, methodology, best practices, and implications of the changing role of the military chaplain in the context of war and diplomacy. This may very well be the first resource of its kind—especially in its multidisciplinary approach—to blend together in one volume political theorists, historians, scholars, and chaplain practitioners in their discussion of religious-leader liaison and religious advisement.

This book is long overdue. Its most immediate didactic value resides in helping the reader to understand the importance of religion and culture as foundational to nations, two key factors that cannot be overlooked when conducting diplomacy, waging war, stabilizing people groups, or securing peace in regions of the world. For that reason alone, this book holds its own sociological interest that can be applied to all facets of the human condition.

In this book we quickly learn the rapidly emerging role of the twenty-first-century military chaplain. Although they continue to serve in their traditional roles as bulwarks of religious liberty on behalf of the members of the Armed Forces, chaplains, whose very ministry of presence reminds our troops of the Holy One with them, have slowly, intentionally, and often out of necessity stepped out from behind the pulpit into an essential posture of liaison to foreign religious leaders and religious advisor to military commanders. It is a new role far removed from the image of the gentle-natured, good-humored Father Mulcahy character in the 1970s television series *M*A*S*H*, but a critical role that the military chaplaincy, and their ecclesiastical endorsing agencies, must accept if chaplains are to remain strategically relevant and invaluable combat multipliers in future conflicts.

Any sincere plea for peace and respect for all people is a worthy and noble plea. Today that quest demands our attention perhaps more than any other time in world history. Toward that end, I highly commend this book to you for your understanding of our quintessential role as peacemakers, regardless of our calling or profession, during our brief journey here on earth.

Douglas L. Carver
Chaplain (Major General)
United States Army, Retired
22nd Army Chief of Chaplains

Preface

In 2009 Georgetown University's Berkley Center for Religion, Peace and World Affairs—where I served as an associate director and faculty member—sponsored its first seminar on "Religion and Security in World Affairs" on the campus of National Defense University. One outcome of that meeting was a series of invitations by military chaplains to provide a variety of tools and seminars to their personnel over subsequent years. Among those tools are a host of educational, cocurricular resources such as a syllabus database, film guides on religion and conflict, and twenty case studies on religion, conflict, and peace. Much of this material was funded by a grant from the Henry Luce Foundation to the Berkley Center, and the materials have been used over time at the National War College, Naval Postgraduate School, Armed Forces Chaplains Center, Marine Corps University (Quantico), U.S. Naval Academy (Annapolis), U.S. Military Academy (West Point), International Military Chiefs of Chaplains Conference (Sarajevo, 2012), and elsewhere.

Our goal in 2008–2009 was to change the way that military officers, diplomats, and aid workers are trained. None of these career fields requires formal training in the religious phenomena that are so prevalent when U.S. government officials travel abroad to engage overseas audiences. Indeed, for a nation so religious at home, our foreign policy is tone-deaf, and usually willfully blind, to the religious dynamics latent among our international counterparts.

The way we sought to change this was to provide curricular materials and training to government-learning institutions, such as the State Department's Foreign Service Institute and many of the military's learning centers. We were not alone: individuals like Chris Seiple, Douglas Johnston, and many others were already laboring in this space. But we had the unique resources of Georgetown University to bring to bear in this arena.

In the process we met with many talented, hard-working Americans serving U.S. interests abroad. We also encountered hundreds of U.S. military chaplains, many of whom had significant training and expertise in pastoral roles but no experience or education in comparative religion. We likewise found that many chaplains had been called upon to do a variety of things outside their normal pastoral duties, such as distribute clothing to the needy "outside the wire" in Afghanistan and Iraq, speak with local Muslim religious leaders in order to dissuade them from giving tacit support to insurgents (i.e., storage of weapons in mosques), train religious leaders in the Afghan military, help develop new chaplaincies (Eastern Europe) or new denominations within existing chaplaincies (Protestants in Latin America), and provide evaluations of the religious context for war-fighting commanders.

In most cases, it seemed as if these chaplains had to make it up as they went along, because there was no training and little documentation about what had occurred previously on the ground, and military personnel also rotate in and out rather quickly. Indeed, for the first decade after 9/11 there was virtually no formal, in-depth preparation of military chaplains for understanding global trends in religion and security and the mechanics of successful religious-leader engagement. Nonetheless, many lessons were learned, and not just by Americans, but also by Canadians, Brits, Australians, and others.

The purpose of this book is to record and reflect on those experiences, lest they be lost. Most of the authors are former chaplains who participated in "religious advisement" and "religious-leader engagement" on the ground in Iraq, Afghanistan, Kosovo, and elsewhere. It is our hope that this book will report on the valiant efforts of our personnel in uniform and serve as a lesson learned for national militaries.

I am grateful for the support of Chip Hauss and Marie-Claire Antoine for this project ever since Chip and I hatched it over lunch in Foggy Bottom in 2011. I also appreciatively acknowledge the valuable research assistance of Bryan Ballas, Linda Waits-Kamau, and especially Alise Krapane.

On a personal note, I have seen these chaplains in action, from Camp Pendleton (California) to Carswell Field (Texas) to Ft. Meyer (Virginia), and I have been in their chapels at military installations in Afghanistan, Kuwait, Iraq, Qatar, and Kyrgyzstan. They are motivated by a love of God and their fellow man. They typically serve long hours with few resources, and I can only surmise that the stress of bearing such a burden would be crushing for most of us. I believe I can speak for all of the contributors in this volume in thanking those chaplains for their service.

Eric Patterson, PhD
Dean, Robertson School of Government
Regent University
Senior Research Fellow, Berkley Center for Religion, Peace and World Affairs
Georgetown University

1

The Modern Military Chaplaincy in the Era of Intervention and Terrorism

Eric Patterson

After twenty-five years of severe rule by Indonesia, a UN-sponsored referendum in 1999 was supposed to settle the question about whether East Timor (Timor-Leste) should be independent and sovereign.[1] That referendum ultimately led to nominal independence under a UN transitional administration for East Timor until full sovereignty as Timor-Leste in 2002.[2]

The year of the referendum, 1999, was violent and chaotic. Jakarta supported a policy of intimidation, but 80 percent of the local populace nonetheless voted for independence. The violence perpetrated by the Indonesian military, police, and especially local armed militias resulted in the deaths of over a thousand people (of a population of just under one million), the destruction of private and public property, and the displacement of hundreds of thousands of people.[3] Sexual violence, arson, and torture were commonplace.[4]

It took a UN-authorized intervention to quell the destruction. The Australia-led intervention force for East Timor (INTERFET), with a robust mandate, acted muscularly. The rules of engagement allowed for greater use of force, curfews, forced disarmament, and other measures that put to shame the toothless measures that had been employed by UN peacekeepers at Srebrenica, Bosnia, and Kigali, Rwanda. And the bulk of military forces were first-rate, modern combat troops from Australia supported by Thais, South Koreans, and others—not barefoot privates from poor countries. James Cotton writes that INTERFET's relative success can be attributed to the rapid insertion of overwhelming force in a context where the political ground had been very carefully prepared.[5] That political ground refers to work at the United Nations and in national capitals—especially Canberra—on the legal basis for and boundaries on the intervention.[6]

When INTERFET arrived, it found a Third World environment burned to the ground, thousands of possible perpetrators lurking on both sides of the border, and nearly half a million people having fled their homes. The environment was macabre: mass graves, burned-out churches full of skeletons, defaced cemeteries, and victims everywhere. Not only was the local citizenry traumatized, but many young soldiers were also deeply affected by the gore and savagery.

What was a chaplain assigned with these military forces to do? In this unique case, the lead INTERFET chaplain was a senior Australian chaplain named Len Eacott. The role his team played went far beyond field-worship services for friendly troops. The INTERFET soldiers, in addition to security and stabilization functions, had a mandate to assist the UN investigation of atrocities. This meant military personnel and uniformed doctors had a role in exhuming bodies, autopsies, assessing probable causes of death, and developing a database of their findings to aid potential investigations for trials addressing crimes against humanity.

In short, military personnel and UN civilians needed immediate pastoral care, as did multitudes of the East Timorese. In many cases, Chaplain Eacott and his colleagues provided Christian burials for local casualties (East Timor is overwhelmingly Catholic). This service was not merely a compassionate act; it was a demonstration of respect for the dead and their loved ones and a marker of the value of human life that spoke volumes to the local citizenry. The chaplains went directly to houses of worship, usually ruined Catholic churches, and sought priests and lay leaders. Furthermore, the chaplains developed trust with local people and often became valued intermediaries between INTERFET and civilian community leaders.

Perhaps the most lasting contribution from Chaplain Eacott's team was the development of a burial registry. Starting with an INTERFET injunction on procedures for processing deceased persons, followed by a subsequent UN high commissioner for human rights directive, the policy was to preserve evidence of the mass killings. It was also an important practical matter to keep a detailed record of the bodies exhumed from hasty graves or scenes of violence. The chaplains maintained this registry. This burial registry became a public record released to local churches, the nascent political leadership of Timor-Leste, the UN Transitional Authority for East Timor, and the international community—including jurists engaged in evaluating whether crimes against humanity had been committed.

The twenty-first-century ministry and service represented in this case by the INTERFET chaplains is what this book is about. Particularly in the past decade, Western military chaplains have been called upon to move beyond the pulpit to promote peace: by engaging with local religious leaders abroad, by advising combatant commanders and senior diplomats on the religious and cultural mores of their area, by serving local civilians in war-ravaged environments, and by being agents for peace in ways not conceived of by past generations of military chaplains. This book reports on chaplains as peace builders in real-world contexts from Iraq to Afghanistan to East Timor to Kosovo since the late 1990s.

THE CONTEMPORARY MILITARY CHAPLAIN

An American military chaplain, like those in other Western militaries, is a trained religious professional who is also commissioned as a military officer. The individual is qualified first as a civilian pastor through seminary and practice in ministry and then voluntarily joins the U.S. military as a representative of a religious organization or denomination ("endorsing agency"). Contemporary chaplains are typically considered noncombatants; yet they do go through the various levels of officer commissioning and military education like other officers.

In terms of duties, chaplains provide religious ministrations first and foremost. Their role in the military is, in part, recognition that military service presents unique challenges for citizens to exercise their First Amendment rights when cloistered on a military base at home or deployed abroad. However, the existence of chaplains also says something about the seriousness of the profession of arms and the way that the ultimate questions of life are raised in situations of stress and violence.

So the first role of a chaplain is to perform or provide religious ministry, both to adherents of his own tradition and to adherents of other traditions. Chaplains must ensure religious requirements are met for all members of the military community—they can do so by opening their rites broadly or by facilitating venues, times, spaces, resources, and personnel to meet the spiritual needs of the troops from outside their own tradition. For example, a Methodist chaplain might bring a civilian Catholic priest and a rabbi to the installation to service Catholics and Jews.

Thus preaching and all the other duties of clerical life belong to the chaplain, including pastoral offices such as individual and family counseling and ceremonial obligations (e.g., providing invocations and benedictions at formal military events). At the same time as all of this, the chaplain is a staff officer supporting his or her commander. This means that the chaplain not only participates in a variety of meetings and events, from weekly commander's meetings to grilling burgers at the annual base family day, but also has a role in providing counsel from his or her unique vantage point to military leaders. Chaplains advise commanders from the top of the chain of command down to subordinate leaders. And chaplains also supervise lower-ranking chaplains from different faith traditions.

This makes for a busy life, whether on "home station" in the United States or abroad, on a navy vessel or while deployed. All of this ministry is valuable, important, and interesting in its own right. Nonetheless, it is not the principal focus of this book. Instead, the new duties of chaplains beyond the traditional roles and duties of religious ministry are the focus in this volume, particularly with regard to deployments to combat zones in places like Kosovo, Afghanistan, and Iraq. More specifically, this book looks at the work of contemporary military chaplains in two key areas: *religious-leader engagement* and *religious advisement*. These two concepts are at the heart of the expanding role of contemporary military chaplains.

Religious-leader engagement, sometimes called religious-leader liaison, is a form of peace building. Some chaplains "liaise" or "engage" with local citizens and/or local religious leaders (e.g., imams, mullahs) to provide charitable goods, prevent or correct misunderstandings, and advance peace and security. Religious advisement formally means all of the preparations necessary and the actual act of providing materials, briefings, reports, summaries, and counsel to war-fighting commanders of the U.S. military and the role that religion and culture play in a specific theater of operations. At times it means being, or becoming, the subject-matter expert on matters of local religious and cultural context. Such information, as described in chapters by Micheal Hoyt, Jon Cutler, and others, is not intelligence gathering. Collecting such information and offering advice need not violate the chaplain's noncombatancy status. What it does do is awaken a commander's situational awareness to the religious and cultural sensitivities of local institutions—the human geography—of a place and its inhabitants.[7] Religious-leader engagement and some elements of religious advisement have been controversial, particularly within the chaplaincy itself, over the past decade.

However, before we look at changing job descriptions and policy documents, it may be best to step back and answer the question: What do chaplains value? That is, what do their mission statements say, and what are their core values? What names are inscribed in places of honor, such as at the memorial at the Armed Forces Chaplains Center at Ft. Jackson, South Carolina? One way to get at this is to consider those chaplains from the past who are the heroes of the modern chaplaincy.

HEROES OF THE CHAPLAINCY

Western military chaplains rightly pride themselves as belonging to a tradition of service to God and their fellow man. By "Western," I mean those countries associated with the United States as part of the Western alliance during the Cold War, where the most mature chaplaincies exist. For this book, chaplains from a half-dozen countries were invited to participate, but only American and Canadian chaplains chose to offer chapters in the end.

Not surprisingly, the logos of the chaplaincies emphasize their core values of faith and service. The motto of the U.S. Army chaplaincy is *Pro Deo et Patria* ("For God and Country"). The Canadian Armed Forces, as well as the U.S. Navy (which provides chaplains for the Marine Corps as well), have as their motto "Called to Serve" (*Vocatio ad Servitium*).[8] The seal of the U.S. Air Force chaplaincy says, "Freedom, Faith, Ministry."

The contemporary chaplain has many heroes to look back upon.[9] U.S. Army chaplains recall the heroism of Union Army chaplains John Milton Whitehead and Francis Bloodgood Hall, who each earned a Medal of Honor by going to the front lines and physically carrying the wounded back for medical attention. They honor Chaplain Francis P. Duffy of the Fighting 69th, who has a statue in New York City's Times Square, for his courage under enemy fire during World War I. It was a chaplain, Howell Fogey, who cried, "Praise the Lord, and pass the ammunition," during the attack on Pearl Harbor. Fogey is one of a small number of contemporary chaplains who, under extremis, have taken up arms to save their mates.

Chaplains of all services venerate the four chaplains who died during World War II when their vessel, the USAT *Dorchester*, was sunk while crossing the Atlantic on February 2, 1943. These four men represented the diversity of the chaplaincy: Lt. George L. Fox was Methodist, Lt. Alexander D. Goode was Jewish, Lt. John P. Washington was Roman Catholic, and Lt. Clark V. Poling was Dutch Reformed.[10] These men not only prayed, sang, and comforted their comrades as the ship was lost, but each also took off his life jacket and gave it to someone else. They were among more than six hundred who perished. Today their heroism is enshrined in beautiful stained-glass windows at the Army War College, the base chapel at Fort Snelling, the base chapel at West Point, and a full display at the Armed Forces Chaplains Center—where all U.S. chaplains are trained—in South Carolina.

One of the famous army chaplains was Charlie Waters of the Vietnam era. The citation for his magnificent action to save human lives and minister to his comrades is summarized in his Medal of Honor citation (see figure 1.1).

Of course, the other services are not without their heroes. During World War II Father O'Callahan, a navy chaplain, earned the Medal of Honor for conspicuous gallantry when he led a firefighting effort when it seemed certain that his ship was lost after the Japanese attacked. A frigate, the USS *O'Callahan*, was named after him. In fact, the U.S. Navy has named several of its ships after chaplains: the USS *Rentz* (Chaplain Rentz gave his life jacket to save a sailor when his ship had sunk), the USS *Kirkpatrick* (named for a chaplain aboard the USS *Arizona* on December 7, 1941), the USS *Schmitt* (Father Schmitt saved twelve men as his ship sank at Pearl Harbor), and the USS *Capodanno* (unarmed Father Capodanno placed his body between attacking enemy forces and a wounded medic while serving with Marines in Vietnam).

The youngest U.S. service, the air force, is not without its heroes. Chaplain Robert Taylor ended his career as chief of Air Force Chaplains. He was a

---

MAJOR CHARLES JOSEPH WATTERS
United States Army

For conspicuous gallantry and intrepidity in action at the risk of his life above and beyond the call of duty. Chaplain Watters distinguished himself during an assault in the vicinity of Dak To. Chaplain Watters was moving with one of the companies when it engaged a heavily armed enemy battalion. As the battle raged and the casualties mounted, Chaplain Watters, with complete disregard for his safety, rushed forward to the line of contact. Unarmed and completely exposed, he moved among, as well as in front of the advancing troops, giving aid to the wounded, assisting in their evacuation, giving words of encouragement, and administering the last rites to the dying. When a wounded paratrooper was standing in shock in front of the assaulting forces, Chaplain Watters ran forward, picked the man up on his shoulders and carried him to safety. As the troopers battled to the first enemy entrenchment, Chaplain Watters ran through the intense enemy fire to the front of the entrenchment to aid a fallen comrade. A short time later, the paratroopers pulled back in preparation for a second assault. Chaplain Watters exposed himself to both friendly and enemy fire between the two forces in order to recover two wounded soldiers. Later, when the battalion was forced to pull back into a perimeter, Chaplain Watters noticed that several wounded soldiers were lying outside the newly formed perimeter. Without hesitation and ignoring attempts to restrain him, Chaplain Watters left the perimeter three times in the face of small arms, automatic weapons, and mortar fire to carry and to assist the injured troopers to safety. Satisfied that all of the wounded were inside the perimeter, he began aiding the medics ... applying field bandages to open wounds, obtaining and serving food and water, giving spiritual and mental strength and comfort. During his ministering, he moved out to the perimeter from position to position redistributing food and water, and tending to the needs of his men. Chaplain Watters was giving aid to the wounded when he himself was mortally wounded. Chaplain Watters' unyielding perseverance and selfless devotion to his comrades was in keeping with the highest traditions of the U.S. Army.

Figure 1.1.

survivor of the infamous Bataan Death March. His official USAF biography relates the following:

> At the surrender of the American forces there, he became a member of that part of the "Death March" which led from Bataan through the streets of Manila, to the prison camp approximately eight miles east of Cabanatuan. He served as chaplain in the prison camp hospital at Cabanatuan where he ministered to more than ten thousand patients. In the summer of 1944, he spent fourteen weeks in solitary confinement for smuggling food and medicine to the patients. He was later taken to Japan and Manchuria on one of the infamous "hellships" which was bombed twice by American planes with a loss of more than a thousand lives. During the second bombing, Chaplain Taylor was struck in the wrist and leg by flying fragments. Ironically he was not awarded a Purple Heart since he was wounded by our own forces.[11]

America's allies likewise have chaplain heroes, such as Canada's Padre Rosaire Crochetiere, of the Royal 22e Regiment. He died during an attack near Flanders in 1918. According to one account, Father Crochetiere was described as "a father, a brother, a confidant, and a friend."[12] Canadians also revere Padre Walter Brown, who landed at Juno Beach on D-Day and was captured and executed by German troops—the only Allied chaplain to be so dealt with in the European theater.[13] The British Army has a long tradition of military chaplains known for sacrifice and heroism. For instance, Reverend Edward Noel Mellish served in both the Boer War and World War I. During the former he escaped when his unit was surrounded by the enemy, went for help, and then returned to encourage his comrades that reinforcements were on the way. During World War I Mellish served in the trenches at Ypres. He earned the Victoria Cross for gallantry during this time. One observer wrote:

> Nothing could be finer than the way Captain Mellish did his duty and more than his duty during the time he was near us. Immediately the troops captured the trenches, and while the wounded were picking their way painfully back, the enemy's guns were turned on full blast and the intervening ground was deluged with shell and machine-gun fire. Into this tempest of fire the brave parson walked, a prayer book under his arm as though on church parade in peacetime.
>
> He reached the first of the wounded and knelt down to do what he could for them. The first few he brought in himself without any aid, and it made us think a bit more of parsons to see how he walked quietly under fire assisting the slow-moving wounded and thinking more of saving them from discomfort than of his own safety.
>
> It was only during a lull in the fighting when the ambulance parties could get out that he finally took a rest. Next day he was out again, unconcerned as ever. Some of the men would not have survived the ordeal had it not been for the prompt assistance rendered to them by Mr. Mellish.[14]

What are we to make of the "parson" Mellish, the "four chaplains," Bataan survivor Taylor, Padres Brown and Crochetiere, and the rest of them? Why are they the "chaplains' chaplains"? What do they represent? Most importantly, as Chaplain Carver said in the foreword and as subsequent chapters suggest, these chaplains represent a ministry of *presence*, of being there in the thick of battle. Even those "fighting chaplains" like the Civil War's Lt. James Hill or Chaplain Fogey are remembered not because they fought but because they were on the very front lines when disaster struck and they did what they could to protect their brother soldiers and sailors. So, too, were Taylor and Waters and others there with the troops in the very worst of times, and chaplains venerate this. Indeed, for Christian chaplains (the vast majority in Western militaries), there is a theological impetus for this based on the doctrine of the Incarnation of Christ, who came to earth in flesh to be with and minister to sinful humanity, face to face. The presence of a chaplain in military life—during its mundane and terrifying moments—remains essentially a human enterprise. Chaplains bring a human focus as clergy, helping the individuals and the institution itself to remain connected to the community "back home." Chaplains don't work to establish a military congregation or denomination, but rather extend a link from the wider communities of faith across the nation.

The ministry of presence begs the question of motivation, and it is clearly the valuing of the *sacred* that is shared by all chaplains. By sacred, I mean that sense of the transcendent, spiritual dimension that is a part of all human reality and that brings humanity into contact with moral teaching and spiritual realities beyond their own limited faculties. The sacred is present in the symbols and offices of religious ministry, and it is the engine and raison d'être for the work of chaplains. In this vein, one chaplain, quoting a former commandant of the U.S. Navy Chaplains School, explained to me that chaplains are "the physical bearers of the presence of God."[15]

Essential to that ministry of presence is a holistic notion of *courage*, physical as well as moral. The first is not raw bravado but the willingness of individuals to face danger even when the situation is hopeless or terrifying. No one claims that the USAT *Dorchester* chaplains or others did not face fear—they were fully human. But they exhibited courage in serving their comrades despite the most horrendous of conditions. So, too, chaplains venerate moral courage—bravery to take the moral high road in all circumstances, to live up to the highest ideals of both one's faith and one's service. Chaplains like Taylor, who broke the rules to feed the starving, or Mellish, who went back to his squad through enemy lines, are heroes. Moreover, they encourage today's chaplains to act courageously in many small but significant ways, such as speaking truth to power behind closed doors or advocating for those who have no advocate.

Chaplains value *freedom*. In particular, U.S. chaplains vaunt their role in providing for the First Amendment "rights" of their parishioners, and most chaplains I know are defenders of their own faith while at the same time advocates for the religious practices of others. This is not always easy, because the onerous demands of the service, even in peacetime, can make military commanders fill up the Sabbath with after-hours work and training for their subordinates. This is even more the case aboard a navy vessel at sea or when deployed "down range." Nonetheless, chaplains attempt to provide a venue for religious participation and worship—freedom of religion—in the most extreme of conditions. Moreover, chaplains value freedom of the mind and conscience. They are one of the few people that military personnel can go to for off-the-record counsel; they are sounding boards for commanders and junior personnel alike when ethical considerations must be weighed.

Chaplains themselves have encapsulated these values into their pithy creeds, emphasizing their *faith* and *service* (or ministry). Chaplains honor those who came before them who were able to be true to the ideals of their faith in practical service despite the terrors of the battlefield. Just as the conditions under which military chaplains serve have changed from the Revolutionary War to the present, so, too, have some of the opportunities for chaplains to make an impact as well as the context in which they work. It is that changing set of opportunities and contextual features that is the general backdrop for this book. Consistent across the ages—even with each evolutionary step of military technology—is that warfare remains an essentially human endeavor. From the invention of gunpowder to the current debates about drone warfare, the obligations, responsibilities, and consequences of war accumulate to human beings, and chaplains provide both a continuing connection to the human (and faith) communities to which military members are tied and a divine connection to something outside the self. Chaplains represent the connections to church/synagogue/mosque and family back home. Chaplains affirm that spiritual aspects of people, or, to borrow some of the language that has surfaced elsewhere, connect the "human dimension" with the spiritual and religious life of individuals and institutions.

BEYOND THE PASTORATE:
ENGAGEMENT, ADVISEMENT, AND THE CULTURE WARS

The purpose of this book is multifaceted. By collecting chapters from experienced chaplains (both U.S. and Canadian), this volume records the changing nature of the military chaplaincy, particularly in the context of the past twenty years. From the perspective of the U.S. military, one immediately becomes aware that some members of the armed forces have been deployed into war zones since 1991. More specifically, whether it was Desert Shield/ Storm followed by allied air forces enforcing the no-fly zones over Iraq, or peacekeeping deployments in Bosnia and Kosovo, or more than a decade of active warfare in Afghanistan and Iraq, the U.S. military and its closest allies have had troops deployed abroad for more than two decades. This does not count large forward-positioned troops in Japan, South Korea, and Europe that are legacies of the Cold War. In every war-zone deployment, military chaplains played a vital role providing religious ministry to the troops. This book reports on the many things military chaplains have done beyond traditional religious ministry and seeks to analyze what these changes mean for the chaplaincy and for the military more broadly.

There are two major areas this book brings into focus. The first is *religious-leader engagement* (or religious-leader liaison), which means chaplains encouraging understanding and peace with local religious interlocutors when deployed. In other words, this is peace building by chaplains. For instance, Chaplains David West and Micheal [*sic*] Hoyt reflect on elite religious-leader engagement in Central Asia and Iraq, whereas Chaplain Jon Cutler discusses grassroots engagement in East Africa.

A key question for all of this engagement is: What does it mean? What are its consequences, both in the local, tactical context and for the chaplaincy and the military more broadly? Are these efforts grounded in theories of conflict resolution and peace building? The chapters in this book will discuss these issues, from chaplain noncombatant status to training and theory to denominational issues to service policy.

The second major area of this book focuses on the expert advice chaplains provide as special staff officers. This role and responsibility encompasses a wide range of obligations contingent on the trust between the chaplain and the person or organizations receiving the chaplain's advice. Providing professional, religious, or staff advice also depends on the credibility and particular expertise of the chaplain.

When chaplains provide such counsel on matters of faith and culture, it is called *religious advisement*. For instance, when a military commander arrives in a highly religious context, such as Herat (less than fifty miles from Iran), Kandahar (birthplace of the Taliban), or Karbala (sacred to Shias), whom is he or she to turn to for counsel about the religious context? This was not a critical issue for military commanders of the Cold War era running U.S. bases in Okinawa, Seoul, and Bavaria, but it has been a matter of life or death for the past decade. This book will illuminate the understanding, or lack thereof, that many chaplains have to provide religious advisement to commanders and how advisement has worked in the field. Various contributors will also speculate about how the U.S. government could do this better, such as by developing a separate religious advisory specialty in the military as well as other government agencies, most notably at USAID and the Department of State.

Both religious advisement and religious-leader engagement are not without their critics inside the chaplaincy. Indeed, there has been a significant debate within the chaplaincy about whether such efforts are appropriate: Does advisement and engagement jeopardize chaplains' noncombatant status, veer chaplains off into doing intelligence work, and rob the troops of desperately needed pastors? Some of the nuances of this debate are reflected in the chapters of this book, particularly in that by Dayne Nix, who looks at the different approaches each service chaplaincy has taken. Nearly half of the chapters refer to a critical joint-services publication (a document spanning the U.S. Air Force, Army, and Navy) issued in late 2009, Joint Publication 1-05, "Religious Affairs in Joint Operations." JP 1-05 provides the definitions and guidance necessary for chaplains who are tasked by their commanders with providing religious advisement or religious-leader engagement.[16]

Some of the contributors will allude to other challenges of context: the tremendous stress on the chaplaincy as an institution under attack by outside forces and a shifting cultural landscape. Prior to 9/11, most military chaplains led a chapel-based community on a military post. This was largely noncontroversial. In contrast, since 9/11 there has been, unique in U.S. history, a determined drive to circumscribe the chaplaincy, and indeed religion itself, from the armed forces. Determined assaults from outside the military (e.g., the Freedom from Religion Foundation) on issues such as the formula for prayer (i.e., "in Jesus's name, amen"), chaplains teaching about the historic just war tradition, and the role of outside groups in on-base chapels have made the senior leadership risk-averse in an increasingly secularized society.[17] Chaplains have been tasked with finding space for religious groups with whom they would normally not associate, such as Wiccans, to practice on their installations.[18] Moreover, the so-called culture wars of the past decade, which are often considered issues of sin and conscience by some individuals of faith, have created a challenge for chaplains. The diversity and even polarizing views within the culture are latent in military chaplaincy. Chaplains of some groups categorize decisions by military and civilian leaders repealing "Don't Ask, Don't Tell" as sinful, while other chaplains view the repeal and increasing acceptance of homosexual people as widening the circle of grace. Vocal critics of the repeal saw danger and warned against the potential for gay marriage rites at military chapels (which became possible in 2012).[19]

How are chaplains dealing with all of this? How does the personal stress of deploying, leaving spouses and family, affect the individual chaplain? How are the troops under their care dealing with all of these stressors? Two of the chapters in this book will look at the stress and context that contemporary chaplains face. This is an important part of the book's analysis because it helps us to locate the chaplaincy within the wider set of issues and controversies in Western societies.

OVERVIEW OF THE BOOK

This book does not easily fit into a single niche in the scholarly literature. It is at once a work of historical reporting while at the same time raising issues critical to U.S. foreign and national security policy, diplomacy, and the social sciences. Some chapters (chapter 3, by Dayne Nix) clearly tie to the literature on conflict resolution and peace building, whereas others are rooted in the social-scientific and behavior-science literatures (chapter 10, by Gary Roberts and L. Diane Hess-Hernandez). Most of the material is historical and qualitative, though there is more formal social-scientific analysis from surveys and interviews (chapter 9, by Eric Wester). In sum, the book attempts to paint a broad, yet deep, portrait of the changing world of Western military chaplains, particularly in the context of the West's decade-long deployment of military personnel to fight wars in the greater Muslim world.

Pauletta Otis has long been a sympathetic, yet critical, observer of the U.S. military, first as an academic at a major public university and later as an advisor to various government agencies and a faculty member at Marine Corps

University in Quantico, Virginia. Thus she is uniquely qualified to present an overview of the history of military chaplains—back to the Crusades—as well as a snapshot of the contemporary chaplaincy and the challenges it faces today. In chapter 2 she reports that there were approximately three thousand active-duty and two thousand reserve/National Guard chaplains in 2013. They served approximately three million members of the armed forces, and although the majority of chaplains are Christian, they represent 175 different religions or denominations. Otis discusses a number of the challenges that the contemporary chaplaincy faces, such as noncombatant status when under fire in the field, U.S. culture wars over "church" and "state," and the radically different expectations chaplains experience from commander to commander. Despite the fact that there are some calls from outside groups to disband the chaplaincy, Otis sees it as vibrant and important to the contemporary military.

Chaplain Eric Wester (ret.) is now a pastor and senior official advising his church, the Evangelical Lutheran Church in America, on military chaplains' issues. In chapter 9 he introduces key army concepts most civilians have not heard of: resiliency and spiritual resiliency. *Resiliency* describes the ability of the individual to rebound and overcome hardship. In the context of the Afghanistan and Iraq wars, Wester writes that "resiliency includes not only sustaining themselves physically and emotionally while in combat but also coming home fit." Certainly resiliency—in the face of a liberated-turned-hostile nation, roadside bombs, IEDs, and the dramatic beheadings and suicide missions of al-Qaeda, not to mention family stress on the home front—has been a critical issue for the U.S. military in the past decade. Wester's chapter provides unique insights derived from analysis of sophisticated surveys of the U.S. Army in the second half of the Iraq War, surveys intended to assess and correlate spiritual resilience with ethical attitudes and actions as well as physical and emotional resilience. For instance, the EXCEL survey looked at "moral courage," "moral efficacy," and "intent to report unethical conduct." Wester also reports on the roles that military chaplains have had in strengthening the ethical and spiritual resiliency of the troops and some of the challenges of doing so in an era of increasing pluralism.

When the U.S. military deploys into a highly secularized theater (e.g., Europe in the 1980s), it is unlikely that military commanders need to concern themselves with the religious profile of the host population. How about when the U.S. military deploys into a highly religious society? Where are military commanders to get the counsel needed in order to act in a manner that will not set off a holy war? And can commanders send their chaplains outside of the wire to engage with local religious officials in the interest of peace? This has been a challenge for the United States in both Iraq and Afghanistan, and in chapter 3 Dayne Nix discusses a model for approaching these questions taken from an influential book, *Religion: The Missing Dimension of Statecraft*.[20] More specifically, Nix discusses efforts in the early 2000s to prepare chaplains to "advise" military commanders on religious dynamics in foreign settings. Nix also describes, however, the tentative steps that the U.S. military has taken toward institutionalizing chaplain training and policy in order to be prepared to provide such advisement. These incremental developments have been controversial, and Nix reports on the different approaches of the different services as well as the latest policy statements by the U.S. Army, Navy, and Air Force on "religious advisement" and "religious-leader engagement."

Chaplain Eric Keller, now a PhD candidate at a major U.S. university, was referred to in this book's foreword. He provided critical state side support within the army chaplaincy in the years following 9/11 (at the same time that Nix was involved with chaplains training for the U.S. Navy). In chapter 4 Keller provides an overview of the scenario in 2001: the military chaplaincies prepared their members for pastoral service, not to be world religions experts or to engage with religious leaders of other faiths abroad. Keller helps us understand both the entrepreneurial spirit of army chaplains who tried to get things done and the bureaucratic hurdles they faced in terms of policy and doctrine. Interestingly, despite interest from the highest levels of government, such as Deputy Secretary of Defense Paul Wolfowitz, it took until 2009 for substantive interservice change to be codified as doctrine in Joint Publication 1-05, calling for chaplains to be ready to provide religious advisement and religious-leader engagement. Keller also describes good-faith efforts to develop relationships with Muslim religious leaders through an exchange program in the early 2000s, but such programs were poorly funded and executed between the Defense Department and the Department of State.

People around the world vividly remember the carnage in Iraq in 2005 and 2006, when it appeared that al-Qaeda shock troops, Sunni tribal sheikhs, and the death squads of the Shia majority would outvie one another in their capacity for destruction. Coalition troops, led by the United States, were constantly under assault as Western governments tried to midwife a representative political system and effective government services. One largely untapped resource in the first years of the conflict was the omnipresent religious faith of the local citizenry, despite the fact that the Coalition ruefully learned the potency of religious authorities, such as when Grand Ayatollah Ali al-Sistani single-handedly forced the Coalition Provisional Authority to hold elections as scheduled (rather than delay), not to mention the constant turmoil surrounding the brash and deadly Muqtada al-Sadr (himself the son of Sistani's mentor). What was unknown to Coalition forces at the time was that a British priest, Canon Andrew White, had served as vicar of Baghdad for years and was a respected religious figure among many rivals. White's peace-building initiatives initially were ignored but later were given serious attention by the Coalition commander, General David Petraeus, and his command chaplain, Micheal Hoyt. In chapter 5 Hoyt himself describes the successful religious diplomacy in 2007 and the formal Baghdad Accords. This agreement became, along with the Sunni Awakening and the troop surge, the third pillar for the transition to peace among many religious factions and the spurning of al-Qaeda.

In chapter 6 Canadian chaplain S. K. Moore provides case studies of chaplains working for peace among warring religionists in the Balkans and in Afghanistan. But first he locates the work of chaplains as peace builders within a wider shift in security approaches in the past decade: from military-only to whole-of-government approaches. The past twenty years have seen a slow shift, accelerated by the wars in Afghanistan and Iraq, to mobilize in a cooperative fashion the various areas of expertise and resources of national governments in pursuit of what is typically called "stabilization and reconstruction operations." In practical terms, this means governments' development, military, and diplomatic agencies working as partners to resolve and ameliorate the effects of conflict. Moore describes how chaplains, often working in coordination with diplomats and aid workers, can be agents for peace by "bridging social capital." He provides examples such as the work by a Canadian military imam (in Kandahar) and a French military priest (in Kosovo), both of whom engaged religion as a "strategic social space" within those societies as a critical lever for peace.

Chaplain Jon Cutler was a Jewish rabbi assigned as the command chaplain for the Horn of Africa, an area long known for its strife between Muslim and Christian populations. He begins chapter 7 with an important argument about the role of religion in African societies that is more widely applicable:

> Religions structure meaning and purpose for billions of people. Religions can serve for both ill and good, catalysts of violent conflicts and potent forces for brokering reconciliation and sustaining peace. Religious-extremist violence may be a backdrop to life today, but it is the countless mundane ways in which people live their lives and demonstrate their religious faiths that are not noticed. For example, every day Africans demonstrate their religious practices and commitment in the public realm. In their culture, religion is not relegated to the margins of society. They live in a world that recognizes no clear distinction between private individual faith and secular, public life.

Cutler goes on to report his surprising, novel work across religious communities to increase understanding in the interest of peace from meetings of religious elites in Ethiopia to youth service projects in Kampala, Uganda.

Within the chaplaincy, a controversy during the past decade has been whether chaplains on deployment should engage with local religious leaders. Throughout this book, this notion of "religious-leader engagement" or "religious-leader liaison" comes up time and again. It was controversial for a number of reasons. Opponents argue that it puts chaplains in the line of fire, into a role they are not trained for, and takes valuable time away from their key functions while deployed (i.e., pastoral ministry to troops in the combat zone). Proponents argue that some chaplains should be prepared to engage local religious leaders if directed by their commander, with the purpose being to promote understanding and peace. Chaplain West participated in religious-leader engagement at an elite level, with the direct support of then–U.S. Central Command (CENTCOM) commander General David Petraeus. As West describes it in chapter 8, the initiative was multifaceted, from bringing social-scientific research to CENTCOM in order to better understand the human geography of the region to engaging with religious clerics. West reports on those efforts, including outreach in the United States to universities, think tanks, and the State Department, as well as meetings abroad with religious leaders, including Wahhabi and Deobandi madrassa leaders from Pakistan.

In a companion essay to that of Chaplain Wester, in chapter 10 Gary Roberts and L. Diane Hess-Hernandez discuss the findings of a series of interviews with military chaplains on occupational stress. More specifically, because military chaplains are the "frontline" spiritual support for men and women in uniform, they are often under tremendous stress themselves. In other words, from the perspectives of psychology and workplace health, the very nature of the chaplaincy presents many unique and profound occupational stress-coping and adaption challenges. This chapter provides an overview of the sources of occupational stress for chaplains and the various strategies for addressing the main stress risk factors with special emphasis on the role of workplace spiritual intelligence (WSI). WSI is the ability to achieve transcendence, enter higher states of consciousness, interject the sacred into everyday events, utilize applied spiritual principles to solve problems, and engage in religiously informed character behaviors, such as forgiveness, love, transparency, and humility. Roberts and Hess-Hernandez's interviews with chaplains find a range of stressors for contemporary chaplains and go on to apply WSI as a mechanism for understanding how chaplains adapt to and overcome those challenges.

Finally, the University of California's Jason Klocek and Ron E. Hassner provide a summative conclusion in chapter 11. Based on their research of religion in foreign militaries, they are uniquely qualified to consider critical elements of religion in the U.S. military, particularly the roles and responsibilities of chaplains over the past decade. Moreover, their chapter links this book on military chaplains to wider currents in the scholarship on international relations, American politics, and the nexus of religion and U.S. foreign and national security policy.

NOTES

1. A UN report documenting the period of Indonesian rule records approximately 180,000 civilian deaths during the time, including many from deliberate starvation

policy. See "UN Verdict on East Timor," *Australian*, January 19, 2006, www.yale
.edu/gsp/east_timor/unverdict/html, accessed March 16, 2009. For a more detailed
history, see James Dunn's *Timor: A People Betrayed* (Sydney: ABC Books, 1996).

2. The author thanks Chaplain Len Eacott for providing this valuable perspective and information. The United Nations' documents (and others) can be found at
East Timor's Commission for Reception, Truth, and Reconciliation (http://www.cavr-
timorleste.org/) and Yale University's East Timor Project (http://www.yale.edu/
gsp/east_timor/).

3. Michael J. Kelly, Timothy L. H. McCormack, Paul Muggleton, and Bruce M.
Oswald, "Legal Aspects of Australia's Involvement in the International Force for East
Timor," *International Review of the Red Cross*, no. 841 (March 31, 2001): 101–39, http://
www.icrc.org/eng/resources/documents/misc/57jqz2.htm.

4. See Sonia Picado Sotela, Judith Sefi Attah, A. M. Ahmadi, Sir Mari Kapi, and
Sabine Leutheusser-Schnarrenberger, *Report of the International Commission of Inquiry
on East Timor to the Secretary-General*, UN Doc. A/54/726-S, January 31, 2000, http://
www.unhchr.ch/huridocda/huridoca.nsf/%28Symbol%29/A.54.726,+S.2000.59.En.

5. James Cotton, "Australia's East Timor Experience: Military Lessons and Security Dilemmas," presentation made at the fifth symposium of the National Institute
for Defense Studies, Tokyo, January 21–23, 2002, available online at http://www
.nids.go.jp/english/event/symposium/pdf/2002/sympo_e2002_10.pdf.

6. Jarat Chopra, "The UN's Kingdom of East Timor," *Survival* 42, no. 3 (Autumn
2000): 27–39; and Carsten Stahn, "The UN Transitional Administration in Kosovo
and East Timor: A First Analysis," in *Max Planck Yearbook of United Nations Law*, vol.
5, ed. Jochen A. Frowein and Rüdiger Wolfram, 105–84 (The Hague: Kluwer Law
International, 2001).

7. Intelligence professionals call their analysis of human geography, particularly
with regard to individual and collective notions of identity, culture, and affiliation,
human terrain. Chaplains typically speak of *religious terrain*, distancing themselves
from intelligence gathering but utilizing a similar term in order to speak a lingo understood by their fellow service personnel.

8. The U.S. Navy writes it as *vocati et servititum*.

9. One website has a publication devoted to chaplains who earned military honors for gallant deeds under fire (see http://theedgeofmadness.com/index.php). The
stories of all of these chaplains can be found there, and many are also available in the
Canadian journal for military chaplains, *Curtana: Sword of Mercy*, available at http://
www.justwar101.com/. However, all of these stories are so famous that they can also
be found more generally, from traditional military histories to Wikipedia.

10. http://www.fourchaplains.org/story.html.

11. http://www.af.mil/information/bios/bio.asp?bioID=7354.

12. http://www.anglican.ca/amo/history/.

13. http://www.anglican.ca/amo/history/.

14. http://www.hellfire-corner.demon.co.uk/coulson.htm.

15. Chaplain (Col.) David West (U.S. Army, ret.) provided this quotation from
Captain Michael Langston (USN, ret.), now professor of Chaplain Ministries at
Columbia International University, Columbia, South Carolina. Langston formerly
served as the commandant of the U.S. Navy School.

16. U.S. Department of Defense, "Joint Publication 1-05: Religious Affairs in Joint Operations," November 20, 2009, http://www.dtic.mil/doctrine/new_pubs/jp1_05.pdf.

17. Todd Starnes, "Air Force Suspends Christian-Themed Ethics Training Program over Bible Passages," *Fox News*, August 3, 2011, http://www.foxnews.com/politics/2011/08/03/air-forces-suspends-christian-themed-ethics-training-program-over-bible/#ixzz2U2SQf5uC.

18. Hanna Rosin, "Wiccan Controversy Tests Military Religious Tolerance," *Washington Post*, June 8, 1999, http://www.washingtonpost.com/wp-srv/national/daily/june99/wicca08.htm.

19. Ed O'Keefe, "Gay Weddings Can Be Performed by Military Chaplains, Pentagon Says," *Washington Post*, September 30, 2011, http://www.washingtonpost.com/blogs/federal-eye/post/gay-weddings-can-be-performed-by-military-chaplains-pentagon-says/2011/09/30/gIQA0hX19K_blog.html; Padmananda Rama, "Military Chaplains Debate Their Role without 'Don't Ask, Don't Tell,'" *CNN*, December 8, 2010, http://www.cnn.com/2010/POLITICS/12/05/dadt.chaplains/index.html.

20. Douglas Johnston and Cynthia Sampson, eds., *Religion: The Missing Dimension of Statecraft* (New York: Oxford University Press, 1994).

2

✝

Understanding the Role and Influence of U.S. Military Chaplains

Pauletta Otis

There are two reasons why the military chaplaincy and the chaplains should be better known: The chaplaincy is one of the most important institutions of the U.S. government and the only institution that wears the insignia of both church and state. And it is always wise, in a democratic state, to be aware of the nexus of religion and the state in order to protect religion from the state and the state from religion.

Most people know of the existence of U.S. military chaplains and generally appreciate their services in times of war, but very little is actually known about their role and influence. From an individual perspective, chaplains seem to be invariably energetic people with unique and important perspectives on current times, issues, and challenges. Although formal doctrine and policy define and restrict chaplains' roles and responsibilities, the daily activities of a chaplain are, in and of themselves, a fascinating study in the influence of faith and spirituality in modern warfare. There are thousands of personal stories of men and women whose lives were touched—physically, mentally, and spiritually—by chaplains during situations of armed combat.

The U.S. military chaplaincy is the embodiment of pluralistic cooperation among religious faiths that serve in defense of the people and government of the United States. According to Joint Publication 105 (JP-105) from the Department of Defense, "The Services maintain chaplaincies to accommodate religious needs, to support welfare and enhance morale, and to help the command understand the complexities of religion with regard to its personnel and mission, as appropriate. As military members, chaplains are uniquely positioned to assist Service members, their families, and other authorized personnel with the challenges of military service as advocates of spiritual, moral, and ethical maturity and resiliency. Uniformed chaplaincies are essential in fulfilling the governments, and especially the responsibilities of the Department of Defense to all members of the Armed Forces of the United States."[1]

With this statement in mind, and against the context of the past decade of active warfare in Afghanistan, Iraq, and beyond, this chapter seeks to provide an overview of the history of U.S. military chaplains, their roots in deeper historical chaplaincies, the context of their current ministry, and some of the most pressing issues that chaplains—as individuals and as an institution—will face in the years to come.

WHAT IS A CHAPLAIN?

The mandate of the U.S. military chaplaincy is to ensure that the free exercise of religion is supported in all military settings. The chaplaincy, as it is organized in each of the services and through individual chaplains, is required to provide basic enabling services to ensure that all military members, regardless of their faith community, are able to maintain their religious practices while serving in the U.S. Armed Forces. Chaplains are advocates of spiritual, moral, and ethical maturity and resiliency and are considered militarily essential and inherently governmental in nature, thus fulfilling the government's robust responsibilities to those who serve. What this means is that the government understands that the chaplain serves the individual military person as well as the national security interests of the United States.

Chaplains are ordained clergy—priests, pastors, rabbis, imams, ministers—who are recommended to the various military services by an "endorsing agency." The endorsing agency is the official religious body that credentials chaplains as representing that faith group. Endorsing agencies are vetted through the Department of Defense and must meet specific criteria—such as number of adherents, history, educational credentials, vesting and ordination (a list of these endorsing agencies and references regarding the process of endorsement is included at the end of this chapter). Chaplains are commissioned military officers and as such are subject to the same requirements for service as other commissioned officers with regard to age, education, and physical fitness. After formal acceptance into the military and then the chaplaincy, they are appointed as officers in the army, navy, Marines, air force, or Coast Guard.

As of the beginning of 2013, there were approximately three thousand active-duty military chaplains (army 1,580, navy 800, air force 549) and two thousand reservists. The U.S. Marine Corps chaplains are part of the navy chaplaincy and are allowed to wear either navy or Marine Corps uniforms when serving in the Marines. Chaplains serve over three million service members and are rather evenly split between land-based and sea-based forces. Women represent approximately 10 percent of chaplains. The most common distinctions between faiths are Catholic and Protestant, but representation is misleading, as there are approximately 175 different religions or denominations represented in the chaplaincy. The percentage of those deployed overseas at any one time is estimated to be approximately 20 percent.[2]

HISTORY

At a fundamental level, the presence of clergy on and off the battlefield in times of war is a very natural association: both religion and war are about life and death. Religion provides reason for life and death. War is about who, or what societies, live or die. Military members are forced to think about *just war, justice in war,* and the law of armed conflict simply as part of their daily work. If there is a dearth of institutionalized handling of the topic of religion and warfare, it is not because there is no logical association or even that individual citizens and soldiers are unaware of the relationship.

The history of war includes the reality that kings, emperors, and warriors often took a sage, religious, or spiritual leader with them into combat. Studies of tribal warfare give primary evidence of the role of a shaman before, during, and after war, a role separate from that of tribal warrior or chief. Advice or counsel for commanders from a spiritual person is also known to be a part of the history of ancient India, China, Greece, and Rome and the Aztec and Mayan empires. An illustration drawn from biblical history is that of Moses, the military commander, and Aaron, the spiritual leader.

In the past, the religious person in warfare generally had the job of advising the ruler prior to war as to whether that war was just and righteous, helping to prepare the leader for war by justifying the war in eternal terms, defining the enemy as against goodness and life itself, sanctifying and blessing weapons, and even going into battle with the warrior-prince. Postwar ceremonies invariably called on the religious personage to cleanse the living warrior who had spilled blood and sanctify the dead. It is a rich, often forgotten history. The chaplain may be the modern version of this, although the places and perspectives have changed.[3]

The formal history of the use of chaplains between the time of Constantine and the Council of Ratisbon in A.D. 742 is either undocumented or unknown. It can be assumed that the religious councilors, pastors, ministers, or priests had a role in military activities. The formal authorization in 742 may have been a nod to that reality. It also signified that clergy could be officially authorized and that their service was recognized as part of the duty of the church. It was recorded that Pope Urban II (b. 1095) assigned Bishop Adhemar to be his personal representative in the Crusades. Throughout those campaigns, religious personages—both formally authorized and volunteers—accompanied the Crusaders and provided solace for the weary, comfort for the dying, relief services for pilgrims, penance for transgressions, cleansing for those who had killed, and hospitals to treat the wounded (notably for leprosy), and they gave sermons to encourage the fighting spirit.[4] Through the Middle Ages, including the tragic period of the Inquisition and again during the European wars of religion, clergy could be found alongside their "flock" or serving the state in a wide range of activities. Motives, whether spiritual or temporal, can only be the subject of conjecture and are assumed to be widely diverse.

As for the United States, chaplains have served in every war that has been fought. From the late seventeenth century onward, clergy or religious personages provided religious observances and counseling during intermittent frontier wars and the French and Indian Wars (1756–1763) and carried both weapons and Bibles. Clergy were present on both sides during the American Revolutionary War. Many served in the Regular Army, but service in militias was also common. Although most signed up in order to spiritually minister to the troops, their service was paid and recognized as that of a soldier or sailor.

The U.S. Army Chaplain Corps was established in July 1775 by the Continental Congress. George Washington issued the order that "the honorable Continental Congress, having been pleased to allow a Chaplain to each regiment, are directed to procure Chaplains accordingly; persons of good character and exemplary lives—to see that all inferior officers and soldiers pay them a suitable respect and attend carefully upon religious exercise."

It is noted that the pay was twenty dollars a month. Regimental commanders were to find their own chaplain, and there were no stipulations as to denomination, church, ordination, or education. Upon being nominated by a unit commander in the Continental Army, a chaplain was issued the commission by Congress. Colonial governors also appointed chaplains to serve in their respective militias. A total of 219 chaplains are known to have served in the revolution on the side of the colonials; 111 were in the Continental Army.

In November of 1775, the Continental Navy established the Chaplain Corps to provide religious services, but the navy itself was disbanded in 1783 as an expendable luxury.[5] The navy was reestablished by the Navy Act of 1794, and Reverend Benjamin Balch is believed to have been commissioned as the first official navy chaplain on October 22, 1799. The second article of the Navy Regulation of 1785 orders that "the Commanders of the ships of the thirteen United Colonies are to take care that divine services be performed twice a day on board, and a sermon preached on Sundays, unless bad weather or other extraordinary accidents prevent." In 1841 general regulations mandated that ordination and good moral character should be the characteristics of navy chaplains, a regulation that still stands. As of 2013, the navy chaplaincy has a mission statement, a list of priorities for service, guiding principles, a vision statement, and a code of ethics.[6]

Historical information for the periods between 1799 and 1880 regarding the number of chaplains, denominational affiliation, and job descriptions is sketchy. The records are unclear possibly because chaplains were commissioned as officers, not chaplains. Evidently the chaplaincy, as an institution, was not centralized enough to maintain a central registry for either the army or the navy.

During the American Civil War, the number of clergy who served unofficially or chaplains who served officially is equally unclear. Yet the historical records indicate that both clergy and chaplains were in evidence at every battle and in every campaign. Religious leaders, like the rest of the country, were split over the issues of secession and slavery and took up the cause on both sides. The clergy in small towns across the United States supported families, communities, and returning veterans and helped provide medical care and education. They took those skills onto the battlefield—but it was generally as clergy in an unofficial capacity. Some served with the units from their own states, others took on hospital and prison duties, and yet others simply buried the dead.[7]

It was not until 1880 that army and navy chaplains started to keep separate military records. The increasing formalization of the U.S. military chaplaincy in the First and Second World Wars resulted in better, but not great, record keeping. The U.S. Army and Marines lost one hundred chaplains in World War II, a casualty rate greater than any other branch except infantry and army air corps, suggesting that chaplains were serving their flocks on the front lines.

The first army chaplain in Vietnam arrived on February 26, 1962, and by 1967 over three hundred army chaplains served in the field. There were seven hundred U.S. Navy chaplains who served in Vietnam, many with Marine Corps units in the midst of combat operations. A total of eighty-two chaplains were awarded Purple Hearts and twenty-six awarded Silver Stars. While ministry to the troops was their overriding concern, the chaplains also aided the Vietnamese people by helping supply clothing, food, and money for schools, orphanages, and medical support. Thanks to the helicopter, chaplains visited the far-flung reaches of the Vietnamese countryside; with portable field kits, they set up and conducted services wherever needed. In essence, the chaplains did whatever they could to support the troops and the people in the wartime environment.[8]

U.S. PUBLIC RELIGIOUS PREFERENCES
AND REPRESENTATION IN THE U.S. MILITARY

This brings us to the following questions: What are the religious preferences of U.S. military personnel? And does the U.S. military chaplaincy reflect the general population's religious preferences? The population of the United States is the most religiously diverse in the world. It stands to reason that the past and present profile of the U.S. military, if it represents demographically the rest of the country, would reflect that same religious diversity. There are few official government statistics available on the religious affiliation of the civilian population, as the government is precluded by law from census and population surveys that inquire about religion. Most statistics concerning the American general public in relation to religious adherence, membership, beliefs, and attitudes are collected by public-research institutes, universities, or religious organizations and subsequently vary in quality.

The original and primary reason for asking individuals for their "religion" was to provide appropriate burial rites (most people are familiar with the "dog tags" that basically required a soldier to choose a religion before going into combat). That was the official rationale until 1984, when statistics on religious affiliation of military members were first collected by the Department of Defense in order to satisfy the new legal requirement within the DOD for "religious accommodation" for all service personnel.[9]

As shown in table 2.1, the religious preferences of U.S. military personnel are roughly equivalent to that of the civilian population.

Table 2.1.　Religious Preferences of the U.S. Population and Military Personnel

Religious Preference	Military	Civilians	
All preferences	100	Ages 20–39	Ages 18+
Protestant	35	45	53
Catholic/Orthodox	22	26	25
Other Christian	11	3	2
Atheist/no religion	21	19	
Jewish	—	1	2
Muslim/Islam	—	1	1
Buddhist/Hindu		2	1
Other religions	11	3	2

Source: DOD Defense Manpower Data Center for the information on military preferences; the civilian preference data is taken from a variety of public and private sources.

THE "JOB" OF THE U.S. MILITARY CHAPLAIN

According to the Department of Defense Instruction (DODI), chaplains "must provide pastoral care, counseling, and coaching which attend to personal and relational needs. This includes relational counseling by chaplains which may be enhanced by their proximity and immediate presence, distinguished by confidentiality, and imbued with professional wisdom and genuine respect for human beings. Such counseling is most effective when based on strong relationships developed in the context of shared life in the same unit. Some examples of care are: work-space visitation, counseling, coaching on military life, pre- and post-deployment training for Service members and their families, crisis prevention and response, family-life programs, memorial observances, and combat-casualty care."[10]

Chaplains have a wide range of responsibilities; some of the responsibilities are inherent in the spiritual nature of the chaplaincy, and some directly related to DOD directives. Those responsibilities related to the chaplain may be preservation and maintenance of a personal spiritual life, continuation of education regarding the changing nature of warfare, and maintenance of communication with the denominational endorser, the "chain of command," fellow chaplains, family, friends, and the soldiers, sailors, and Marines whom the chaplain serves.

A religious congregation in the United States assumes a congregation with commonalities; in the Department of Defense, no such assumption is possible. The chaplain is responsible for provision of services to all religions, denominations, and faith groups. For instance, a Jewish chaplain must see to it that the Baptists in his military unit have what they need to ensure their "free exercise of religion." This often requires not only a great deal of education but also imagination, cooperation, and coordination between and among the faith groups. But the overall idea is that the individual soldier, sailor, Marine, guardsman, or airman has spiritual needs that can and should be met.

Military ministry is different from "church" or other types of parochial ministry. Chaplains rotate in and out of chapel (church) leadership based on military priorities, not congregational preference. The chaplain is not "called" by a church as such, but is instead under contract with the U.S. government. Chaplains must minister to service personnel and their families regardless of their particular church affiliation, making it by design a more global, diverse, and pluralistic ministry. Funding for the chaplains is not dependent on denominational or individual contributions, but rather on the U.S. taxpayer (the chaplaincy is funded by appropriated and nonappropriated dollars through the Department of Defense). Commanders have the official responsibility to provide for the free exercise of religion for all service personnel and must budget accordingly for facilities, programs, and materials. Service members and their families may contribute at their discretion to a special fund to support chapel activities and beneficent activities.

The chapel, generally located on a military base, is legally a "community" building and not designated as a religious facility. But military chaplains do not minister from a single, stationary location. Formal chapel-worship events and services are scheduled to support the particular regimens of duty stations and training regimes or the operational tempo. Services may be held in tents, from the backs of pickup trucks, underground, and in a variety of other places.

Church governance in the civilian sector varies considerably, but the chaplaincy is constrained by statutes and directives of the U.S. government.

Religious programs are required to meet the needs of all assigned person-nel regardless of their faith group. Chaplains are accountable for ministry practice to all faiths while serving as commissioned officers under the rank, structure, and authority of the Department of Defense, their commander, the endorsing agency, and the supervisory chaplain. The military chaplain is unique and remarkable in that he or she is committed to serve God and man in the most variable and difficult of circumstances. The word *pluralism* does not begin to cover it.

Military duties for chaplains include (but are not limited to) provision of liturgical services, music, literature, counseling, marriages, burials, hospital duty, prison duty, humanitarian projects, and provision of ministry to de-pendents. Chaplains serve as a conduit of information between individual service personnel and their homes and families. Incredibly, they carry out these duties willingly and for a wide diversity of believers.

Chaplains also provide professional guidance and advice to commanders, staff, and all military personnel on issues of spirituality, religious dynam-ics, ethics and morality, armed-conflict regulation, resiliency, and personal well-being. Chaplains serve under the command of a senior officer and are required to protect freedom of religion and freedom of worship while avoid-ing activities that create a preference for any specific religion.

In addition, it must be remembered that the chaplain serves the command and commander. The commander may task the chaplain with other respon-sibilities or restrict the chaplains in areas where military necessity requires such restrictions. There is a delicate balance here: sometimes the command-ers do not know the abilities and restrictions of chaplains. In a combat zone, the chaplains are simply expected to "do their job" in the same way a logistic officer or fire officer is doing theirs—without much direct supervision other than "commander's intent." In areas of operations where an indigenous religion is a primary concern, chaplains often have the position and skills to engage (with the commander's guidance) in negotiations, conversations, and community interaction. (It is important to note that the chaplain is part of a team that advises the commander and that the commander is under no obligation to take the chaplain's advice.)[11]

CHALLENGES OF WORKING IN A
WAR ZONE WITHOUT A WEAPON

The Geneva Convention, Article 24, and the Geneva Protocols of 1977 identify chaplains as protected personnel in their function and capacity as ministers of religion. If chaplains are captured, they are expected to continue in their religious capacity as "retained personnel," not as prisoners of war, and are to be repatriated as soon as is possible. That said, *noncombatant status does not abrogate the right to "self-defense."* In fact, most U.S. military chaplains carried weapons up to and during World War I. However, JP 1-05, "Religious Affairs in Joint Operations," specifically precludes any activity taken by a chaplain that would undermine the noncombatant status. This includes anything related to direct targeting—that is, intelligence collection and analysis, wearing or using a weapon (except in self-defense), and direct conversation or negotiation with indigenous leaders except at the direct request of the commander.

CHALLENGES INHERENT IN THE
RELATIONSHIP BETWEEN CHURCH AND STATE

On the surface, it would seem that the U.S. military chaplaincy is dangerously close to being a religious institution established by the state. Yet this would be a serious misreading of both policy and practice. The chaplaincy is in direct support of free exercise and presents no threat to the establishment clause.

Nevertheless, some argue that the United States is a secular state and that the military should reflect the secular arrangements as codified in the U.S. Constitution with the concomitant principle of separation of church and state. They hold that since the chaplaincy is established by the state (through the DOD), it, in effect, represents the establishment of religion.[12] The chaplaincy thus oversteps Constitutional boundaries. Another side argument is based on the tagline "freedom *from* religion" and holds that the Constitution should protect citizens from all religion and advocate for a secular—that is, atheistic or a-religious—government.

Others hold that the writers of the U.S. Constitution were extremely careful not to establish an official church that would link the power and resources of the government with the power and resources of a specific church or religion but wanted to ensure that citizens could have freedom of religion—that is, that they were able to "freely exercise." It was the government's responsibility to ensure that this freedom was supported. To this way of thinking, the chaplaincy ensures that everyone in the U.S. military has religious support sufficient to ensure his or her right to worship. This debate will not be settled in these pages, but suffice it to note that the military, including the chaplaincy, has had to defend its role as providing for the free exercise of religion and is extremely sensitive to overstepping its boundaries.

There are, of course, risks associated with a government-supported chaplaincy. One set of problems comes from those who would leverage the chaplaincy to support DOD programs. Another group would like to leverage the position of the chaplaincy to support specific religious agendas. There is another group that seems to be simply antireligion and has become noise in the system. The countermeasures come from the chaplaincy itself: if it were to engage in overtly political or religious agendas not in support of "free exercise," the very existence of the chaplaincy would be in jeopardy.

A more serious and perplexing question is whether the chaplaincy brings the blessings of religion to the war. Do chaplains, simply by being there, encourage, support, or "bless" war?[13] The chaplains generally contend that they are not there to bless war itself but to support the individual right of constitutionally guaranteed freedom of religion. Nevertheless, it is a difficult question. In his book *The Faith of the American Soldier*, Stephen Mansfield, for one, seems to support the idea that God is on the side of the United States, its mission, and, therefore, the soldiers.[14] Pictures of chaplains blessing helmets, tanks, and battlefields lend credence to his argument. Most chaplains struggle with this question and practice discretion in their daily activities.

UNEQUAL TREATMENT OF RELIGIOUS MINORITIES

There is a perception that service personnel from some religions fare better than others insofar as advancement and promotion. There is no concrete evidence of this, in part because complaints are handled by commanders, not chaplains, and settled as military issues. Although religious diversity has been a reality since 1775, religious differences have been downplayed in favor of military discipline throughout the course of U.S. military history. The codification of the accommodation of differing religions was only officially institutionalized in 2009 with DOD Directive 1300.17, which required that the DOD "promote an environment free from personal, social, or institutional barriers that prevent Service members from rising to the highest level of responsibility possible. In this environment, Service members shall be evaluated only on individual merit, fitness, and capability. Unlawful discrimination against individuals or groups based on race, color, religion, sex, or national origin is contrary to good order and discipline and counterproductive to combat readiness and mission accomplishment and shall not be condoned."[15] Quite simply, the commander is focused on "military necessity" and is not in any way a "social engineer."[16]

LEVEL OF PRESSURE BY
COMMANDERS REGARDING RELIGION

Many of the recent controversies have focused on whether individuals in command positions have been too aggressive in urging others to participate in religious activities. These activities may be individual (such as invitation to a prayer meeting) or group (such as seeming to endorse a religious music festival or participating in prayers at burial ceremonies or other events where religion is peripheral rather than a central aspect of the event). In a 2002 interview with the Pew Forum on Religion and Public

Life, law professor Robert W. Tuttle suggested that "when thinking about these controversies, it's important to distinguish between mandatory and voluntary religious activities. All service academies used to require everyone to attend religious services. Although the U.S. Court of Appeals for the District of Columbia Circuit found this requirement unconstitutional in *Anderson v. Laird* (1972), the Naval Academy still holds pre-meal prayers, and attendance at these meals is required." The chaplains are often called up to give "official prayers" at various times, including promotions, special presentations of honors, graduations, and internments. The practice varies widely across the services and often depends on whether the units are in deployed areas.[17]

Section 5.2 of DOD Directive 1304.19 stipulates that the secretaries of the military departments shall provide "pertinent guidance to ensure that persons appointed as chaplains meet the minimum professional and educational qualifications prescribed in reference (d) and other pertinent guidance. The Secretaries of each of the military services may impose additional requirements."[18] The army and navy websites list the pertinent professional and educational requirements in addition to the standard eligibility requirements for any other military officer. Some of the major denominations report difficulty in finding clergy to serve in the military as a result of disapproval of the wars in Iraq and Afghanistan and a general unfamiliarity with serving in a military environment, as well as the physical rigors of military life.

ASSESSMENT AND EVIDENCE

One of the major problems facing the chaplaincy is the lack of scientific evidence that spirituality is directly related to ethical or moral behavior or resiliency. There is no specific research on whether a self-defined spiritual or religious individual is more moral or behaves more ethically than one who is not. Academics, commanders, and chaplains pontificate as if it were axiomatic, but the evidence is not there. However, chaplains work by faith grounded on the premise that spirituality supports life forces, that the social and cultural aspects of worship support hope and strength, and that the counseling aspect provides someone who cares.

DISBANDING THE CHAPLAINCY

The final challenge to military chaplaincy comes not from within but from without—namely, from those who believe that the chaplaincy should be civilianized. The argument is that it would reduce the problem encountered by church-state controversies, that civilian chaplains would be less expensive, and that the number of chaplains would be of a higher quality because they would not have to sign up for a career but for short-term service. This would mitigate the costly effects of burnout and career stagnation. Two major arguments against civilianization have thus far won the day: (1) the business of war is difficult and not meant for amateurs, and (2) the services require a stable, trained, professional clergy willing and able to take on some of the nation's most difficult problems. There is another, perhaps more subtle, argument constructed from both history and experience: that commanders who are responsible for war and the conduct of war can use the presence of spiritually minded men and women, personally and professionally.

No one would argue that the U.S. chaplaincy is a perfect institution manned by perfect individuals, but in the view of those who serve with them, they may be some of the country's finest professionals. As with any human institution, there are problems. Most of the problems of the chaplaincy, like the problems faced by many others, are rooted in the nature of bureaucratic institutions and simply need integrity and stamina and intelligence to solve. Under any situation of change, institutional inefficiency, or public concern, the U.S. chaplaincy must maintain a foundation of religious integrity. That spiritual, moral, and ethical leadership is foundational to support for the free exercise of religion. However, the chaplaincy also needs to be adaptable, flexible, and responsive in order to adapt to the changes and challenges of modern warfare.

CHAPTER SOURCES

References: Department of Defense

1. Federal Statutory Laws
   a. Goldwater-Nichols Department of Defense Reorganization Act of 1986, Public Law 99-433 (codified in various sections of Title 10 USC, especially Sections 164 and 167).
   b. Title 10, USC, "Armed Forces," Sections 3073, 3547, 5142, and 8067.
   c. Title 14, USC, "Coast Guard," Part I, Chapter I, Section 3, and VII, Section 145.
   d. Title 32, USC, "National Guard," Section 502 (f).
   e. Title 50, USC, "War and National Defense."

2. Department of Defense Directives and Instructions
   a. DODI 1300.17, *Accommodation of Religious Practices within the Military Services.*
   b. DODD 1304.19, *Appointment of Chaplains for the Military Departments.*
   c. DODD 3000.5, *Military Support for Stability, Security, Transition, and Reconstruction (SSTR) Operations.*

    d. DODD 5100.01, *Functions of the Department of Defense and Its Major Components.*

    e. DODI 1000.1, *Identity Cards Required by the Geneva Conventions.*

    f. DODI 1300.19, *DOD Joint Officer Management Program.*

    g. DODI 1304.28, *Guidance for the Appointment of Chaplains for the Military Departments.*

    h. DODI 5100.73, *Major DOD Headquarters Activities.*

    i. DODI 5120.08, *Armed Forces Chaplains Board.*

3. Chairman of the Joint Chiefs of Staff Instructions and Manuals

    a. Chairman of the Joint Chiefs of Staff Instruction (CJCSI) 1301.01C, *Individual Augmentation Procedures.*

    b. CJCSI 1800.01C, *Officer Professional Military Education Policy.*

    c. CJCSI 3150.25D, *Joint Lessons Learned Program.*

    d. CJCSI 3500.01E, *Joint Training Policy and Guidance for the Armed Forces of the United States.*

    e. CJCSM 3122.01A, *Joint Operation Planning and Execution System (JOPES), Volume I: Planning Policies and Procedures, Enclosure R.*

    f. CJCSM 3122.02C, *Joint Operation Planning and Execution System, Volume III: Crisis Action Time-Phased Force and Deployment Data Development and Deployment Execution.*

    g. CJCSM 3122.03C, *Joint Operation Planning and Execution System, Volume II: Supplemental Planning Formats.*

    h. CJCSM 3500.03B, *Joint Training Manual for the Armed Forces of the United States.*

    i. CJCSM 3500.04E, *Universal Joint Task Manual.*

4. Joint Publications

    a. JP 1, *Doctrine for the Armed Forces of the United States.*

    b. JP 1-02, *Department of Defense Dictionary of Military and Associated Terms.*

    c. JP 3-0, *Joint Operations.*

    d. JP 3-08, *Inter-organizational Coordination During Joint Operations.*

    e. JP 3-16, *Multinational Operations.*

    f. JP 3-27, *Homeland Defense.*

    g. JP 3-28, *Civil Support.*

    h. JP 3-29, *Foreign Humanitarian Assistance.*

    i. JP 3-33, *Joint Task Force Headquarters.*

    j. JP 3-57, *Civil-Military Operations.*

    k. JP 3-61, *Public Affairs.*

    l. JP 4-06, *Mortuary Affairs.*

    m. JP 5-0, *Joint Operation Planning.*

5. Army Publications

   a. Army Regulation 165-1, *Chaplain Activities in the United States Army.*
   b. FM 1-05, *Religious Support.*

6. Navy Publications

   a. Secretary of the Navy Instruction 1730.7, *Religious Ministry Support within the Department of the Navy.*
   b. Naval Warfare Publication 1-05, *Religious Ministry in the United States Navy.*
   c. Chief of Naval Operations Instruction 1730.1D, *Religious Ministry in the Navy.*

7. Air Force Publications

   a. Air Force Policy Directive 52-1, *Chaplain Service.*
   b. Air Force Instruction 52-101, *Chaplain Service Planning and Organizing.*
   c. Air Force Instruction 52-104, *Chaplain Service Readiness.*

8. Marine Corps Publications

   a. Marine Corps Manual, *Chaplains and Religious Affairs.*
   b. Marine Corps Warfighting Publication 6-12, *Religious Ministry Support in the USMC.*
   c. Marine Corps Reference Publication (MCRP) 6-12B, *Religious Lay Leaders Handbook.*
   d. MCRP 6-12A, *Religious Ministry Team Handbook.*
   e. MCRP 6-12C, *Commanders Handbook for Religious Ministry Support.*

9. Coast Guard Publication

   Commandant, United States Coast Guard Instruction M1730.4B, *Religious Ministries within the Coast Guard.*

Proceedings

International Society of Military Ethics, Conference Proceedings, "Religion and the Military," January 25–26, 2007, http://isme.tamu.edu/ISME07/isme07.html.

Table 2.2.   Religion of Active-Duty Personnel by Service (No Coast Guard) as of March 31, 2010

Total (Officer and Enlisted)	USA	USN	USMC	USAF	Total
Advent Christian Church	204	115	113	107	539
Jehovah's Witnesses	172	113	93	82	460
Native American	0	41	246	0	287
Seventh Day Adventist	1,829	1,032	570	971	4,402
Adventist Churches	0	10	12	0	22
American Baptist Churches in the USA	2,733	383	378	869	4,363
Baptist Churches	74,921	34,992	18,905	40,208	169,026
Southern Baptist Convention	7,220	2,318	1,343	5,614	16,495
Free Will Baptist Churches	690	340	103	171	1,304
General Association of General Baptists	512	9	0	40	561
National Baptist Convention of America	133	6	4	16	159
Progressive National Baptist Convention, Inc.	16	5	1	7	29
General Association of Regular Baptist Church	198	13	21	43	275
American Baptist Conference	172	23	39	160	394
National Baptist Convention, USA, Inc.	93	6	3	27	129
Catholic Churches	0	1,054	5,626	0	6,680
Roman Catholic Church	105,457	67,206	42,591	67,621	282,875
Church of Jesus Christ of Latter-day Saints	7,324	2,706	2,451	5,797	18,278
Reorganized Church of Latter-day Saints	74	36	18	42	170
Anglican Churches	0	29	45	0	74
Episcopal Church	3,150	1,984	1,226	1,917	8,277
Episcopal Churches	0	53	373	0	426
Reformed Episcopal Church	117	69	44	176	406
Independent Churches Affiliated	19	9	2	16	46
Independent Fundamental Bible Churches	7	18	22	67	114
Independent Fundamental Churches of America	38	2	3	11	54
Fundamentalist Churches	0	3	5	1	9
Associated Gospel Churches	23	2	1	5	31
Christian Church and Churches of Christ	7,342	770	92	2,466	10,670
Christian Church Disciples of Christ	4,031	2,063	964	441	7,499
Tioga River Christian Conference	0	0	0	1	1

(continued)

Table 2.2. *(continued)*

Total (Officer and Enlisted)	USA	USN	USMC	USAF	Total
Church of Christ	6,385	1,495	683	2,176	10,739
Church of God (Anderson, IN)	10	16	22	54	102
Churches of Christ in Christian Union	224	15	9	6	254
Holiness Churches	0	18	33	0	51
Church of the Nazarene	703	252	172	522	1,649
Salvation Army	37	27	33	25	122
Islam	1,827	739	437	650	3,653
Judaism (Jewish)	1,869	1,047	722	1,141	4,779
Buddhism	2,024	1,174	927	1,387	5,512
Baha'i Faith	0	20	19	0	39
Hinduism	456	207	86	200	949
Eastern Religions	0	6	15	0	21
Evangelical Lutheran Church in America	500	172	255	843	1,770
Lutheran Churches	10,957	6,375	3,860	8,093	29,285
Lutheran Church Missouri Synod	408	187	409	1,168	2,172
Christian Methodist Episcopal Church	220	139	154	455	968
African Methodist Episcopal Church	511	207	138	472	1,328
Methodist Churches	13,488	18,533	3,588	6,071	41,680
Free Methodist Church of North America	172	12	16	67	267
Moravian Churches	42	17	17	33	109
United Methodist Church	734	339	376	4,172	5,621
Wesleyan Church	64	34	32	78	208
African Methodist Episcopal Zion Church	72	16	33	114	235
Christian, No Denominational Preference	105,039	48,841	51,912	79,167	284,959
Eastern Orthodox Churches	482	260	209	275	1,226
Orthodox Churches	86	157	45	53	341
Assemblies of God	1,422	564	436	1,567	3,989
Church of God in Christ	847	237	144	504	1,732
Full Gospel	6,650	47	27	47	6,771
International Church of the Foursquare Gospel	37	14	13	37	101
Church of God and Prophecy	32	13	19	28	92
Pentecostal Holiness Church International	648	188	209	500	1,545
Pentecostal Church of God	251	85	118	161	615
Pentecostal Churches	2	2,524	1,860	2,896	7,282
Open Bible Standard Churches, Inc.	11	4	2	29	46

Total (Officer and Enlisted)	USA	USN	USMC	USAF	Total
Churches of God					
(Cleveland, TN)	1,079	386	192	544	2,201
United Pentecostal					
Church International	122	46	83	153	404
Brethren Churches	157	195	92	70	514
Friends (Quakers)	40	39	85	96	260
European-Free Churches	0	0	4	0	4
Schwenkfelder Churches	2	1	2	0	5
Cumberland Presbyterian					
Church	14	8	4	19	45
Congregational Churches	146	91	21	47	305
Christian Reformed Church					
in North America	278	49	113	152	592
Reformed Church in America	21	8	7	35	71
Churches of God General					
Conference	26	4	11	17	58
Presbyterian Church in					
America	106	120	172	823	1,221
Presbyterian Church (USA)	197	301	120	2,595	3,213
Reformed and Presbyterian					
Churches	4,454	2,151	1,227	182	8,014
United Church of Christ	199	110	58	252	619
First Church of Christ Scientist	381	116	59	84	640
Protestant, no denominational					
preference	13,666	5,709	4,743	14,646	38,764
Protestant, other churches	3,704	1,436	957	1,727	7,824
Unitarian Universalist	168	123	49	188	528
Asbury Bible Churches	0	0	4	1	5
Plymouth Brethren	5	2	3	4	14
Evangelical Covenant Church	71	35	10	42	158
Evangelical Free Church					
of America	193	145	59	240	637
Christian and Missionary					
Alliance	136	23	63	156	378
Bible Protestant Church	44	29	42	138	253
Evangelical Churches	240	124	41	122	527
Iglesia Ni Christo	0	25	20	0	45
New Age Churches	0	8	0	0	8
Unclassified religions	4,082	1,346	745	1,769	7,942
Wicca (Witchcraft)	399	264	490	1,443	2,596
Magick and Spiritualist	2	55	2	5	64
Atheist	2,520	695	1,479	2,766	7,460
Agnostic	0	282	1,249	0	1,531
No religious preference	103,207	90,518	32,185	59,583	285,493
Unknown	47,505	20,457	16,251	3,720	87,933
Total	**555,849**	**324,292**	**202,966**	**331,486**	**1,414,593**

Source: Active Duty Personnel Inventory File. Produced by DMDC on May 12, 2010. DRS# 24012.

Table 2.3. Religion of Active Duty Personnel by Service (No Coast Guard) as of September 30, 2010

Total (Officer and Enlisted)	USA	USN	USMC	USAF	Total
Advent Christian Church	205	120	113	101	539
Jehovah's Witnesses	164	113	96	83	456
Native American	0	42	227	0	269
Seventh Day Adventist	1,829	1,025	577	947	4,378
Adventist Churches	0	10	12	0	22
American Baptist Churches in the USA	2,660	350	349	850	4,209
Baptist Churches	73,790	33,796	18,394	38,850	164,830
Southern Baptist Convention	7,101	2,248	1,295	5,479	16,123
Free Will Baptist Churches	672	326	93	170	1,261
General Association of General Baptists	499	11	0	39	549
National Baptist Convention of America	136	6	4	17	163
Progressive National Baptist Convention, Inc.	16	7	1	6	30
General Association of Regular Baptist Churches	199	17	20	41	277
American Baptist Conference	172	21	37	150	380
National Baptist Convention, USA, Inc.	93	6	3	29	131
Catholic Churches	0	1,479	5,401	0	6,880
Roman Catholic Church	106,211	66,070	42,117	66,639	281,037
Church of Jesus Christ of Latter-day Saints (Mormons)	7,455	2,723	2,416	5,821	18,415
Reorganized Church of Latter-day Saints	74	37	17	42	170
Anglican Churches	0	34	41	0	75
Episcopal Church	3,108	1,940	1,167	1,821	8,036
Episcopal Churches	0	59	357	0	416
Reformed Episcopal Church	113	67	43	167	390
Independent Churches Affiliated	17	9	2	18	46
Independent Fundamental Bible Churches	10	21	19	74	124
Independent Fundamental Churches of America	34	3	3	9	49
Fundamentalist Churches	0	4	5	2	11
Associated Gospel Churches	20	3	1	5	29
Christian Church and Churches of Christ	7,170	847	87	2,501	10,605
Christian Church Disciples of Christ	4,110	2,473	955	435	7,973
Tioga River Christian Conference	0	0	0	1	1

Total (Officer and Enlisted)	USA	USN	USMC	USAF	Total
Church of Christ	6,402	1,417	659	2,139	10,617
Church of God (Anderson, IN)	12	20	20	51	103
Churches of Christ in Christian Union	219	15	7	5	246
Holiness Churches	0	20	30	0	50
Church of the Nazarene	696	248	173	503	1,620
Salvation Army	37	27	38	26	128
Islam	1,838	750	433	643	3,664
Judaism (Jewish)	1,869	1,074	691	1,137	4,771
Buddhism	2,113	1,214	934	1,363	5,624
Baha'i Faith	0	20	19	0	39
Hinduism	515	214	97	194	1,020
Eastern Religions	0	8	14	0	22
Evangelical Lutheran Church in America	530	173	243	848	1,794
Lutheran Churches	10,859	6,291	3,763	7,852	28,765
Lutheran Church Missouri Synod	424	196	408	1,188	2,216
Christian Methodist Episcopal Church	237	134	159	470	1,000
African Methodist Episcopal Church	503	196	134	443	1,276
Methodist Churches	13,288	17,558	3,414	5,874	40,134
Free Methodist Church of North America	164	12	15	62	253
Moravian Churches	41	14	14	30	99
United Methodist Church	767	372	362	4,036	5,537
Wesleyan Church	61	37	28	77	203
African Methodist Episcopal Zion Church	72	16	37	108	233
Christian, no denominational preference	110,930	51,335	53,177	80,961	296,403
Eastern Orthodox Churches	487	255	217	268	1,227
Orthodox Churches	82	159	44	52	337
Assemblies of God	1,428	539	416	1,524	3,907
Church of God in Christ	846	229	141	487	1,703
Full Gospel	6,517	51	28	42	6,638
International Church of the Foursquare Gospel	37	13	13	34	97
Church of God and Prophecy	31	12	21	29	93
Pentecostal Holiness Church International	643	178	201	473	1,495
Pentecostal Church of God	255	97	119	155	626
Pentecostal Churches	2	2,394	1,771	2,809	6,976
Open Bible Standard Churches, Inc.	9	3	3	27	42

(continued)

Table 2.3. *(continued)*

Total (Officer and Enlisted)	USA	USN	USMC	USAF	Total
Churches of God (Cleveland, TN)	1,136	340	181	528	2,185
United Pentecostal Church International	120	47	86	148	401
Brethren Churches	149	181	99	67	496
Friends (Quakers)	36	37	87	99	259
European-Free Churches	0	0	2	0	2
Schwenkfelder Churches	2	1	2	1	6
Cumberland Presbyterian Church	15	9	5	18	47
Congregational Churches	136	118	19	44	317
Christian Reformed Church in North America	280	46	115	153	594
Reformed Church in America	21	8	8	35	72
Churches of God General Conference	25	5	11	18	59
Presbyterian Church in America	104	139	167	816	1,226
Presbyterian Church (USA)	194	386	113	2,540	3,233
Reformed and Presbyterian Churches	4,424	1,996	1,185	182	7,787
United Church of Christ	206	106	54	243	609
First Church of Christ Scientist	398	105	55	78	636
Protestant, no denominational preference	13,593	5,613	4,574	14,163	37,943
Protestant, other churches	3,625	1,367	947	1,639	7,578
Unitarian Universalist	157	136	49	183	525
Asbury Bible Churches	0	0	5	2	7
Plymouth Brethren	4	2	3	4	13
Evangelical Covenant Church	67	34	10	38	149
Evangelical Free Church of America	199	142	55	235	631
Christian and Missionary Alliance	149	21	58	167	395
Bible Protestant Church	50	31	39	142	262
Evangelical Churches	245	128	39	120	532
Iglesia Ni Christo	0	30	21	0	51
New Age Churches	0	6	0	0	6
Unclassified religions	4,060	1,309	740	1,763	7,872
Wicca (Witchcraft)	407	281	454	1,417	2,559
Magick and Spiritualist	2	63	2	4	71
Atheist	2,594	720	1,487	2,931	7,732
Agnostic	0	417	1,247	0	1,664
No religious preference	103,808	89,330	32,255	59,759	285,152
Unknown	48,001	20,827	16,743	3,896	89,467
Total	**561,979**	**323,139**	**202,612**	**329,640**	**1,417,370**

Source: Active-Duty Personnel Inventory File. Produced by DMDC on November 9, 2010. DRS# 24012.

Department of Defense Directive Number 1304.19

June 11, 2004
Certified Current as of April 23, 2007
USD(P&R)
SUBJECT: Appointment of Chaplains for the Military Departments
References:

(a) DOD Directive 1304.19, "Appointment of Chaplains for the Military Services," September 18, 1993 (hereby canceled)
(b) DOD Directive 1332.31, "Administrative Separation of Chaplains Upon Loss of Professional Qualifications," October 16, 1981 (hereby canceled)
(c) DOD Instruction 1330.7, "Visits of Civilian Religious Leaders to Military Installations in Overseas Areas," April 26, 1974 (hereby canceled)
(d) DOD Instruction 1304.28, "Guidance for the Appointment of Chaplains for the Military Departments," June 11, 2004
(e) DOD Directive 5100.73, "Support of Headquarters of Combatant and Subordinate Joint Commands," November 15, 1999

1. REISSUANCE AND PURPOSE
   This Directive:
   1.1. Reissues reference (a) to update policy and responsibilities.
   1.2. Cancels references (b) and (c).
   1.3. Continues the educational and ecclesiastical requirements for appointing military chaplains.

2. APPLICABILITY
   This Directive applies to the Office of the Secretary of Defense, the Military Departments, (including the Coast Guard when it is operating as a Military Service in the Navy), the Chairman of the Joint Chiefs of Staff, the Combatant Commands, the Defense Agencies, the DOD Field Activities (hereafter referred to collectively as "the DOD Components"). The term "Military Departments," as used herein, refers to the Department of the Army, the Department of the Navy, *DODD 1304.19, June 11, 2004*, and the Department of the Air Force. The term "Military Services" as used herein refers to the U.S. Army, Navy, Air Force, and Marine Corps.

3. DEFINITIONS
   Terms used in this Directive are defined in DOD Instruction 1304.28 (reference (d)).

4. POLICY
   It is DOD policy that the Chaplaincies of the Military Departments:
   4.1. Are established to advise and assist commanders in the discharge
        of their responsibilities to provide for the free exercise of religion
        in the context of military service as guaranteed by the Constitu-
        tion, to assist commanders in managing religious affairs (DOD
        Directive 5100.73 (reference (e))), and to serve as the principal
        advisors to commanders for all issues regarding the impact of reli-
        gion on military operations.
   4.2. Shall serve a religiously diverse population. Within the military,
        commanders are required to provide comprehensive religious
        support to all authorized individuals within their areas of respon-
        sibility. Religious Organizations that choose to participate in the
        Chaplaincies recognize this command imperative and express
        willingness for their Religious Ministry Professionals (RMPs) to
        perform their professional duties as chaplains in cooperation with
        RMPs from other religious traditions.
   4.3. Requirements and details addressing the Chaplaincies of the Mili-
        tary Departments are found in reference (d).

5. RESPONSIBILITIES
   5.1. The Under Secretary of Defense for Personnel and Readiness shall
        issue additional implementing guidance, as appropriate.
   5.2. The Secretaries of the Military Departments shall adhere to this Di-
        rective, reference (d), and other pertinent guidance to ensure that
        persons appointed as chaplains meet the minimum professional
        and educational qualifications prescribed in reference (d) and
        other pertinent guidance. The Secretaries of the Military Depart-
        ments may impose additional professional requirements.

NOTES

1. U.S. Department of Defense, "Joint Publication 1-05: Religious Affairs in Joint Operations," November 20, 2009, http://www.dtic.mil/doctrine/new_pubs/jp1_05.pdf. See also Secretary of the Navy, "SECNAV Instruction 1730.10," January 23, 2009, available online at http://doni.daps.dla.mil/Directives/01000%20Military%20Personnel%20Support/01-700%20Morale,%20Community%20and%20Religious%20Services/1730.10.pdf.

2. Kim Philip Hansen discusses how chaplains handle religious diversity in *Military Chaplains and Religious Diversity* (New York: Palgrave Macmillan, 2012).

3. For a brief introduction to the history of chaplains, see Dennis R. Hoover and Douglas M. Johnston's *Religion and Foreign Affairs: Essential Readings* (Waco, TX: Baylor University Press, 2012), 264–65.

4. Ibid., 265.

5. E. B. Potter and Chester W. Nimitz, eds., *Sea Power* (Englewood Cliffs: Prentice Hall, 1960), 189.

6. America's Navy, "Chaplain Corps," http://www.chaplain.navy.mil/.

7. Randall M. Miller, Harry S. Stout, and Charles Reagan Wilson, eds., *Religion and the American Civil War* (New York: Oxford University Press, 1998).

8. First Battalion, 50th Infantry Association website, http://www.ichiban1.org/, accessed March 10, 2013.

9. This number does not include the business, intelligence, and nongovernmental organizations or academic institutions that directly or indirectly support the military forces of the United States.

10. U.S. Department of Defense, "Instruction 1304.28: Guidance for the Appointment of Chaplains for the Military Departments," June 11, 2004, updated March 20, 2014, available online at http://www.dtic.mil/whs/directives/corres/pdf/130428_2004_ch3.pdf.

11. The role of "chaplain as advisor to the commander" is discussed by some of this book's other chapter authors.

12. Isaac Kramnick and R. Laurence Moore take the view that the U.S. Constitution is a strictly secular document in *The Godless Constitution* (New York: Norton, 1997).

13. Stephen Mansfield, *The Faith of the American Soldier* (New York: Jeremy P. Tarcher/Peguin, 2005).

14. Ibid.

15. U.S. Department of Defense, "Instruction 1300.17: Accommodation of Religious Practices Within the Military Services," February 10, 2009, updated January 22, 2014, available online at http://www.dtic.mil/whs/directives/corres/pdf/130017p.pdf.

16. In an informal survey of twenty U.S. Marine Corps personnel ranking from first lieutenant to colonel, none of the respondents said that their promotion or selection was in any way related to religious adherence. In fact, most were completely taken aback by the question and responded that military competence was not related to faith traditions.

17. "Accommodating Faith in the Military," Pew Research Religion and Public Life Project, July 3, 2008, http://www.pewforum.org/2008/07/03/accommodating-faith-in-the-military/.

18. U.S. Department of Defense, "Directive 1304.19: Appointment of Chaplains for the Military Departments," June 11, 2004, updated April 23, 2007, available online at http://www.dtic.mil/whs/directives/corres/pdf/130419p.pdf.

3

✛

Chaplains Advising Warfighters on Culture and Religion

Dayne Nix

My military assignments took me around the world to Europe, Japan, South Korea, and Hong Kong, first as a U.S. Marine officer and then, beginning in 1986, as a U.S. Navy chaplain. During a visit to South Korea as command chaplain on the USS *Frank Cable*, a wardroom dinner with a South Korean commander and his officers resulted in invitations to preach at a local South Korean chapel and church, as well as the opportunity for our ship's praise team to lead in worship. These activities provided wholesome off-duty activities for our crew members, benefit for the local congregations, and positive international relations between our commands.

I was reflecting on this experience when, in late 2001, I attended the Navy Chaplain Corps' annual Professional Development Training Course[1] on the chaplain's role in religion and statecraft. The title of the four-day seminar was "The Impact of Religion on Culture and Politics across the International Spectrum." Much of the conference was influenced by Douglas Johnston's critique of American diplomacy, titled *Religion: The Missing Dimension of Statecraft*.[2] Johnston argued that American foreign policy had neglected religious and cultural factors in international relations, to the detriment of U.S. national interests. Part of the problem identified by Johnston was that neither diplomats nor politicians were comfortable in dealing with religion and religious actors. He argued that military chaplains could potentially assume a role in the international sphere and become agents of peace and understanding. The conference examined many of these ideas as they applied to the chaplaincy. For instance, in addition to the traditional chaplain role of

providing religious ministry for military members and advising commanders on the religious needs of their commands, chaplains were informed they
were now to serve as advisors on religion and statecraft—or religion and
culture, as it came to be known. The subject of religion in international affairs was foreign to many of the conference participants; yet it was to become
a major focus for many of us following the events of September 11, 2001.

Advisement on religion, a term of art for chaplains advising commanders,
and its impact on friendly military operations is a core capability and responsibility of the military chaplain. As professional military officers and
members of commanders' staff (at any level), chaplains are responsible for
assisting the commander in mission accomplishment. For chaplains, this has
traditionally been understood to consist primarily of caring for the spiritual
needs of military personnel and their families, to "provide, care, and facilitate" where their religious needs were concerned. Advising commanders on
the religious climate and morale of the command has always been a part of
the chaplain's responsibility. Since 2001, however, the advisement responsibility has taken on new meaning, relating to the impact of local religions
on military operations when deployed. This responsibility brings new challenges for members of the clergy who come to the Chaplain Corps expect-
ing to simply serve the religious needs of their personnel. In this chapter I
discuss the impact of this thinking on Chaplain Corps roles since that 2001
training, relate my own experience in both training and practicing advisement and liaison in support of the war fighter, contrast and compare Joint
Publication 1-05 and the various service policies on religion and culture
advisement and liaison, and list some professional competencies required to
effectively accomplish that role while providing specific examples from my
own and other's experiences.

THE IMPACT OF RELIGION ON CULTURE AND ON
POLITICS ACROSS THE INTERNATIONAL SPECTRUM

The 2001 annual Chaplain Corps Professional Development Training Course
titled "The Impact of Religion on Culture and Politics across the International Spectrum" served as a watershed for the Navy Chaplain Corps, introducing new requirements and professional expectations for Navy, Marine
Corps, and Coast Guard chaplains. The goal, or projected student outcome,
of that training was stated as follows: "As a result of participation in this
year's Professional Development Training Course (PDTC) chaplains will be
equipped to serve as primary staff officers trained to advise their command
on the complex and profound role of religion in statecraft as it shapes both
cultural and political attitudes toward war and peace across the international geopolitical spectrum."[3]

Douglas Johnston, the lead subject-matter expert and developer of the training event, expanded on this goal in one of the reading assignments.

With an expanded mission statement and proper training, chaplains can serve an invaluable early warning function for their commands based on personal interactions with local (overseas) religious communities and with religious-based, nongovernmental organizations. Not only will they be able to develop a grassroots understanding of the religious and cultural nuances at play, but they will be able to pass on the concerns of indigenous religious leaders about threats to stability posed by ethnoreligious demagogues. At times, they may also be in positions where they can provide a reconciling influence in addressing misunderstandings or differences with these communities. Finally, they can advise their commanders on the cultural aspects of decisions that are being taken (or that should be taken). In other words, Chaplains can become an important tool in preventing [conflict's] eruption in the first instance.[4]

For many of us, the course content was a dramatic departure from previous training and took us out of our comfort zone. The course presented a discussion of globalization, the continuing role of religion in world politics, instruction in general peacemaking and conflict-resolution principles, and a number of case studies in which religious leaders played a role in conflict resolution. Finally, participants worked in small groups on challenging scenarios they might encounter when deployed at potential trouble spots with their ship or unit around the world.

Doug Johnston saw chaplains as being able to fulfill the role he'd envisioned for a number of reasons, chief among them that chaplains represent a group of potential religious peacemakers that, when "properly trained and supported, can add a critically important dimension to the work of diplomats and nongovernmental organizations in addressing ethnic conflict and other problems of communal identity that are proving beyond the reach of traditional diplomacy."[5] Religious peace makers can assist in providing a "transcendent environment for dealing with secular obstacles and an improved ability to identify and deal with any deep-seated religious issues."[6]

Of course, chaplains are not the only professionals within the U.S. government with the responsibility for understanding and providing advice about religion and culture to government leaders and military commanders.

- Intelligence officers are responsible for collecting and briefing the commander and staff on cultural issues that will impact an operational area, including religion and religious leaders.
- Civil-affairs personnel are relied on to understand an operational area and how indigenous cultural issues (including religion) will impact the commander's mission. They are also expected to interact with all segments of civil population in order to facilitate that mission.

- The U.S. State Department has no set policy regarding interaction with indigenous religious groups. The matter is largely left up to each chief of mission. Some are comfortable engaging religious leaders and groups; others are not. Douglas Johnston's nearly twenty-year-old suggestion that the State Department develop "religious attachés" has not been acted upon. The State Department's International Religious Freedom office has repeatedly requested that a military chaplain be routinely detailed to them. To date, this has not been accomplished.
- USAID regularly engages with religious groups in order to facilitate international aid projects. But these interactions are often limited by the fear of possibly transgressing the Constitution's Establishment Clause in the First Amendment and individual discomfort with the subject of religion. To its credit, USAID has developed a "religion and conflict toolkit" and provides instruction to USAID personnel on effective religious engagement in conflict environments.

Chaplains, however, hold a singular position in the U.S. government. Unlike most diplomats, politicians, and military leaders, chaplains operate within the religious dimension and are comfortable with it. Chaplains also serve as both commissioned military officers and fully qualified religious professionals. Their uniqueness is a function of the American constitutional system and the First Amendment clause that states that "Congress shall make no law respecting an establishment of religion, or prohibiting the free exercise thereof." The chaplaincy "walks a narrow line between 'free exercise' and 'nonestablishment' of religion."[7] They do so because our military men and women face the danger of having their free exercise of religion denied while fighting in defense of that constitution and the freedoms it guarantees. Chaplains exist to guarantee those rights. This position presents them with unique challenges while allowing them to develop some unusual skills that make them effective interpreters of religion and culture within the military.

The challenges chaplains experience are a function of the diverse and pluralistic environment they must operate in. It is not unusual for a junior evangelical chaplain to find herself working for a Catholic or Jewish senior chaplain. For some, this is a real challenge. Chaplain ministry includes providing for, facilitating, and caring for the religious needs (and many nonreligious needs) of every command member regardless of faith group, even those who claim no religious faith or affiliation. On a given day, a chaplain may lead a Bible study for members of his own denomination, facilitate the religious needs of a Catholic, Hindu, or Buddhist, and then provide counseling to an individual who claims no religious faith. Prior to entering the military, many chaplains may have considered these religious bodies to be ecclesiastical competition or even cults. The successful chaplain learns to appreciate the diversity of religious belief while also remaining grounded in their own belief system, to cooperate without compromise.

One important role that chaplains fulfill is to assist with the command's responsibility to accommodate the religious needs of the many faith groups found in the Navy, Marine Corps, and Coast Guard. In doing so, they must be educated in and sensitive to the practical needs of these very diverse faith communities. It is not unusual for a Christian chaplain to facilitate Jewish worship requirements or Muslim dietary restrictions.[8] But accommodation also requires advocacy, as most military commands are not tuned to the religious dimension and might even be antagonistic to practices considered extreme or unusual. The effective chaplain learns to facilitate and accommodate diverse religious practices in ways that also promote mission accomplishment. This skill enables chaplains to develop an understanding and appreciation for religious diversity beyond mere sensitivity that can be helpful when he or she is called on to serve as an advisor or liaison in the international arena.

In international contexts, many religious leaders are highly regarded and possess significant moral authority as a result of their religious positions. They often hold public offices and political positions that play significant roles in daily community life. In these cultures, military chaplains, by nature of their religious position, may possess authority and legitimacy not enjoyed by other military or diplomatic personnel. Chaplains may also have a natural relationship with nongovernment organizations (NGOs), many of which are faith based, that operate in these environments and are often hesitant to work with the military. Since 9/11, chaplains have served effectively as liaisons with religious leaders in both Afghanistan and Iraq, mitigating conflict and resolving thorny issues that might have otherwise escalated out of control. It is likely that U.S. forces will be engaged in similar locations for the foreseeable future and that chaplains will continue to serve effectively in these roles.

These essential qualities guarantee that chaplains play an important and expanding role in the U.S. military. The conference leaders of that 2001 PDTC believed that chaplains' new roles could include service as intercultural interpreters to U.S. military personnel, provision of cooperative engagement and service as ambassadors of goodwill, service as collaborators and catalysts with extramilitary agents (diplomats, NGOs, and other non-American actors in local situations, including peacekeeping forces of the United Nations and other coalitions), and service as worship leaders vis-à-vis the peacekeeping context. In sum, they could serve as agents of reconciliation in providing their unique perspective to military and governmental leaders. The events of September 11, 2001, served to emphasize the timeliness of that 2001 PDTC and how important the subject of religion in international relations had become.

TRAINING AND EXPERIENCE IN
RELIGIOUS ADVISEMENT AND LIAISON

In a 2002 U.S. Navy *Proceedings* article, Douglas Johnston reported that all Navy, Marine Corps, and Coast Guard chaplains had been trained in the complex role of religion in statecraft and should be provided "expanded rules of engagement commensurate with the training they have received."[9] I recall reflecting that the course had been good but that more preparation was required before chaplains would be fully ready for the role Johnston envisioned. At best, we had been introduced to the subject, made aware of the possibilities, and given some very basic tools. Success in these areas would require additional education as well as judicious application of the insights we had gained.

I believe my own journey reflects the evolution of the Chaplain Corps on the subject of religion and culture. Beginning in April 2001 I was given the opportunity to train chaplains as well as line officers on this subject when I was assigned to the Navy Chaplain's School in Newport, Rhode Island, as the advanced-course officer under the leadership of Chaplain David Atwater. Our curriculum included much of Johnston's material on religion in world politics, religious ministry in military operations other than war, ethics in strategic ministry, and a session on religiously inspired terrorism.

One of the highlights of our curriculum was a two-hour presentation by Lieutenant Colonel (LTC) Joe Anderson, who had commanded U.S. Army forces in Kosovo. His objectives for his chaplains are instructive:

- Provide religious support in the area of operations to include enemy prisoners of war, civilian detainees, and refugees.
- Advise and coordinate with the operations officer on the impact of faith and practices of indigenous religious groups in the area of operations.
- Provide liaison to indigenous religious leaders.
- Assist the plans officer and the civil-affairs officer with humanitarian assistance operations.[10]

To illustrate the liaison objective, this decorated commander discussed how his chaplain had served as liaison with a local Orthodox priest who was fomenting conflict in the area. The chaplain had served as a communication link between the commander and the priest, with very positive results. The priest began to support NATO operations, and the U.S. commander attended services at the local Orthodox parish church. LTC Anderson was enthusiastic regarding chaplain capabilities in the international arena.

I also had the honor of teaching the "Faith and Force" elective at the Naval War College. The class addressed (and still addresses) the basic tenets of the major world religions and how they each deal with the subjects of war and peace. The class was always oversubscribed, requiring a lottery to determine who could enroll. Participants included chaplains, members of all the military services, State Department and other government personnel, and officers from foreign militaries. The discussion was always illuminating, especially when foreign officers provided insights and perspectives on the subject of their own faith. For instance, when discussing Islam and the differences between the Sunni and Shia, a Muslim officer informed us with some emotion that there is no division within Islam, that "the Shia are not of the true faith."

In late November 2003 I was assigned to U.S. Central Command (CENTCOM) forward, at Doha, Qatar, for a six-month tour. I was to serve as one of three deputies to Captain Philip Gwaltney, the CENTCOM chaplain. During my six-month deployment, I had the opportunity to observe chaplains in the roles envisioned by Douglas Johnston. In Afghanistan, the army command chaplain at Bagram Airfield briefed us on a mullah-engagement program being conducted in his region. He showed us pictures of groups of twenty or more Afghan mullahs who met regularly with his chaplains. Later, Dr. Pauletta Otis, author of chapter 2 in this book, traveled to Bahrain, where she provided training to CENTCOM chaplains on cultural issues within the region. During the battle for Fallujah, the CENTCOM forward logistics section received a request from the Marines for guidance on proper Muslim burial practices. Our chaplain department provided the required information along with the recommendation that the Marines work with the local hospital to provide appropriate services. It's instructive that the Marines had the wisdom to ask and that guidance was sought from the chaplain.

My next assignment took me to Naval Air Station Keflavik in Iceland. As part of my duties as command chaplain I provided ministry for the U.S. embassy at Reykjavík. The ambassador and deputy chief of mission both valued the religious dimension and planned and participated in a number of events with local religious leaders as well as special religious and cultural observances (for example, the embassy conducted an annual Eid dinner for local Muslims). I participated in a number of these events, and my advice on issues of culture and religion was sought and welcomed. I also served as liaison with the head of the Evangelical Lutheran Church of Iceland, that nation's established religion. This assignment provided numerous opportunities to foster international dialogue and understanding.

My personal experience relating to this subject crystallized in 2008 with my retirement from the navy. I was asked to serve as the lead subject-matter expert for the 2010 PDTC on the new SECNAVINST 1730.10, titled "Command Advisement and Liaison." Later I accepted a position at the Naval War College (Monterey Campus) as associate professor of national security decision making. An important part of my research and writing has focused on religion and security in international relations. My comments relating to chaplains as staff officers are informed by my current teaching and research responsibilities.

CHAPLAIN ADVISEMENT AND LIAISON
IN JOINT DOCTRINE AND SERVICE POLICY

Today's military structure is very different from the one that won World
War II in the 1940s and that fought in Vietnam in the 1960s. As a result of
the Goldwater-Nichols Act of 1986, our services train and fight in a "joint,"
or multiservice, environment. This means that the geographic combatant
commanders (U.S. Central Command, U.S. European Command, etc.)
direct U.S. forces in combat and peacetime (while deployed or stationed
under their command), while the services (Navy, Army, Air Force, Marines) provide trained and equipped personnel and combat units to the
combatant commanders.

Joint doctrine guides U.S. forces as they work together to accomplish
U.S. national objectives around the world. The writing of joint doctrine is a
collaborative and, sometimes, competitive effort. Joint doctrine is updated
and rewritten on a five-year cycle. Guided by the Joint Staff at the Pentagon, one branch of the military ("service") is designated as the lead or
responsible service while each of the other services collaborates to produce
a completed document. The result is representative of the most recent field
experience and reflects common agreement on the issues. *Joint doctrine* is
senior to and guides *service doctrine*. However, *service policy* trumps *joint
doctrine*. Members of a particular service cannot be forced by joint doctrine
to perform duties that their service's policy prohibits them from performing.[11] This background is necessary to understanding the following discussion on joint and service doctrine.

Joint Publication 1-05, "Religious Affairs in Joint Operations" (2009)

Joint Publication 1-05, "Religious Affairs in Joint Operations," provides the
doctrine and guidance for all the services concerning joint religious ministry
in the combatant command or joint arena. The document was updated in
2009, and all of the service chaplaincies were involved in the update. The
2004 version had introduced the subject of chaplain advisement and liaison
in joint operations, even quoting Douglas Johnston's works. However, it
had never been popular with either the services or the agencies that endorse
chaplains for military ministry.[12] This is due to a number of service disagreements but also grows out of the nature of joint doctrine itself.

The 2009 version of JP 1-05, as it is known, is comprehensive in its description of the roles and duties of chaplains who serve in the joint arena. The
document provides definitions of religious ministry in the joint arena and
assigns responsibilities for the provision of religious ministry: "This publication establishes doctrine and guidance for the Armed forces of the United
States regarding religious affairs in the joint-force environment and joint
operations. It describes the major responsibilities and functions of the joint-

force commander, joint-force chaplain, enlisted religious-support personnel, and religious-support teams regarding religious affairs in joint-force settings and operations."[13]

Advisement on religion's impact on military operations and liaison are a significant part of those duties.[14] It describes *religious advisement* as "the practice of informing the commander on the impact of religion on joint operations to include, but not limited to: worship, rituals, customs, and practices of U.S. military personnel, international forces, and the indigenous population. Chaplains provide religious advisement consistent with their noncombatant status."[15]

In an earlier paragraph, the document states that, "additionally, based on the particular knowledge and experience of the individual, and consistent with their noncombatant status, chaplains may advise the commander and staff members on various religious dynamics within the operational area. On occasion, they may be tasked with accomplishing certain liaison functions, particularly with indigenous religious leaders and faith-based nongovernmental organizations (NGOs) operating in the operational area."[16]

The remainder of the document details the duties of the joint-force chaplain and support staff at the different echelons of command. Each includes language describing the advisement role. The common language includes two important phrases: The chaplain

> Provides strategic and operational level advice and situational awareness for the Combatant Commander and staff on all matters related to religion, ethics, and morale.[17]
>
> . . . Engages with senior military chaplains and local religious leaders and others as directed by the Combatant Commander.[18]

JP 1-05 also provides specific guidance regarding the protection of chaplains' noncombatant status: "Chaplains may not advise on religious or cultural issues in the operational area where the law of armed conflict specifically prohibits such activities. Chaplains must not function as intelligence collectors or propose combat target selection. However, chaplains can provide input as to what constitutes religious structures or monuments of antiquity in a particular designated area but do not advise on including or excluding specific structures on the no-strike list or target list."[19]

A later section on military-engagement operations expands our understanding of chaplain liaison. When chaplains pursue religious liaison, their sole purpose is to "ameliorate suffering and to promote peace and the benevolent expression of religion. It is a focused and narrow role that addresses religion in human activity without employing religion to achieve a military advantage." Chaplains should not engage in manipulation or deception operations, take the lead in formal negotiations for command outcomes, or identify targets for combat operations. Chaplains are also directed to coordinate their activities with other staff and nonstaff agencies of their command.[20]

JP 1-05 closes with two pages of questions intended to guide joint-force chaplains in the production of a religious estimate for a joint-operational area. These questions are included at the end of this chapter. It assumes knowledge of joint doctrine and practice, characteristic of those who have completed Joint Professional Military Education.

In summary, JP 1-05 is a comprehensive document that addresses the requirements for religious advisement and liaison in a broad and general way. It does not provide explicit guidance regarding how chaplains will accomplish this aspect of their mission, instead leaving most of the details to the individual chaplain as he or she is guided by their particular service policy under the guidance of their commanding officer.

SERVICE INSTRUCTIONS RELATING TO CHAPLAIN ADVISEMENT AND LIAISON

In this section I address the policy documents that each of the services has published. As I worked with the Navy Chief of Chaplains' Office to develop the 2010 PDTC, I was advised that each of the services had very different viewpoints regarding the role of the chaplain as advisor on religion and its impact on military operations. The army had completely embraced this role, with the understandable proviso that chaplains maintain their noncombatant status. The navy had taken a middle-of-the-road approach, recognizing the need for and possibility of advisement on religion but choosing to establish very strict guidelines in its application. The air force seemed to take the most conservative approach, largely rejecting a role for chaplains in international religious engagement.

U.S. Air Force Instructions

As mentioned above, the U.S. Air Force adopted the most conservative approach regarding their chaplains' involvement in religious engagement in the international sphere. A thorough search of their instructions regarding the subject results in only one comment on the subject of chaplain advisement in the most general of terms. Chaplains are to provide "advice to leaders on spiritual, ethical, moral, morale, and religious-accommodation issues."[21] Note that this comment is contained in a document that predates the 2009 JP 1-05 and has not been recently updated.

The air force chief of chaplains did publish a policy paper in October 2009 stating that religious engagement by chaplains should be restricted only to U.S. citizens, but that paper expired after six months and has not been reissued or updated. The Air Force Culture and Language Center, based in Montgomery, Alabama, currently sends instructors to the Air Force

Chaplains' College to conduct cultural-awareness training. That training, however, is intended for chaplains headed for combatant command billets.

U.S. Army Instructions

Army chaplain policy relating to chaplain advisement on religion and culture is contained in "Army Regulation 165-1: Religious Support" (December 3, 2009) and "FM-1-05: Religious Support" (October 5, 2012). The army's approach to religion and culture is perhaps the most robust of all the services. The language contained in these publications is similar to that found in JP 1-05 and seems matter of fact in its acceptance of the role of chaplain as advisor on religion and its impact on military operations. In addition to the normal chaplain-advisement activities regarding religious issues relating to command personnel, chaplains provide advice on:

(g) Ethical, moral, and humanitarian implications of operational decisions.
(h) Analysis of the impacts of indigenous religions on military operations.[22]

The army's operational instruction, FM 1-05, clarifies the advisement responsibility, dividing it between internal and external advice. The internal advice pertains to religious issues within the command. Externally, "the chaplain advises the command on the specifics of the religious environment within the area of operations that may impact mission accomplishment. This may include indigenous religions in the area of operations, holy days that may impact military operations, and the significance of local religious leaders and structures. Chaplains and Unit Ministry Teams can work within boards, bureaus, centers, cells, and working groups to integrate their respective expertise and knowledge with the collective expertise of the staff in order to focus on specific problem sets to provide coherent staff recommendations to the commander."[23]

It is obvious that the army values this chaplain role and expertise. At the corps level, provision is made for a world-religions chaplain. This staff position is established to provide a "world-religions advisor to the corps commander on cultural and religious networks for current and future operations" who also participates in operational- and strategic-level planning by providing a religious-impact analysis. This staff member additionally supervises religious-leader liaison and works with the key leader workgroup.[24]

Army chaplains also engage in liaison with local religious leaders, always under the auspices of their commanding officer and ensuring they do not violate their noncombatant status. At the tactical and operational levels, chaplains are expected to establish liaison with local or host-nation religious leaders "in order to build mutual trust, promote human rights, and develop appropriate command relationships within an operational area."[25]

Army policy also recognizes the interagency and multinational realities of contemporary national security engagement, increasingly characterized by irregular warfare. Chaplains at the theater strategic echelon are encouraged to "develop opportunities in support of combatant-commander objectives to enhance chaplain contacts and mutual projects with foreign chaplaincies that build trust and confidence, share information, and maintain influence with American allies."[26] In support of these objectives, the army maintains a Center for World Religions at its Army Chaplaincy Center.[27]

U.S. Navy Instructions

Secretary of the Navy David Winter signed the Navy's updated SEC-NAVINST 1730.10, "Chaplain Advisement and Liaison," on January 23, 2009. The document had been in preparation and staffing within the navy for nearly two years. I was brought on board in late 2008 to prepare a course that would introduce the new instruction and the subjects of "advisement and liaison" to the Navy, Marine Corps, and Coast Guard chaplains of the Navy Chaplain Corps. In the summer of 2008 I was given a draft of the document and began my preparations, which were closely supervised by the Chief of Chaplains' Office. The process was somewhat daunting, however, for the document was still unfinished. I was informed that navy lawyers were heavily involved, with the chief sticking point being the protection of the chaplain's noncombatant status.

General navy policy guiding chaplain activities is contained in SEC-NAVINST 1730.1D. In that document, the Navy Chaplain Corps' four core capabilities are defined as facilitating the religious requirements of authorized personnel, provision of faith-specific ministries, caring for all, and "advising commanders on the impact of religion on military operations, within the boundaries of their noncombatant status."[28] SECNAVINST 1730.10 focuses specifically on the chaplain's advisement role, stating that its purpose is to provide "policy on the role of chaplains as advisors to commands and their derivative tasks as command liaisons."[29]

The navy divides chaplain advisement into three distinct categories—*essential, executive,* and *external. Chaplain liaison* is defined as inherent and distinct within each category: "The chaplain advises the command in three distinct ways. The chaplain strengthens the chain of command and assists in the development of leadership by providing advice to leaders at all levels (essential advice). The chaplain serves as the principal advisor to the commander for all matters regarding the Command Religious Program (CRP) (executive advice). The chaplain serves as an advisor to the commander regarding the impact of religious and humanitarian matters on military operations (external advice). The nature of each type of advice drives concomitant liaison work."[30]

Most of the guidance of this document describes ministry that chaplains conduct on a regular basis under the core capabilities of "facilitate, provide, and care."[31] Essential advisement includes the counseling and advice provided to all members of the command, whether spiritual or secular in nature. This includes the guidance chaplains provide to command members on personal and career-related questions, issues of morality, as well as those of a religious nature. *Liaison* in this case refers to the coordination the religious-ministry team may make with other helping professionals—lawyers, doctors, career counselors, and so on—as they assist military personnel and their families.

Executive advisement is that advice the chaplain provides the commander "on all issues regarding the impact of religion on military operations when the impact is upon the command itself."[32] This includes the command religious program, which the chaplain manages and for which the commander is responsible. Chaplains keep the commander informed of the religious needs of military personnel, morale, and the status of the command religious program. Executive advisement also includes the conduct of humanitarian operations and community-relations projects. Liaison in this role includes the relationships the Religious Ministry Team must maintain in the daily conduct of the CRP as well as those persons outside the command who might provide religious ministry or assistance to members of the command. For instance, in 2007 the commander of the Navy South-West Region directed his chaplain to call a meeting with San Diego–area civilian clergy to discuss the religious needs and resources available for military members residing in the San Diego metropolitan area. Meeting with local religious leaders to plan and coordinate humanitarian operations and community-relations events also falls under this rubric.

The navy directs that external advisement and liaison take place under limited situations, that being combat or "conditions in which the law of armed conflict applies." This section specifically states that "chaplains shall be permitted to perform only duties that will not jeopardize their noncombatant status."[33] Chaplains will provide for, facilitate, and care for members of their commands during combat operations. Beyond those efforts, their advisement and liaison activities during combat must be limited to those that provide "amelioration of suffering and the direct pursuit of humanitarian goals."[34]

Additional guidance states that chaplains may provide advice relating to religious considerations in building and maintaining coalitions, the religious considerations of humanitarian-assistance support, and the benevolent expression of religion within the area of responsibility. The instruction goes on to prohibit participation in targeting boards under any circumstance, guidance more restrictive than that in JP 1-05. The prohibitions extend to providing advice on psychological operations, providing military intelligence, or providing information regarding the enemy to the command's combat decision-making process or the use of religion as a weapon. Liaison efforts are similarly limited, with all efforts specifically related to religious and/or humanitarian purposes approved or directed by the commander. Information conveyance to or from key leaders is similarly limited to religious and humanitarian purposes as directed by the commander.[35]

It was made clear to me during the development of the 2010 PDTC on the Navy Chaplain Corps' new instruction that a primary goal was to communicate how restrictive this new policy was. Chaplain Corps leadership was especially concerned about "chaplain loose cannons." Navy chaplains are well known for their independence, and the Chief of Chaplains' Office wanted to emphasize that chaplain advisement and liaison must always occur under the guidance and supervision of commanding officers.

U.S. Marine Corps Doctrine

As noted earlier, the Marine Corps is a part of the Department of the Navy, and its chaplains are provided by the navy. As such, they are governed by the navy policy discussed above. However, Marine Corps chaplains have a different mission and operational experience than chaplains assigned to navy commands. The Marine Corps exists to provide amphibious forces that project U.S. military power onto foreign shores. Chaplains assigned to Marine Corps units will find themselves in circumstances similar to army chaplains, conducting operations that come into direct contact with indigenous cultures and religions that will inevitably impact military operations.

The document that guides Marine Chaplains is "Marine Corps War-Fighting Publication 6-12: Religious Ministry in the U.S. Marine Corps." Consistent with navy policy, advisement is listed as a core capability of "some" Marine chaplains. "Within the boundaries of their noncombatant status, some chaplains are trained to advise on the impact of religion on military operations."[36] Later, the document seems to expand advisement as a core competency for all chaplains. They must advise their commanders on the following:

> *Religion and cultural impact on operations.* At the tactical, operational, and strategic levels of war, advise on religious and/or cultural issues (external to the command) related to unit operations.
> *Religious-leader engagement.* As part of the theater security cooperation program, assist the command, as directed, in engagement with local religious leaders to enhance communication and understanding (without violating noncombatant status).[37]

Marine Corps chaplains are also expected to participate in the planning process and provide some level of expertise on the religion and cultural practices within the area of operations. In a section on chaplain training in preparation for deployment, a lack of knowledge of local religions is noted as a problem.

> *Local religions.* A lack of awareness of local religious sensitivities could create significant problems with allies. It is imperative that Religious Ministry Teams obtain an understanding of the religious environment prior to deployment and entering a combat situation. . . . [During] Operation Iraqi Freedom some chaplains were not as prepared as they should have been to teach classes on and support requirements for the religious and cultural aspects of Islam.[38]

It appears from these comments that the Marine Corps is very well aware of the requirement to include religion and culture in its operational planning and that its chaplains play a key role in advisement and liaison activities.

As is evident from the above discussion, each of the services has its own policy and doctrine relating to its approach to religion and culture in the operational environment. Each has been forced to grapple with contemporary realities and the influential role that religion plays on the international stage. It must be remembered, however, that JP 1-05 is the senior doctrine and will guide their efforts when deployed in a joint environment.

CONCLUSION: RISING TO THE CHALLENGE

Chaplains are a unique and sometimes unpredictable force within the military. This is due to their unique source and experience. They come from the churches, synagogues, mosques, and religious institutions of America. They come to the military as fully qualified professional clergy persons of their own faith community. Each of the services has an initial training program to orient new chaplains to the military and prepare them for ministry within it. Chris Seiple, president of the Institute for Global Engagement, identifies a problem caused by this unique characteristic of chaplains. "I've talked with numerous line officers who have commanded troops in the last four to five years, from all branches of service," he says. "There is a common thread among their debriefs: Chaplains are unpredictable. They are all different with a wide range of capabilities. You never know what you're going to get. They [line commanders] tell me they hold their breath as the new chaplain reports aboard."[39]

"Because the nature of chaplain expertise varies so greatly," Seiple continues, "commanders simply do not know what to expect professionally from their chaplains."[40] I would suggest that this problem is not unique to chaplains. However, when assigning them to duties as advisors on culture and religion, unpredictability does present a problem. While they generally do possess a sensitivity and understanding of religion, they may not possess the knowledge, skills, and abilities necessary to serve effectively in this new role.

Douglas Johnston's 2001 PDTC on religion and statecraft in the international arena was a first step in the process of preparing chaplains for their new role. But additional training and education are required before chaplains are thoroughly prepared to fulfill that role in the contemporary global environment. JP 1-05 and the various service publications provide a first step in addressing the training and education issue, as they provide an identified capability that the services must provide and train their chaplains to fulfill.[41] The navy's concept of the Professional Naval Chaplaincy is a service approach that further defines the knowledge, skills, and abilities required of chaplains in fulfilling the advisement responsibility.[42] Proposed advisement tasks are outlined in figure 3.1, taken from the navy's Chaplain Corps Strategic Plan.

ADVISE
Strategic/operational requirements *
Impact of religious ministry
Impact of religion
Role of culture
Moral advice
Ethical advice
Communications
Theater Security Operations
Morale
Spiritual well being of Command
Family issues
Measure Performance
Conflict Resolution (within Command)
COMRELS (Theater Service Cooperation)
Support of returning IAs
Faith Based Initiatives
GO religion based advice

Figure 3.1.

Of course, this list only includes the tasks that religious-ministry teams are expected to accomplish, not the training and education required to prepare them to do so. I will conclude this chapter by addressing each of four general-competency areas on culture and religion that are a challenge to the contemporary chaplaincy: religion and constitutionality, staff effectiveness and credibility, joint-professional military education, and world religions, globalization, and international ethics.

First, as discussed above, chaplains fill a unique role within the U.S. government, walking that fine constitutional line delineated by the First Amendment's Establishment Clause and Free Exercise Clause. Chaplains must understand that role and how it guides their ministry within the U.S. military.

They serve as representatives of their religious groups as well as commissioned military officers, responsible to both to fulfill specific duties and roles. They must walk that line carefully, ensuring that they serve the needs of all military personnel by caring, facilitating, providing, and advising within the command echelon to which they are assigned, all the while cognizant of the fact that they are noncombatants. Commanders may not understand the difference, and it is incumbent upon the chaplain to explain the nuances.

Second is the issue of staff-officer effectiveness. In all candor, chaplains have not always served effectively as staff officers. This can be attributed to a number of causes, most importantly the expectations of the commander. Many expect that the chaplain will, at best, fit the good-natured but bumbling role played by Father Mulcahy on the popular television series *M*A*S*H*. Contemporary roles require a chaplain who can serve effectively as a special staff officer, "assigned to a commander to assist him or her in the administration and operation of his or her command."[43] Staff are provided to the commander as an aid to command, with the understanding that the best solution to a problem is derived from the knowledge, experience, study, and foresight of the entire staff working together. Contemporary chaplains must do well in this area if they are to be taken seriously as advisors and confidantes.

Related to this is training and experience at various levels of command and training in the joint-operational planning process. Too often chaplains become fixated on the job in front of them (today's ministry) without taking seriously the requirements of the next, mandatory round of professional military education as well as how to prepare for wider levels of influence at the operational and strategic level. In sum, chaplains must work hard to not be parochial when it comes to moving beyond pulpit ministry to advisement of commanders and engaging leaders, whether they wear an American military uniform or are foreign religious elites.

Finally, there is much work to be done in preparing chaplains in the nexus of world religions, globalization, and international ethics. Unfortunately, chaplains are simply not well prepared for this, either before or after they enter military service. Systematic change in both the expectations of chaplains and their training is necessary, and this spans the course of their careers. In sum, it is incumbent on the services to provide the training and education that will enable them to accomplish the tasks and roles they are expected to fulfill, especially that of advisor on religion and culture. Education and experience in the competencies discussed above, as well as others, will prepare chaplains to serve successfully and enhance mission accomplishment.

APPENDIX: RELIGIOUS ESTIMATE (FROM JP 1-05)

When developing the religious estimate, the joint forces chaplain (JFC) may receive assessments and input relative to religious advisement from various subject-matter experts. Chaplains participate in the development of religious estimates consistent with their noncombatant status. The following considerations can be used to develop the religious estimate to be used in religious advisement.

1. How do U.S. political goals for this situation interface with the religious sensibilities of the host nation concerned and the local communities in the operational area?
   a. How is the host nation affected by the religious preferences of regional neighbors or global religious perceptions and pressures?
   b. What host-nation cultural-religious perceptions or practices conflict with U.S. positions on democracy, personal dignity, religious tolerance/pluralism, or separation of religion/state?
   c. How is the host nation's political and diplomatic process influenced by religious persuasion?

2. How does religious liaison facilitate the commander's intent, end state, and operation or campaign-plan objectives?
   a. Which lines of operations can religious liaison support?
   b. What are the measures of effectiveness for religious-liaison initiatives?
   c. How are the objectives of religious liaison communicated to other levels of command?
   d. How can U.S. military policies in the host nation support or offend religious preferences?
   e. How can religious liaison be reinforced by interagency organizations, IGOs, or NGOs?
   f. What is the type, amount, and duration of religious liaison that the command will support?
   g. How do branches/sequels address ongoing operations and religious liaison? What is the chaplain's role in the plans and preparation? What accurate and timely advice can be offered? Where is the best information and wisdom to be found?
   h. What religious practices (or religions) directly affect the host-nation decision-making process?

NOTES

1. The annual Professional Development Training Course (PDTC) is intended as a training opportunity for all navy chaplains who also serve the U.S. Marine Corps and the U.S. Coast Guard. It is offered at nine or ten U.S. locations and two or three overseas sites. It also serves as an opportunity for Chaplain Corps leadership to meet

with chaplains as well as for chaplains to socialize with one another. While some deployed chaplains may miss the event, most attend.

2. Douglas Johnston and Cynthia Sampson, eds., *Religion: The Missing Dimension of Statecraft* (New York: Oxford University Press, 1994).

3. Professional Development Training Course FY01 course material, 3.

4. Douglas Johnston, "Religion, Culture and Globalization," presentation made as part of the PDTC FY01 course material, 34.

5. Ibid., 33.

6. Ibid.

7. "An Expanding Role for Chaplains," PDTC FY01 course material, 131.

8. *Facilitation* does not mean that chaplains conduct religious services for faith groups other than their own. Instead, they provide the resources for those faith groups to conduct their own religious observances—a location, candles, and prayer books, among other things, and perhaps arrangements for a contract priest, rabbi, or minister.

9. Douglas Johnston, "We Neglect Religion at our Peril," *Proceedings Magazine* 128, no. 1 (January 2002): 52.

10. LTC Joe Anderson, "Peace Operations in Kosovo," PowerPoint presentation given during a Staff and Leadership Course, session 4.4, slide 48.

11. Both the army and the navy published their own policies on the subject nearly concurrently with the publication of Joint Publication 1-05.

12. Each chaplain must be endorsed by their religious organization for service within the military. These agencies also meet with the Service Chiefs of Chaplains annually to discuss policy and are very influential.

13. U.S. Department of Defense, "Joint Publication 1-05: Religious Affairs in Joint Operations," November 20, 2009, http://www.dtic.mil/doctrine/new_pubs/jp1_05.pdf, xiv.

14. Note that the term *culture* is not used in any of the joint or service documents but, I believe, is understood.

15. U.S. Department of Defense, "Joint Publication 1-05," II-2.

16. Ibid.

17. Ibid., II-5.

18. Ibid., II-6. This is actually a typo; it should read *GCC* instead of *Combatant Commander* to be consistent with the paragraph it is in.

19. Ibid., I-2.

20. Ibid., III-5. This section reflects the fact that the joint pub is the result of interservice collaboration. These prohibitions could have been included earlier in the section regarding the noncombatant status of chaplains. This section seems out of place in a section that deals with military engagement, the "routine contact and interaction between individuals or elements of the Armed forces of the U.S. and those of another nation's armed forces." This language is very similar to that found in SECNAVINST 1730.10.

21. Secretary of the Air Force, "Air Force Policy Directive 52-1," October 2, 2006, 1, available online at http://www.militaryatheists.org/regs/AFPD52-1v2006.pdf.

22. U.S. Department of the Army, "Army Regulation 165-1: Religious Support; Army Chaplain Corps Activities," December 3, 2009, 12, available online at http://www.apd.army.mil/pdffiles/r165_1.pdf.

23. U.S. Department of the Army, "FM 1-05: Religious Support," October 5, 2012, 3-1, available online at http://armypubs.army.mil/doctrine/DR_pubs/dr_a/pdf/fm1_05.pdf.

24. Ibid., 3-3.

25. Ibid., 3-5.

26. U.S. Department of the Army, "Army Regulation 165-1," 52.

27. "This enabler provides the U.S. Army with relevant, timely, and accessible resources to address the impact of religion in the conduct of unified land operations. The center is designed to facilitate Army-wide analysis, product dissemination, learning and advisement on religion." U.S. Department of the Army, "FM 1-05," 3-4.

28. U.S. Department of the Navy, "SECNAVINST 1730.1D: Religious Ministry in the Department of the Navy," August 8, 2008, 5-6.

29. U.S. Department of the Navy, "SECNAVINST 1730.10: Chaplain Advisement and Liaison," January 23, 2009, 1, available online at http://doni.daps.dla.mil/Directives/01000%20Military%20Personnel%20Support/01-700%20Morale,%20Community%20and%20Religious%20Services/1730.10.pdf.

30. Ibid.

31. Chaplains provide religious ministry for members of their own religious denominations, facilitate the religious needs of other denominations, and care for all military members and their families, regardless of religious affiliation.

32. U.S. Department of the Navy, "SECNAVINST 1730.10," 2.

33. Ibid., 3.

34. Ibid.

35. Ibid., 4.

36. U.S. Marine Corps, "MCWP 6-12: Religious Ministry in the U.S. Marine Corps," December 16, 2009, section 5-5.

37. Ibid., sections 5-5–6.

38. Ibid., section 6-5.

39. Chris Seiple, "Ready . . . Or Not? Equipping the Military Chaplain for Interreligious Liaison," *Review of Faith and International Affairs* (Winter 2009): 47. The quotation is from M. R. Ferguson, former chaplain at the Joint Chiefs of Staff.

40. Ibid.

41. Requirements drive budgetary, manpower, and training issues within the military.

42. "The concept of 'Professional Naval Chaplaincy' has been developed to describe some of the unique characteristics of what it means to be chaplains and RPs in the U.S. Navy. It includes developing and articulating professional standards and expectations as well as processes for developing our future leaders." Rear Admiral Mark Tidd, chief of "Chaplains Guidance" for 2011, November 28, 2010.

43. U.S. Department of the Navy, "United States Navy Regulations, 1990," September 14, 1990, article 0710, available online at http://www.cs1dino.com/uploads/3/0/4/3/3043921/U.S.%20NAVY%20REGULATIONS%5B1%5D.pdf.

4

✛

Beginnings: The Army Chaplaincy and the War on Terror, 2001–2005

Eric Keller

The attacks on September 11, 2001, that struck the World Trade Center and the Pentagon (as well as the foiled attack that ended in Pennsylvania) also struck the U.S. Army chaplaincy like a thunderbolt. The chaplains serving at the Pentagon immediately provided direct care for the many casualties created by the plane slamming into the building near their office. All over the world, the U.S. Army and its chaplains reacted with stunned anger as well as with the grim realization that a new type of war had descended upon the United States. The purpose of this chapter is to examine the earliest days of the post–9/11 U.S. Army chaplaincy as it struggled with a new type of war and dramatically increasing calls for religious expertise: not only with providing care and comfort but also in understanding and interacting with Islam. Of course, this mission, in many ways, was certainly not new to the army chaplaincy, and from Vietnam to Bosnia army chaplains and chaplain assistants have provided religious analysis as well as on-the-ground interactions with local religious leaders. However, in its very long history, the U.S. Army chaplaincy had never before confronted a war that placed religion in the very center of the conflict, and this very important dynamic changed how the U.S. Army chaplaincy would define itself in its evolving role as religious liaison with local and national religious leaders abroad. More specifically, this chapter outlines the path after 9/11 that led U.S. Army chaplains with little experience, expertise, and policy (doctrine) on how to engage foreign religious leaders to a heightened awareness and reformed doctrine that allowed them to support the cause of peace and security by religious advisement to their commanders as well as engaging foreign religious leaders in the context of the conflict.

U.S. ARMY CHAPLAINS AND
RELIGIOUS-SUPPORT TEAMS ON 9/11

U.S. Army chaplains consist of one half of the *religious-support team* (abbreviated to RST in conversation), while a trained enlisted soldier consists of the other half. The enlisted soldier, many times a noncommissioned officer, is trained as a *chaplain assistant* to provide security, coordinate movements, offer assistance in religious-support planning, and fulfill numerous other duties. The chaplain is the clergy representative from a particular faith tradition as well as an army officer. Each chaplain (not the chaplain assistant) is endorsed by an endorsement agency that represents a particular denomination or group of denominations, and thus each chaplain has a responsibility to follow the religious doctrine of their endorsement agency. As such, the chaplain provides religious support to the military members assigned, attached, or in direct support to the area of operations as well as serves as the religious advisor to the commander. Consequently, the U.S. Army religious-support team (called the *unit-ministry team* in army doctrine and the *religious-support team* in joint or interservice doctrine)[1] normally consists of these two individuals providing support within a specified unit's area of operations.[2] When deployed to a combat zone, this team works under a whole host of army regulations, field manuals, joint publications, operation orders, standing operating procedures, and, for the clergy member, the particular standards of their faith tradition. For example, a chaplain who is a Roman Catholic priest must follow all the standards dictated by his denomination, such as the sanctity of the confessional, and so on. In addition, the religious-support team is under the direct command of a unit commander (normally no lower than battalion, which is about five hundred to eight hundred soldiers, depending on the type of unit) and is obligated to follow the legal orders of that commander.

The U.S. Army Chaplain Center and School is where new chaplains and chaplain assistants are trained as well where they receive ongoing training throughout their career cycles. Indeed, army chaplains receive a significant amount of ongoing training throughout their career, returning to the "schoolhouse," as it is often called, every two to four years. One such training process, the Chaplains' Advance Course (as it was called in 2001), took chaplains nearing the end of their time at the rank of captain (0-3) and brought them to Ft. Jackson, South Carolina, for a six-month school on learning to be a field-grade army officer (major through colonel) as well as a middle-grade chaplain. This course was taught in a small-group format and lead by an experienced chaplain, normally one who had graduated from the in-residence Army Command and General Officers Staff Course at Ft. Leavenworth. Before 9/11, the tactical portion of this course consisted of a made-up heavy battlefield scenario using fictional nations and armies. The students were learning how to lead junior chaplains in war as well as their role as religious advisors to brigade-level commanders. Ironically, one group was in their tactical phase when the planes went into the buildings on 9/11; they instantly knew they were going to go to war sometime in the near future.

After a laborious effort was made to send this group to a six-week course at Ft. Leavenworth (a resident phase of ongoing continuing training all army captains undergo), the director of training, Chaplain (Colonel) Hank Steinhilber, directed one of his small-group instructors to rewrite the scenario to better reflect the new reality of war. This effort created a simulated campaign for the 2001–2002 academic year using real tribes, religions, terrain, cities, and leaders currently in Afghanistan. This was a first for the chaplain school in recent memory (even the training for Bosnia deployments had used fictitious countries). The intent was to prepare these mid-level chaplains to provide religious support in this new environment. As chance would have it, then–Brigadier General Mark Hertling had been asked to speak on his experiences with the digital transformation of the army. En route to the Pentagon to work in information operations, he had been invited to the school by his former brigade chaplain, Doug Fenton. Before he spoke to us about transformation, he decided to take a moment and observe the Afghanistan simulation. After the training event, he wrote an e-mail to the chief of staff of the army, General Eric Shinseki, CCing the training-command commander and the chief of chaplains. In his e-mail Hertling discussed the Afghanistan simulation and how engaged the chaplaincy was with the new (and then still only possible) operational environment. He provided a series of observations and recommendations, speaking to "the role of the chaplain on the CMOC/CA [Civil-Military Operations Center/Civil Affairs] . . . and how they might assist the S5/G5 in accomplishing the mission . . . the intricacies of this current war on terrorism, and how 'men and women of God' can assist the 'warriors' fight in this context."[3] Hertling went on to mention a brief conference he'd had with the current director of combat developments (Chaplain Greg Hill) about the use of world-religion chaplains (a small group of chaplains sent to civilian universities to receive masters degrees in the study of world religions) on the joint staff, primarily with information operations. However, this concept of using world-religion chaplains in information operations or with civil affairs was not without controversy within the U.S. Army Chaplain Corps because of the perception it might violate the noncombatant status of the chaplains.

GOING TO WAR WITH THE ARMY YOU HAVE

Secretary of Defense Donald Rumsfeld famously quipped that the country goes to war with the army it has, not the army it envisions. So in late 2001, the existing army chaplaincy rules, regulations, and training structures were informed by the Cold War and deployments to the Balkans in the 1990s. The Army Chaplain Corps updated its materials, using multiple reference documents to determine their religious-support mission as discussed in some detail above. On top of the army documents, there were joint documents that take priority over a specific service document, which meant an additional layer of instruction was given to the army chaplaincy. This bewildering maze of instructions, requirements, and "best practices" meant a unit-ministry team would very potentially be confused about their role with local religious leaders when deployed abroad. To be clear, no one disputed the role of chaplains as pastors to their flocks and as ethical advisors to commanders. What was in dispute—and continues to be controversial even as of the writing of this book—was the role of chaplain as religious affairs expert (religious advisement) on the religious context of the battlefield and the role of chaplain in religious-leader engagement (often called *religious-leader liaison*): direct outreach to indigenous religious leaders (i.e., mullahs and imams) outside the military cantonment.

The fast-paced response to 9/11 left little time for deliberate reflection about this, since very soon after the September attacks the United States responded with a military operation designed to overthrow the Taliban and replace them with a democratic government that would be friendly to the United States. Previously, religious-leader liaison had not been given a central role in the activities of an army unit-ministry team, and thus regulation and doctrine were vague on the requirements for conducting this mission. The field manual in effect in 2001 ("FM 16-1: Religious Support") had been published in 1995, while the army regulation ("AR 165-1: Chaplain Activities in the United States Army") had been updated in 1998. As a result, both had already incorporated the lessons learned from the Balkans operations as they pertained to religious-leader engagement; those experiences had been fairly limited in scope and had certainly not been conducted in a hostile combat zone. Each focused on the traditional role of the unit-ministry team, which was to "nurture the living, care for the wounded, and honor the dead."[4] The core concept for the chaplain and the chaplain assistant, according to doctrine in 2001, was to provide religious support to U.S. military forces while other missions would take a far lesser priority. However, the early guidance did provide some direction for those U.S. Army unit-ministry teams that deployed in 2002 and 2003 to Afghanistan and Iraq, respectively.

Looking specifically at Iraq, U.S. intervention in 2003 found a cauldron of Islamic faith groups that had the potential to either explode into violent conflict or learn to work within a pluralistic framework. According to the analysts at the United States Institute of Peace, the religious environment in Iraq after the downfall of Saddam Hussein was one in which Shia, Sunni, and Kurdish clerics had begun to play a role in the political spectrum (while there are Sufi Muslims and even Christians in Iraq, they play a minimal role in politics). Sunni Islamism had two major political and religious strands beginning in 2003 that endured in part until the end of U.S. military operations in December 2011. The dominant Muslim Brotherhood provided a relatively moderate influence on Sunni followers, while Wahhabism and the Salafi methodology preached a radical rejection of the West (and the American occupation), which included violent resistance.[5] The majority Shiites had then, and still have, a wide range of political participation, which included the Quietists of Ali al-Sistani, the more radical al-Sadr faction, the SCIRI (Supreme Council for the Islamic Revolution in Iraq) faction of al-Hakim, and the traditional Islamic Dawa Party (which had actually been started by al-Sadr's father). These groups waxed and waned in dominance from late 2003 to 2011 while the insurgency and counterinsurgency raged. However, as explained by political analyst Graham Fuller, "to a major extent, Shiite politics is religious politics. Politics among the Shia in the Muslim world is typically characterized by the central role of the clergy."[6] Again, doing justice to Islamic politics in the Iraqi context is beyond the scope of this chapter. It is sufficient to note the large influence of the clergy in both Sunni and Shiite groups, as well as the central role of religion in determing their political stances on virtually all issues. This role of the cleric is dominant from the village to Baghdad, with mullahs (religious teachers and respected scholars) and imams (worship leaders and religious leaders) determining matters of justice, norms, values, and cultural expression. The political parties mentioned above for the Sunni and the Shiite are, in essence, religious parties that work in the political system.

Given their central role in the Iraqi system, it seems reasonable to expect that cooperative relationships between these Islamic clerics and U.S. Army religious-support teams would have some influence on overall metrics of cooperation. As Johnston states, the clergy "can serve as instruments of change by exercising their moral authority, their commitment to nonviolence, and the ability to inspire their communities."[7] In theory, commonalities in theology between those religions in the Judeo-Christian culture could perhaps serve as the lubricant.

From the beginning, commanders on the ground in both Afghanistan and Iraq knew religion had a central focus in these conflicts. Thus the chaplaincy (as an institution) would receive urgent requests from commanders as well as chaplains on how to engage the local religious leaders—who were primarily Islamic but adhered to a minority of other religions as well. Joint religious-support doctrine was also beginning to grapple with this issue, since navy (which includes the Marines) and air force chaplaincies were confronted with these same issues—although on a far more limited scale than was the army. The central question, simply stated, was this: What is the role of a ministry team when deployed to the theater of operations as it pertains to local religious engagement? The Balkans certainly had religious leadership among the various populations there and, in fact, had religious authorities from three different faith groups—Muslim, Orthodox, and Roman Catholic. Senior chaplains and their chaplain assistants had also engaged in various councils, meetings, and one-on-one liaison with these leaders with the intention of creating goodwill between American forces and the local population. Due to this reality, U.S. Army combat-training centers in the 1990s provided some training in this area. For example, toward the end of 1992 the United States Forces commander in Europe ordered every maneuver battalion to undergo training at what was then called the Combat Maneuver Training Center in preparation for possible missions to the Balkans. Role players from military-intelligence battalions as well as from the U.S. Army unit that performed the opposing-force mission would replicate the Balkan experience using fictitious countries and cultures that happened to be identical to those in the Balkans. The junior member of the observer-controller chaplain team was assigned to provide scenarios for the chaplains and chaplain assistants undergoing training. Using the opposing-forces chaplain, the scenarios would focus on several "traps" that an unsuspecting chaplain might fall into while working with the local religious leader. The training goal was to help the chaplain learn to sidestep a natural inclination to take sides and to not violate U.S. Army doctrine specifically forbidding the ministry team from gathering intelligence. Without going into the details of the scenarios, it is important to note that the unit-ministry teams learned these lessons well and soon were able to work with the local religious leaders despite the vagueness of army doctrine and regulation. Thus informal lessons learned were passed down from unit to unit as they deployed to the peacekeeping mission in the Balkans, which served the U.S. Army chaplaincy well.

Almost ten years later, after 9/11, the early doctrine for religious-leader engagement for U.S. Army ministry teams required the chaplains to provide commanders with a religious analysis of the local population that was extensive in historical dimensions as well as culture, customs, and local religious requirements (regardless of whether the chaplain had this expertise). The doctrine also stated that the chaplain and chaplain assistant would not initiate religious-leader liaison and would only engage while supporting civil military affairs. Nor was the team to gather any intelligence or violate privileged communications if the situation called for it. They were strictly to play a support and advisory role, with strong boundaries placed on their activities due to their noncombatant status. However, this limited doctrine soon proved to be inadequate when commanders would either keep the ministry teams away from the local religious leaders due to a fear of casualties or lack of training within the ministry team or, conversely, order the ministry teams to engage with the local religious leadership with the mission of building goodwill as well as gathering information as to the "friendliness" of the local religious leadership. At the same time, the U.S. Army chaplaincy itself was in a vociferous internal debate between those who supported an active role in religious-leader liaison versus those arguing for a more passive role with an emphasis on supporting U.S. forces only. The formal documents used by unit-ministry teams (UMTs) in both Afghanistan and Iraq provided little help as the wars continued.

The primary statement found in most army religious-support doctrine simply states that "the UMT is responsible for advising the commander regarding the impact of religions on military operations."[8] In a training circular designed for unit-ministry teams to take to the field for training as well as into war, the religious area and impact assessment provided the only doctrinal guidance for the deploying chaplains and their chaplain assistants. It goes into great detail on how to assess the area of operations so that the chaplain can "explain religious/spiritual beliefs and practices of the people they encounter to commanders and soldiers in their unit."[9] Beyond some instruction on information gathering and providing briefings to soldiers, there was virtually no guidance on how unit-ministry teams were supposed to conduct—or even on whether they should conduct—religious-leader liaison. As mentioned above, there was some regulatory guidance (to support civil-military operations, for example), and certainly each deploying unit had an operations plan or operations order offering more specific guidance. As the theater headquarters became more robust and theater chaplains began to create standard operating procedures, the deploying unit-ministry team would be able to receive the guidance they needed. However, it is important to note that there really was not any systemic doctrinal document coordinating the entirety of the various unit and theater documents that referred to religious-leader liaison. Much of this was word-of-mouth, shared from unit to unit over time. Predictably, this created some confusion.

IRAQ: THE CHALLENGE OF LOCAL ENGAGEMENT, ATTEMPTS AT NATIONAL RECONCILIATION

In an unclassified history of religious-support-liaison (or engagement) operations, a chaplain assistant—then–Master Sergeant and now–Sergeant Major Johnny Procter—wrote of his experiences right after the march to Baghdad with the 2nd Brigade Combat Team, 82nd Airborne Division, from April 2003 to January 2004.[10] In 2003 Major General Petraeus ordered the religious-support teams under his command to begin working with the local clerics to build relationships while the 101st occupied Mosul and began building trust with the occupants. This initiative was expanded by Major General Sanchez in the 1st Armored Division and then by the Combined Joint Task Force 7, which mandated religious-leader engagements with the purpose of assessing the local religious needs, building relationships with the very powerful clerics in Iraq, and assisting in building bridges between the various religious groups in Baghdad.

However, as conditions on the ground changed, the opportunities for engagement changed as well. Coalition forces began moving out of civilian population centers and consolidated into what were called forward-operating bases. For chaplains and civil-affairs experts, this meant that aggressive reaching out degraded. As the war continued in intensity, force protection became important, and by 2005 and 2006 many religious-support teams were ordered to focus solely on providing religious support to their units because it was simply too dangerous to go "outside the wire." While this hindered tactical and even operational units' ability to liaison with religious leaders in their particular areas of operation, a strategic-level effort continued with the State Department, creating a unique program designed to influence key religious leaders in Iraq into accepting a more pluralistic viewpoint.

In 2004, as the Iraq war intensified, then–Deputy Secretary of Defense Paul Wolfowitz established in Department of Defense Directive 1304.19 that chaplains "serve as the principal advisors to commanders for all issues regarding the impact of religion on military operations."[11] At this time the State Department gathered influential Iraqi religious leaders from multiple religious faith groups and brought them together for a conference in the United States hosted by the Department of Defense. State and Defense both hoped to expose these religious leaders to the religious pluralism found in the United States so that they could then lead their followers in Iraqi along a more peaceful route. After this conference, the clerics were taken to places around the United States where they were shown this pluralism in action.

As the State Department action officer was coordinating this program, he would routinely walk by the U.S. Army Chief of Chaplains' Office in the Pentagon. Almost by impulse, on one occasion he asked the army chaplain who worked operations there if the chaplaincy might have something to offer. It is noteworthy that prior to this serendipitous moment chaplains had not had a major role. After consulting with the army chief of chaplains, the operations chaplain gathered a panel of active and reserve chaplains to meet with the clerics during the conference. This included an imam, an Orthodox rabbi, a Roman Catholic priest, and two Protestants—all army chaplains. The Iraqi participants represented Sunnis, Shias, Kurds, Christians, Yezidis, Sufis, and secular groups, and all were intensely interested in how the U.S. chaplaincy managed to care for soldiers with all the varied religious traditions found in the U.S. Army. During the panel, the U.S. Army chaplains discussed pluralism in the U.S. Army as well as how they conducted religious support. Many of the clerics responded strongly when the Jewish rabbi shared that he would pray over the dead and wounded regardless of the soldier's religion but would attempt to pray in that soldier's tradition. Both the Sunni and the Shiite clerics were visibly moved by this knowledge, which contradicted their previous understanding of the Jewish faith. They asked several incredulous and penetrating questions until they were satisfied that this was a normal action for any chaplain. Most had little understanding of the differences between the various denominations in the Christian faith (and frankly were not very interested in learning more about them). Many challenged the Muslim army chaplain (an American convert to Islam) but were generally content with his training. Again, they marveled at the idea of a Muslim chaplain caring for Jewish and Christian soldiers. While the chaplains spoke, the Iraqi religious leaders just smiled and nodded their heads in agreement. They were already there in many ways, but the chaplains did not see it yet. The Iraqi religious leaders spoke about their faith and their fervent belief that all of the participants sitting in the room were children of God who wished to serve God, which was the pursuit of peace among all people.

The mere presence of a panel of multifaith leaders gathering peacefully in the same room demonstrated this faith statement, the very concept of pluralism and acceptance the chaplains were hoping to teach. Sadly, in the following years of insurgency and counterinsurgency, many of the faith leaders gathered in the room that day were undoubtedly killed trying to live out this dream of pluralism and peace. But the success of that first meeting soon led to several others like it, eventually including religious leaders from a variety of Muslim-majority countries. However, these visits by several dozen clerics petered out over the next eighteen months, and there was never a systematic, wide-scale effort to sustain future meetings.

2010 AND BEYOND: JOINT DOCTRINE, SHARED EXPERIENCES, AND COIN

The reality on the ground in Iraq and Afghanistan, and a half-decade of debate and equivocation among the chaplaincies, meant a clearer doctrine was required for the systematic performance of religious-leader liaison activities at all levels. Whereas the tactical level, battalions, brigade combat teams, and divisions would primarily follow their particular command's operational orders, the higher-level commands at theater and joint forces needed to synchronize the many liaison activities being conducted by ministry teams from all military services and at all levels. The rewritten Army Regulation 165-1 required that "chaplains plan, coordinate, execute, and supervise all religious-support activities and resources for the commander, including, but not limited to . . . (a) Religious Leader Liaison (RLL), religious analysis, and religious-support products for all plans and orders."[12] This regulation is worth quoting to show the regulatory authority granted to the chaplain for religious-leader-engagement operations (RLEOs).[13] In addition, another fundamental document was updated, Joint Publication 1-05,[14] which provided a more detailed account of possible ways to perform religious support to include RLEOs. JP 1-05 carefully describes the duties of the civil-affairs team in contrast to the religious-support team as both conduct various operations with the local population. This is important to delineate, since each team provides formal and informal contact with indigenous people, which might make it problematic to differentiate between the two in assessing RLEO effects on cooperation. For example, a religious-support team might work with a mullah to rebuild a mosque using U.S. funds and local labor. The coordination with local labor might be through the civil-affairs team, while the mosque-rebuilding coordination might be through the religious-support team. One can see how, on the one hand, good-faith efforts were being made by both civil affairs and the chaplains. On the other hand, it is obvious that for a variety of reasons—not least of which was the inclination of a given commander regarding safety and the appropriate role of the chaplains—the situation on the ground was confusing in terms of policy as well as practice.

The updated JP 1-05 finally provided a common, joint definition of RLEOs, stating that one of the duties of the religious-support team, "when directed by the commander, [was] establishing relationships with appropriate local religious leaders in consultation with the combatant command chaplain."[15] Obviously the religious-support team labored under a tremendous amount of constraint and with heavy requirements while performing its duties during support and stability operations in dangerous environments. Yet in most circumstances there is enough room for the chaplain to determine the best way to perform all those various duties to execute the religious-support mission, especially as they conduct RLEOs. Thus there was considerable variance in the actual performance of RLEOs during Operation Iraqi Freedom/ Operation Enduring Freedom, with some religious-support teams conducting extensive RLEO activities while others, for various reasons, did little despite doctrine. Often this had to do with the local threat perception (e.g., the difference between the largely stable Kurdish north versus the deadly Sunni Triangle). There was also large variation in the type of these engagements, with some religious-support teams working closely with Islamic religious leaders on various projects with a high degree of personal contact while others were less engaged, with minimal contact. Finally, there was variance due to the possible command level where battalion religious-support teams would conduct microlevel RLEOs and the Multi-National Force–Iraq religious-support teams would conduct RLEO activities that might involve the most influential clerics in Iraq.[16] Despite these diverging factors, by 2010 common joint doctrine JP-105 was able to finally provide clear guidance for the religious-support teams regardless of location or level of command.

Despite the primacy of joint doctrine, the reality is that chaplains and chaplain assistants work within the setting of their service—in my case, the U.S. Army. Its regulations and doctrine provide guidance as well as constraints, limitations, and obligations to all soldiers. To best understand this reality is to understand army doctrine as it relates to support and stability operations as well as to counterinsurgency operations. The cornerstone document for army operations is, appropriately enough, "Field Manual 3-0: Operations," which provides doctrinal guidance for the combatant commander. As a result of the persistent state of war over the last decade, there have been several dramatic changes to this doctrine. One such change is to the operational art, which, among other things, gives guidance on stability mechanisms. In this section the most recent edition—approved in 2008—added that "in the context of stability mechanisms, *influence* means to alter the opinions and attitude of a civilian population through inform and influence activities, presence, and conduct . . . it reflects the ability of friendly forces to operate within the cultural and societal norms of the local populace while accomplishing the mission."[17] This same type of guidance is also found in "Field Manual 3-24: Counterinsurgency" (which is also MCWP 3-33.5 of the Marine Corps), a pivotal doctrinal document produced in 2006 under the guidance of Lieutenant General David H. Petraeus, which launched the transition to counterinsurgency (COIN) (from traditional battlefield and counterterrorism) operations. The manual focuses on those things leaders and their soldiers need to know, think, and do to conduct successful counterinsurgencies. One of the most important tasks is summarized in the overused phrase, "winning hearts and minds"; yet this does indicate the critical importance to both understand and work with the local population.[18] One of the foundational tenets of counterinsurgency operations is that all elements of national power are applied to the political, military, economic, social, and informational infrastructure of the host nation as well as to the insurgents.[19] This is to offset the primary strategy of the insurgents, which is to undermine the legitimacy of the host government along with those coalition forces engaged in the counterinsurgency. Hence the insurgency forces tend to be hidden within the population of the cities and villages where they receive logistical and tactical support for their cause. This requires the combatant commander to use all resources available to delegitimize the insurgent's cause as well as build strong connections with the populace to deny the insurgents the succor of the local inhabitants. One such resource is the religious-support team, which can engage the local religious leaders to enhance coalition legitimacy and thus contribute to the ultimate goal of peace.

COIN was used extensively during the mid- to final phases of the Iraq War and to a more limited degree in the War in Afghanistan. As this brief chapter has noted, the military services' chaplaincy doctrine evolved during the early years of the wars to one that fully supported COIN with religious-leader-liaison programs at all levels. Grand religious councils at the strategic level and a battalion chaplain working with a village imam are all part and parcel of a more mature doctrine of religious-leader liaison. However, it is important to remember the path that brought the chaplaincy to this place, since lessons learned tend to be forgotten and every war tends to be radically different from the one right before it. Thus to know the path preceding the current religious-leader-liaison doctrine is to know how to navigate future paths that call upon the military chaplaincies to serve, as the U.S. Army Chaplain Corps motto says, God and country.

NOTES

1. I will continue using *religious-support team* (RST) in keeping with joint doctrine despite this chapter's focus on army operations. To those unfamiliar with the military, this term is less confusing in describing the composition of the team.

2. See U.S. Department of the Army, "Army Regulation 165-1: Religious Support; Army Chaplain Corps Activities," December 3, 2009, 12, available online at http://www.apd.army.mil/pdffiles/r165_1.pdf; U.S. Department of Defense, "Joint Publication 1-05: Religious Affairs in Joint Operations," November 20, 2009, http://www.dtic.mil/doctrine/new_pubs/jp1_05.pdf; and U.S. Department of the Army, "FM 1-05 (FM 16-1): Religious Support," April 18, 2003, available online at http://www.globalsecurity.org/military/library/policy/army/fm/1-05/fm1-05.pdf.

3. M. Hertling (2001, November 1), "Chaplains Advance Course" (email message to U.S. Army Chief of Staff).

4. U.S. Department of the Army, "FM 16-1: Religious Support," May 26, 1995, available online at http://www.militaryatheists.org/regs/ArmyFM16-1v1995.pdf.

5. G. E. Fuller (2003), *Islamist Politics in Iraq After Saddam Hussein* (Washington, DC: United States Institute of Peace), and A. Baram (2005), *Who Are the Insurgents? Sunni Arab Rebels in Iraq* (Washington, DC: United States Institute of Peace).

6. Fuller 2003, 3.

7. Douglas M. Johnston, *Religion, Terror, and Error: U.S. Foreign Policy and the Challenge of Spiritual Engagement* (Santa Barbara: Praeger, 2011), 56.

8. U.S. Department of the Army, "Army Regulation 165-1," DD-1.

9. Ibid.

10. J. Proctor (2009), *A Short History of Religious Leader Engagement Operations in Operation Iraqi Freedom* (Washington, DC: Headquarters, Department of the Army).

11. Paul Wolfowitz, Department of Defense, "Directive 1304.19," June 11, 2004, updated April 23, 2004, http://www.dtic.mil/whs/directives/corres/pdf/130419p.pdf.

12. U.S. Department of the Army, "Army Regulation 165-1," 12.

13. *Religious-leader-engagement operations* (RLEOs) is a joint-force term, while *religious-leader liaison* (RLL) is specifically an army term.

14. U.S. Department of Defense, "Joint Publication 1-05."

15. Ibid.

16. G. Adams (2006), *Chaplains as Liaisons with Religious Leaders: Lessons from Iraq and Afganistan* (Washington, DC: United States Institute of Peace), I. Houck (2012, February 13), U.S. Army Chaplaincy Director of World Religions (E. Keller, interviewer), and Proctor 2009.

17. U.S. Department of the Army, "Field Manual 3-0: Operations," February 27, 2008, 7–8, available online at http://www.ssi.army.mil/ncoa/AGS_SLC_ALC_REGS/FM%203-0.pdf.

18. U.S. Department of the Army, "Field Manual 3-24 (MCWP 3-33.5): Counterinsurgency," December 15, 2006, available online at http://www.fas.org/irp/doddir/army/fm3-24.pdf.

19. U.S. Department of the Army, "Field Manual 3-24," 1-1.

REFERENCES

Adams, G. (2006). *Chaplains as Liaisons with Religious Leaders: Lessons from Iraq and Afganistan.* Washington, DC: United States Institute of Peace.

Alger, C. (2002). Religion as a Peace Tool. *Global Review of Enthopolitics,* 94–109.

Baram, A. (2005). *Who Are the Insurgents? Sunni Arab Rebels in Iraq.* Washington, DC: United States Institute of Peace.

Chairman of the Joint Chief of Staff. (2009, November 13). Joint Publication 1-05. *Religious Affairs in Joint Operations.* Washington, DC: U.S. Printing Office.

Department of the Army. (2005). *Religious Support Handbook for the Unit Ministry Team TC 1-05.* Washington, DC: U.S. Government Printing Office.

Fox, J. (2000). The Ethnic-Religious Nexus: The Impact of Religion on Ethnic Conflict. *Civil Wars,* 1–22.

Fuller, G. E. (2003). *Islamist Politics in Iraq After Saddam Hussein.* Washington, DC: United States Institute of Peace.

Hertling, M. (2001, November 1). Chaplains Advance Course (email message to U.S. Army Chief of Staff).

Houck, I. (2012, February 13). U.S. Army Chaplaincy Director of World Religions (E. Keller, interviewer).

Johnston, D. M. (2011). *Religion, Terror, and Error.* Santa Barbara: Praeger.

Joint Publication 1-05. (2009). *Religious Affairs in Joint Operations.* Washington, DC: Department of Defense.

Krulak, C. C. (1999). The Strategic Corporal: Leadership in the Three Block War. *Marines Magazine,* 1–2.

Mackay, A., and Tatham, S. (2009). *From General to Strategic Corporal: Complexity, Adaptation, and Influence.* Shrivenham: Defense Academy of the United Kingdom.

Proctor, J. (2009). *A Short History of Religious Leader Engagement Operations in Operation Iraqi Freedom.* Washington, DC: Headquarters, Department of the Army.

Snyder, J. (2011). Introduction to Religion and International Relations: History and Theory. In J. Synder, *Religion and International Relations* (1–23). New York: Columbia University Press.

Thomas, S. (2005). *The Global Resurgence of Religion and the Transformation of International Relations: The Struggle for the Soul of the Twenty-first Century.* New York: Palgrave Macmillan.

Toft, M. (2011). Religion, Rationality, and Violence. In J. Snyder, *Religion and International Theory* (115–39). New York: Columbia University Press.

U.S. Army Field Manual 16-1. (1995). *Religious Support.* Washington, DC: Headquarters, United States Army.

U.S. Army Field Manual 16-1. (2003). *Religious Support.* Washington, DC: Headquarters, United States Army.

U.S. Army Field Manual 3-24. (2006). *Counterinsurgency.* Washington, DC: Headquarters, United States Army.

U.S. Army Field Manual 3.0. (2008). *Operations.* Washington, DC: Headquarters, United States Army.

U.S. Army Regulation 165-1. (2010). *Army Chaplain Corps.* Washington, DC: Headquarters, United States Army.

Wolfowitz, P. (2004, June 11). *Appointment of Chaplains for the Military Departments.* Washington, DC: U.S. Government Printing Office.

5

The Iraqi Inter-Religious Congress and the Baghdad Accords

Micheal Hoyt

Former Secretary of State Madeleine Albright writes, "It is not possible to separate what people feel and believe in the spiritual realm from what they will do as a matter of public policy . . . this is an opportunity."[1] Opportunity? In the current maelstrom of global conflict associated with religious groups, the thought of religion inspiring concrete opportunities for peace seems like an oxymoron. Examples abound of people claiming perverse religious sanction for what are really criminal and merciless acts of violence. The notion of "opportunity" seems to be more closely aligned with preemptive strikes or political sanctions as some form of neocontainment strategy than providing a sense of religious-motivated promise. In Western societies, where religion-inspired violence is less prevalent, shrill, antireligious rhetoric and public policy attempts to limit the scope of individual religious freedom. In short, there is nothing neutral about religion.

Albright goes on to argue, that "religion at its best can reinforce the core values necessary for people from different cultures to live in some degree of harmony; we should make the most of that possibility."[2] The opportunity and possibility of which she speaks is precisely the topic of this chapter. More specifically, this chapter discusses the 2007 Iraqi Inter-Religious Congress (IIRC) and subsequent Baghdad Accords, a religious framework for peace among the sectarian groups killing one another in Iraq at that time. Although missed by the mainstream media, the IIRC was the third pillar of efforts that coalesced to reinforce security in Iraq at the time (the other two being the troop surge and the Sunni Awakening).

This chapter will report how senior military leadership came to appreciate the role that religion played in Iraqi society and its role in the conflict, as well as the practical efforts by senior military leaders—represented by me, command chaplain for the Multi-National Force–Iraq—in tandem with the work of NGOs, faith leaders, and senior Iraqi clerics to bring an end to sectarian violence sanctioned by religious elites. It was grueling, perilous work that was a unique opportunity for peace, and it has lessons to teach us applicable to other theaters of conflict.

BACKGROUND: IRAQ ON THE VERGE OF CIVIL WAR

In June 2006, when I arrived in Baghdad for my second tour in support of Operation Iraqi Freedom, many experts outside government were labeling conditions on the ground an Iraqi civil war. Religious opportunity was defined by al-Qaeda in Iraq, Shia militias, and others as they manipulated mob terror and extortion for their own sectarian ends. Indeed, a document from (Sunni) al-Qaeda in Iraq that was made public in early 2004 indicated this was precisely their strategy: hit the Shia population hard and create a civil war.[3] Their most brazen act was to attack the golden-domed mosque in Samarra in February 2006. The site is among the most sacred of religious spaces to Shia Muslims, the majority population in both Iraq and neighboring Iran. As State Department advisor David Kilcullen writes in *The Accidental Guerrilla*, local Iraqis immediately realized that as an escalation to the point of civil war.[4]

Militias and tribes were using social services, kinship networks, and religious-ethnic fault lines to exacerbate circumstances, callously utilizing provocative religious actors, language, sermons, and violence. Coalition forces were battling a growing insurgency fed by foreign fighters, criminal interference, massive population upheaval, and spiraling U.S. military and Iraqi civilian casualties. When I arrived, the third version of an Iraqi government was less than thirty days on the job, as was the third prime minister in as many years.

The Iraqi Constitution was untried; there was no national judicial system or functioning police force. There was no operating national banking system, national budget, or government-purchasing authority. Public utilities were sporadic at best. All means of travel became an adventure between militia and criminal-extortion checkpoints and random shootings. Security was a combination of vigilante, mercenary, sanctioned terror, and Coalition force activities. The brave Iraqis trying to achieve normalcy were rewarded for their success with murder, family kidnappings, torture, and intimidation. Progress, when it occurred, did so only through the heroic efforts of sacrificial politicians, diplomats, military and security forces, tribal sheikhs . . . and one other extremely influential group—religious leaders.

AN OPPORTUNITY FOR BUILDING BRIDGES:
FRRME AND THE IIRC

I was assigned as the command chaplain on the Multi-National Forces–Iraq (MNF-I) staff. This placed me in a unique position: the senior chaplain for all U.S. forces in Iraq. I worked directly for MNF-I Commanding General George Casey and, later, General Dave Petraeus. The assignment placed me at a strategic and national level of influence and allowed me access to positions of power, strategic dialogues, national-level planning, and, eventually, world leaders of Sunni and Shia Islam. Over the next fifteen months I balanced my duties between three primary jobs: the traditional role of a military chaplain ensuring the free exercise of religion for U.S. forces, advocacy for soldiers and civilians in crisis and in need of pastoral care, and "making the most of the possibilities" to create an opportunity for religion to work for peace. The religious opportunity became known as the Iraqi Inter-Religious Congress (IIRC), and toward that end, the remainder of the story unfolds.

The IIRC represented a peace process, and not a single event, although there was a critical three-day congress of religious leaders in late June 2007 to which all effort was turned. The IIRC was necessary to breaking the cycle of vitriolic rhetoric and self-fulfilling violence that most religious authorities agreed needed to cease but none could stop. Shortly after being elected prime minister in May 2006 Nouri al-Maliki announced a multistep national-reconciliation plan oriented on conferences with tribal, civil, religious, and political leaders as the centerpiece of the forming Government of Iraq (GOI). The plan stalled as all energies turned toward keeping the nascent GOI literally alive and solvent. Everyone (the GOI, MNF-I, local leaders) agreed that national reconciliation was essential to recovery and stability, but no one could devote the energy or muster the resources to make or fund a sustainable plan.

The context is important here. In January 2007, seven months after we began the IIRC process, the special commission known as the Iraq Study Group (led by former secretary of state James Baker and former congressman Lee Hamilton) produced its findings. Recommendations 35 and 36 addressed the issue of reconciliation:

> The United States must make active efforts to engage all parties in Iraq, with the exception of al-Qaeda. The United States must find a way to talk to Grand Ayatollah Sistani, Muqtada al-Sadr, and militia and insurgent leaders. The very focus on sectarian identity that endangers Iraq also presents opportunities to seek broader support for a national-reconciliation dialogue. Working with Iraqi leaders, the international community and religious leaders can play an important role in fostering dialogue and reconciliation across the sectarian divide. The United States should actively encourage the constructive participation of all who can take part in advancing national reconciliation within Iraq. . . .[5]

The United States should encourage dialogue between sectarian commuities, as outlined in the New Diplomatic Offensive above. It should press religious leaders inside and outside Iraq to speak out on behalf of peace and reconciliation.[6]

I spent my first month in Iraq learning everything I could about the detailed theater campaign plan, meeting with and listening to MNF-I staff members, and attending significant meetings involving mission analysis, effects synchronization, Iraqi governance and transition, and the daily operational- and battle-assessment briefings. In my first meeting with General Casey I explained my job as including everything I could do to improve conditions. Wherever my presence could help lighten the load mentally, emotionally, physically, or spiritually, I was committed to spend myself, and to do so in a way that generals Casey and later Petraeus would not have to worry about. I requested and received permission to attend any briefing I thought relevant to my mission as the senior chaplain or as a personal staff officer to the MNF-I commander. In addition, General Petraeus told me "to get all over the theater . . . take care of soldiers; tell me what they need and what I need to know."

During my initial three weeks in country I developed a task list to organize my efforts around that third part of my job, "making the most of the possibilities." The focus of effort provided some direction about what I was up to for my very capable office team of chaplains, chaplain assistants, and religious-program specialists. The tasks, as ultimately elaborated in a series of briefings, were as follows:

1. Determine connect points to Strategic Effects cell and Gen. Petraeus, U.S. Mission–Iraq Ambassador level, Government of Iraq Ministers, Council of Representatives, and endowment heads.
2. Find out how to advise Gen. Petraeus, Chief of Staff, J-2 (Intelligence), on *uniquely religious aspects* of ongoing policies, concerns, plans, focus, and GOI dialogue.
3. Highlight the nature of the problems in Iraq in context with Islamic and other religion's practices/issues. Involve the right level of religious leaders to warrant an audience and credible ideas.
4. Make religious concerns relevant to the Campaign Plan: relevance, collaboration, synchronization with broadest spectrum of agencies to mass effects to meet campaign end state [*end state* is a term of art used by the military to identify the preferred future picture, or desired outcome of action plans].
5. Keep it all spiritually distinct and guard against politicizing or militarizing the intent and outcome.
6. Keep this an Iraqi initiative. We facilitate, but Iraq must solve, innovate, fund, perform, and follow through. We can start the dialogue but must carry GOI message, Iraqi solution.

The army uses the term *doctrine* to refer to that standardized body of information that provides the common point of reference and standards for planning, training, and employment of capabilities. *Chaplain doctrine* means the same thing and does not refer to religious doctrines or theological statements. The above tasks were not part of existing chaplain doctrine in 2006.[7] However, keeping the commander informed through one's staff area of expertise was considered part of the staff-estimate process and certainly expected. My challenge was to keep religious interests relevant to the campaign plan as a means of lightening the load even while expending theater resources.

As I continued to learn the theater, I came in contact with a special Anglican clergyman named Canon Andrew White from the United Kingdom. We met during a worship service we both were attending on the grounds of the Presidential Palace now serving as the U.S. Mission–Iraq (Embassy) and Iraqi and Coalition-government administration offices. Canon White was the Sunday speaker that morning, and we met for lunch in the mess hall after service. White had been working in Iraq since 1998 and was the most well-connected Western religious figure in Iraq. He was the president and founder of an NGO called the Foundation for Relief and Reconciliation in the Middle East (FRRME) and was legendary for his charity to all and bravery and dedication to his faith.

Canon White was known to all the Iraqi politicians (including the former dictator) and had been asked by the interim Prime Minister al-Jaafari to form a series of reconciliation initiatives among Iraq's religious leaders to stem the sectarian violence and achieve support for the new GOI. As early as 2003, White had approached the UK government about such an initiative, only to be rebuffed. Canon White was still committed to the task but did not have the means (e.g., funds, transport) to follow through at a national level. He did have, however, personal access and credibility to work with the warring religious factions and their leaders and almost every GOI official. Canon White and I agreed to work together to present a plan for an Iraqi-led national religious-reconciliation peace initiative. He would use his endless contacts to bring the right actors together, and I would find the way to leverage the operational capabilities of MNF-I to plan, conduct, secure, and integrate the actions with the campaign-plan end state.

True to his word, one week after our first meeting and plan of mutual assistance, Canon White took me with him for his weekly private late-night meeting at the home of the Iraq national security advisor, Dr. Mowaffak al-Rubaie. After some discussion concerning the work of FRRME and the Iraq Institute for Peace (a unique Iraqi NGO Canon White had helped found), the topic of our reconciliation plan emerged. National Security Advisor al-Rubaie was immediately supportive and welcomed MNF-I's interest and support at whatever level could be managed. We spoke for another hour on possible delegates, themes, and dates for a conference. The meeting ended well past midnight, as most of our meetings would over the next year, and White and I both left with a clear sense of shared purpose to facilitate a GOI reconciliation process.

There were two immediate problems to work within in order to gain the momentum to carry the proposal forward to Iraq's prime minister and to MNF-I's commander, General Petraeus. One was a nonfunctioning GOI, and the other an overtasked MNF-I trying to pick up the slack. The new al-Maliki government was literally fighting for survival every day. Most days the Council of Representatives could not muster a quorum to pass business. The strategic issues at MNF-I were mammoth as well. Coalition casualties, especially U.S. losses, were too high. The eight-billion-dollar-a-month war costs were unsustainable.[8] Political alliances within the Coalition were straining to an unknown limit. Public opinion at home was turning negative. The lack of a functioning host government was reversing military tactical successes and formal Iraqi training efforts. Success was vague. The risk for more religious failure was too severe to chance, as was the risk for maintaining the status quo. The conditions were right for a breakthrough, but how to accomplish it?

The *challenge*, not only in Iraq but also in Afghanistan and the Balkans and much of Africa, lies in translating authentic religious understanding and actions into measurable effects while protecting the integrity of religion from being used or perceived as some reinvented version of social-political or military art. The *science*, in this case, was to identify the main interests of the parties involved and offer a practical platform for those interests to be intelligently and peacefully discussed. The *art* was orchestrating this kind of exchange by appealing to and representing the best of faith as the motive for gathering together, communicating, and carrying out the results. This religious peace initiative needed to remain an authentic expression of faith even as it worked within the restraints of government and martial power.

Working in religion demands an awareness and commitment to continuity of informed religious thought, respect, and action. On a personal level this required a daily deeply personal reliance on piety, theological integrity, submission, and patience. On the professional level it required strategic vision, intellectual consistency, adaptability, and honesty in a cycle of purpose/follow-through/feedback. In short, the entire process of working toward conflict resolution from a religious framework requires keeping it authentic as a religious act or function. Religious initiatives are not sociology, civil affairs, or a hybrid of political action and crisis management. Religious initiatives put beliefs into action and frame the practical concepts of faith by and through persons committed to serving in their religion to the betterment of common social values that religious behavior can influence. Anything outside of that becomes fertile ground for fanaticism or disrespect.

The center of gravity for religion is its own integrity. Religious actors may be summoned to another stage—namely, politics or education or military command—but they always take with them their religious script. The more that original script (religion) is used or acted upon or perceived as "leverage" for some other agenda, the greater the pressure on its integrity to adapt (or resist). The greater the perception of the perversion of religion, the greater the stimulus to either abandon it entirely or defend the orthodoxy in the extreme. The more perverted the religion, the less authentic its message. The more damaged the message, the more damaged the followers. The more damaged the followers, the greater the loss of respect. Loss of respect increases desire to settle the score by either discounting the entire religious effect or igniting a new appeal of religious fervor to stop the perverting influence. Religion is not neutral. Religion across Iraq was volatile, and time was running out for all concerned.

Canon White spent his time visiting prospective delegates and maintaining his vast array of contacts across Iraq and the Middle East. I began the work of presenting a national religious-reconciliation plan in useable campaign-plan concepts and strategy. We adopted an end state for the reconciliation initiative: religious understanding and leadership cooperating to prevent terrorism and support GOI sovereignty. I presented the strategic-level main interests of each of the participating parties: the United States (political), the GOI, the FRRME, and religious leaders. We outlined the expectations and where they diverged and converged between the coalition forces, the IIRC, and the GOI. We then examined the large-scale issues using a comparison of vulnerabilities and challenges and agreed on four themes for the conference: deny terror, denounce sectarianism, demonstrate religious cooperation, and display democratic values. The entire conference outcome was to forward three purposes: promote religious acceptance, open a channel of dialogue among all religious expressions and to the GOI, and assist the GOI as an Islamic government. Finally, I aligned our objectives under four of the five campaign-plan lines of operation and demonstrated the risks, resources, and actions we would need to succeed.

I briefed the plan to the MNF-I chief of staff and the director of strategic effects in August 2006 and received permission to move forward as the MNF-I action officer to coordinate the event between MNF-I, FRRME, the GOI, and any other necessary entity, including (and especially) religious leaders. I presented the plan again with Canon White to Dr. al-Rubaie, and he accepted it without change and scheduled us for a one-hour session to brief Prime Minister al-Maliki. Two weeks later our little four-man staff—Canon White, his brilliant Iraq operations officer Pete Maki, our FRRME Iraqi interpreter Samir, and I—spent a very pleasant and focused hour in the prime minister's office with the prime minister and the national security adviser. The prime minister gave his full and immediate support, approved the delegate list, and ordered Dr. al-Rubaie to serve as the GOI point of contact for the detailed planning, appointing Deputy Prime Minister Dr. Barham Salih as his personal representative to work through the political issues as they surfaced. The first conference was scheduled to occur in mid-October 2006.

The immediate issue was funding and location. The location very quickly took a back seat to funding as political intrigue and sectarianism appeared in the various Iraq cabinet positions. The minister of the Office of Reconciliation agreed to work on the plan in principle, but in reality he did absolutely nothing and let it languish in a shuffle of unfulfilled commitments. When we finally wrested the funding request from that office and presented it to the minister of finance, he ignored it for additional weeks, eventually telling us he could not fund it unless we could pay him to do so. The delays in GOI funding that was ultimately never forthcoming caused the conference to be postponed to mid-November. This first cancellation disappointed the delegates but did not discourage any of them, and they all agreed to recommit to the November date.

I began pursuing stop-gap alternate funding from a special source of money called interim Iraqi government (IIG) funds, reserved expressly for GOI events. After some days of careful legal analysis it was determined the funding source could be used for the prime minister's reconciliation event, and it was approved for funding through the same minister of finance as before. The only thing that changed on this denial was the increased amount needed to pay him to release the funds. We did not. He did not. The conference was postponed for a second time and rescheduled for mid-December. This was a frustrating time but illustrative of the difficulties plaguing the fledgling GOI. The prime minister's personally directed reconciliation program could not be supported by the Ministry of Reconciliation. The funding, although immediately available with Iraqi funds, could not be released by Iraq's own minister of finance, and there was no alternative. The idea of an Iraqi-led solution was caught between a prime minister's directive and unwilling administration officials.

Civil strife was continuing to mount. In October 2006 over three thousand Iraqi civilians were killed. November would be no better. The need to break the cycle of violence was great, and religious militias stood at the center of the massacres. Tempers and accusations were out of control almost everywhere in Iraq. Patient conference delegates who had been hoping for a breakthrough—especially the Sunnis, who had now been rebuffed twice by the Shia-led Iraqi government they'd boycotted—grew even more hostile. Sunni delegates began to drop off; so did some Shia delegates. The conference was coming apart before we'd even had one meeting, and the country was spinning into chaos; Iraq's clerics were either contributing to the unrest or overwhelmed in trying to serve the needy or targeted victims themselves.

In November I began to seek U.S. funding though MNF-I dollars. The MNF-I comptroller and staff worked tirelessly to try and find the method to fund the conference, but for all the right reasons no legal remedy could be found. We made an appeal to the Department of Defense comptroller for assistance, and after some weeks of legal scrutiny a funding source became available, but it would be too late to fund a December event. For the third and last time in 2006, Canon White had to call the remaining delegates with the sad news.

This was a dramatic blow for the conference. We had hoped to get at least one conference conducted in December just before the delegates would begin the hajj—the pilgrimage to Mecca. Tactically, if all had gone according to plan with a successful conference, the timing would have been excellent. With most of the Middle East Islamic leaders converging on Mecca and reuniting in their annual pilgrimage any good religious news out of Iraq would have been exponentially dispersed across the region. The hope had been that the good news of the beginning of reconciliation talks would create a signal of hope, and perhaps have a calming effect among Iraq's neighboring states, which in turn might have many positive effects on the insurgency. Instead, the news of December was "two more months like October!"

In between the funding follies, Canon White and I met with Council of Representative (COR) members to try and build their support for a national religious-leader-led reconciliation opportunity. We spoke with the leaders of the six political parties holding seats in the COR, all of whom were directly allied with one senior religious leader or another. Those meetings were often very tense and filled with political statements that had nothing to do with our agenda on the surface. What I came to find out later was that our conduct (and mine specifically) was being carefully measured. I met these COR persons wherever and whenever I could. Sometimes we met in the International Zone at the palace. Sometimes we met in the home of one COR member or another, hosting several others. Sometimes we met in an abandoned hotel lobby. I was always in uniform and traveled in some war-torn civilian version of what passed in Iraq as a car.

Our party consisted of just Canon White, Samir, Peter, and me. My uniform and credentials would get us through the Coalition security points. Samir's local knowledge and unsurpassed translating skills got us around town. Canon White's many friendships and vast FRRME generosity cast a wide blanket of popular support that discouraged rival militia attacks. Peter's impeccable coordination kept us at the right place and time. I would later find out that the story of the "occupier's chaplain" willing to risk going anywhere, without armored escort, was getting around, and it would come to make a difference later in the game.

The meetings were unpredictable in frequency, content, and, most especially, mood. I went to the meetings specifically to speak as a man of faith about the religious principles of faith, charity, forgiveness, sacrifice, social order, and communal support. I found these encounters to be stimulating, crazy, humorous, and sometimes wonderfully hospitable. They were always personally and spiritually very challenging. I prayed privately on the way, often during the meetings while I was being verbally assaulted, and on the way back. Prayer was (and remains) my centering spot. It is essential in all theologies, a great common reference point and a truly miraculous power.

Prayer affects the heart and mind. I mention this to hearken back to my earlier comment that religious work must remain an authentic expression of faith with a continuity of thought, action, and respect. Respect is perhaps the biggest influence over what may or may not happen next. All religious peace work requires it, and I think faithfulness demands it. Respect is also one of the first things to diminish among people who are in power. Oftentimes an occupying force loses sight of this fact after years of continual presence.

These meetings served to preserve delegates, recruit new ones, and test the themes of our reconciliation message. It also prepared us—me especially—for the conference challenges of debate, conferring, note taking, and relationship building in a foreign culture and unknown language. In a country full of violence, where everybody has lost something, symbols and small gestures of gracefulness or assistance or generosity will say more than hours of intelligent discourse. It is essential to communicate this up the chain of command.

Religious actors deal in the areas of intentionality, authenticity, credibility, and integrity. It is more than an assessment of "Can one be trusted?" Religion is not a gimmicky "goodwill gesture." When the chaplain—or commander—fails to follow through on a task, breaks appointments, does not keep promises, or appears prejudicial, the observant religious leader sees a breakdown on two levels: individual character and the value of the spiritual message represented. If the character does not match the message or vice versa, then both are rejected.

When a chaplain fails in either character or commitments, the logic flows like this: *The chaplain did not keep his word. The chaplain is either unreliable or a liar. The spiritual message or faith group (or command) is unreliable, and the message is false. Further engagement with this faith group (or command) is not helpful. Any future engagement will occur against a backdrop of deceit, because there is no need for honest and open exchanges. Americans can't be trusted, because their spiritual leaders (or official promises) are untrustworthy, just like their religion.* Strange as it sounds, religious systems can prove unforgiving. Religious people have to prove otherwise.

In January 2007 the national security advisor gave us an entirely new delegate list. Political situations were changing. Canon White secured a fourth venue as well as the personal support of UK prime minister Tony Blair to hold the IIRC at a secluded and gated facility in the United Kingdom perfect for our needs. All the delegates concurred, as traveling and meeting in Iraq was too dangerous. The meeting was set for mid-February amid much skepticism and Sunni threats to abandon the process if this got canceled. This time the funding issues were solved by the DOD, and the deposits were made and the final plans put in place. Three days before we were to host the conference, all the visas were denied. In a weird turn of events, the money we finally received was forfeited in lost deposit fees and the meeting did not happen. Again.

This fourth cancellation nearly destroyed all the goodwill remaining for a reconciliation event. Even Canon White's unquestioned credibility began to weaken. To further complicate matters, Prime Minister al-Maliki made a speech in late January declaring that "from now on all important meetings about the future of Iraq must occur in Iraq." Not only was the event postponed, but it was now going to be rescheduled for Baghdad, one of the deadliest and most dangerous cities in the Middle East. The senior Iraqi Sunni delegates planning to attend the UK event were living in exile out of the country. Without credible Sunni representation, there could be no reconciliation conference. They either would not or could not come, and so nothing looked remotely possible now.

Canon White and I met with Deputy Prime Minister Salih to determine his willingness to let the exiled Sunni religious leaders reenter the country for this conference. He assured us some could reenter without prejudice, but after four cancellations the credibility of the GOI was strained to its limits. The Sunni religious leaders had no one to trust but Canon White and demanded a preconference meeting in April in Amman, Jordan, to discuss the entire IIRC opportunity. A further condition for this meeting was that the "occupiers' chaplain" attend this meeting with Canon White. The Sunnis despised the GOI and MNF-I. However, MNF-I was the real power broker in the country, according to them, and my presence was their assurance of two things: they were talking with the seat of power that could probably get something done, and they were speaking with a fellow cleric as someone they could trust to carry the message and respect their religious positions on the matters at hand.

Symbols are important, including such gestures as traveling unprotected and speaking words of faith—even a different faith. All of these things spoke to our intent more effectively than the dilemmas of canceled venues. I knew from my months of previous dealings with religious leaders that a business suit and tie represented a government official and engendered distrust and animosity. Samir was kind enough to get a couple of clerical-collar shirts made for me in Baghdad, and I wore a sports coat and clerical collar to all the meetings in Amman, the IIRC, and Cairo—despite the fact that this is not the common "uniform" for Baptist ministers of my tradition at home! It was fascinating to see the power of religious preference at work. Islamic religious leaders had no problem dealing with the Christian chaplain of the occupying forces in overtly Christian clothing. I was supposed to be Christian, and that is what they respected. Yet everyone had a problem with a fellow Muslim government leader in a business suit!

The Amman conference went on for three days. It was hosted by Sheikh Dr. Abdul Latif Humayeen, the head of the Iraqi Scholar's Group, the most influential Sunni organization in Iraq. The membership of the ISG included every major mosque in Iraq—counting over seven hundred Sunni religious leaders—and was the leading political anti-Shia and GOI voice. Abdul Latif was the former personal imam to Saddam Hussein. The attendees were the most influential religious leaders in and out of Iraq. Together these men controlled much of the Sunni response to sectarian violence, militias, and the insurgency against the "occupiers." The content was generally free from accusations and focused on the practical matters of religious ethics, social justice, causes and remedies for violence, and personal theology. Basically it was their test to see how "religious" this IIRC idea was and whether Canon White or I had been co-opted to some GOI or MNF-I nonreligious agenda. The meeting ended with promises to reconsider attending in Baghdad. The last week of April, one week later, Sheikh Dr. Abdul Latif informed Canon White that he would send his senior representatives to the meeting but that he and the other top Sunni leaders would await the outcome of the IIRC to decide further action.

THE IIRC FINALLY MEETS: THE BAGHDAD ACCORDS

We had tentatively scheduled the middle of May for the IIRC, but the problems in surmounting security, travel, the delegate list, the agenda, and the usual funding loomed too large to accomplish in the three weeks available. So the IIRC was scheduled for the fifth and final time for June 11–13 at the only working hotel in Baghdad, the Al Rasheed. This time the game was on, and there would be no "next" opportunity. Final planning began in earnest and consumed huge amounts of effort and resources for the next month. The actual planning and coordination details are an entire story unto themselves.

The IIRC was one of the most complicated, resource-intensive interagency and international efforts conducted in postwar Iraq. The security package for the three-day conference included an American infantry battalion, Iraqi special-forces company, helicopter gunships, an artillery firing and counter-fire battery, military-police units, canine bomb-sniffing and personal-search units, medical-evacuation assets, and a large number of increased pedestrian and vehicle checkpoints, guard posts, and surveillance technologies. We coordinated movement plans from Baghdad International Airport, securing delegate holding areas for our arrivals and departures. Every arrival and departure required special armored convoys for ground transportation, en-route emergency-response plans, and helicopter VIP movements to and from the conference site.

In all I worked with three private-contractor security firms, four U.S. federal agencies, three Iraqi airport authorities, two UN organizations, two private air-flight services for diplomatic and cultural exchange, the Al Rasheed Hotel management and full staff, ten different MNF-I staff agencies, three separate U.S. commands, three agencies in the Department of Defense and the Office of the Secretary of Defense, four national ambassadors, the Office of White House Liaison, and the Offices of the Prime Minister, Deputy Prime Minister, and Vice President of Iraq, Iraq Council of Representatives, and Chief of Staff of the Army of Iraq. Canon White worked with the fifty-five delegates and seven COR members to keep them all interested in attending, and staying, at the conference.

The conditions at the Al Rasheed were warlike. The outside temperature averaged 115 degrees Fahrenheit, and inside there was no working air conditioning. Electricity was unreliable and operational for only an hour a day. There was no running water except for the toilets. No elevators in the ten-story hotel functioned. The individual room temperatures reached 120 degrees each day. We could not go outside in groups of more than five and could not stay out longer than ten minutes because the sniper and mortar or rocket attacks were too prevalent. No delegate could leave the hotel grounds for the entire duration of the conference because there was no way to secure their safety or movement in Baghdad. The hotel food came in varying states of preparedness because the electricity and water were so sporadic. We ate one plenary "social" dinner in complete darkness after the light went out while we were being served. It was like eating in a cave . . . at 110 degrees.

Yet the delegates stayed, formally attired in their flowing robes and tribal headdresses. No one complained—except for one incident that nearly closed the conference. On the second day, some of the delegates threatened to walk out if they did not get enough water to perform ablutions before the afternoon-prayer recess. The hotel could not supply the water. I ended up acquiring hundreds of individual bottles of water from MNF-I sources, and Samir and I spent a very hurried and sweat-soaked hour personally delivering a dozen bottles of water per man to each delegate. Ten flights of stairs with a flashlight, a dozen bottles at a time, to fifty-five delegates. We laughed about it later.

The IIRC itself convened in the large banquet hall in the interior of the hotel. There were no windows to minimize any blast effects or sniper attempts. The room never got below 100 degrees. During the first day, the delegates screamed at one another, denouncing one another's factions as murderers. Much of this was heartfelt bitterness, but some of it was posturing. By the end of the first day of obligatory accusations, a change began to take place, and conversations in the following days focused on substantive discussion of problems, committee work, and consensus. The IIRC concluded with an amazing set of accords. What was most important, and enduring, about the entire event was the event itself: for the very first time since the sectarian mess had begun in 2006, actual opposing forces had met. Many of the delegates were personally involved in planning or conducting violent attacks against one another. Now they were engaging on a personal level—devoid of stereotype, absent public, contrived rhetoric, focused on the common dilemma of being a victim—and gathered to personify not their individual religions per se, but rather the best side of a practical faith. It was a historic opportunity to find the "excuse" to begin to walk away from the terrible escalation of which they were all casualties outside those walls. The conference was cochaired by respected Shia and Sunni leaders. They modeled how to disagree and agree. The factions assembled followed their lead.

All the delegates accepted this humble beginning as their best chance to move to a different conclusion than anarchy and regain some badly needed constituent trust after sixteen months of mayhem and conflicted religious messaging. It was their solution, not the government's, but they had the government's attention. The second day of the conference Prime Minister al-Maliki spoke with the IIRC cochairs and COR members in attendance. He expressed his complete support for their efforts, bravery, and tenacity in sticking to the issues. He made no particular promise (and no one sought any) but did say the eyes of the country were watching the effort. Almost none of the delegates favored the al-Maliki government, but all wanted the GOI to acknowledge the importance and essential role religion and religious leaders must play in an Islamic state. That much was accomplished, and it was enough for the time being.

The conference concluded with a planned live press conference. Two minutes before the press conference, cell phones began chirping among the assembled speakers. The sacred golden mosque in Samarra had been bombed a second time, destroying much of the remaining structure. The first bombing, eighteen months earlier, had nearly initiated civil war. But this time, instead of recrimination and calls to violence, the delegates issued a unanimous plea for calm, nonviolent responses. These formerly violent protagonists appealed to the unity of Islam and the bombing as an attack on all and therefore a requirement of all to unite in a common response of repose and order. Then they began speaking about the conference. The result was that nothing marked the second bombing except disappointment in the destruction of such a historical site. A transformation was already occurring.

The IIRC focused on methods for reducing violence through tribal and religious leadership. The delegates, many of whom came together as current warring enemies, began to see each other as "under the same sun," and active discussions resulted in lively debate on key issues such as militias, education and rhetoric in places of worship, protection of worship sites, and the spread of unauthorized weapons. The shared abysmal conditions of the conference accommodations, the mutual risk of mortar and rocket attack, and the common dangers of traveling to and from the meetings placed everyone on similarly vulnerable footing and humanized the entire delegation. The accords occurred as a result of a degree of personal "heart" change borne in part of desperation and exhaustion but transformed by religious commitments and interpreted by the practical imposition of faith. It wasn't the accord per se, but rather the events that made the IIRC real.

The words came from clerics representing the broadest representation of religious leaders (both by sect and by geography) held in Iraq in the prior thirty-seven years, including religious leaders of the Sunni, Shia, Chaldean, Armenian, Yazidi, and Mandaean traditions, from Baghdad, Basra, Tikrit, Sulaymanyah, Fallujah, and Kurdistan. Sessions concluded with the drafting and signing of a final statement pledging to actively work to reduce violence, protect and restore holy religious sites, and form a series of committees to ensure implementation of the points agreed.

The accords received the personal endorsement of the prime minister and his directed signature by Sayyid Dr. Fadel al-Shara, his personal representative and advisor on religious affairs. It was the first broad-based religious accord to recognize the government of Iraq and call for integration and action by the Iraqi government on all previous and future tribal or religious formal conferences to achieve reconciliation. The accords were the first religious document to publicly renounce al-Qaeda by name and declare the spread of arms and unauthorized weapons as a criminal act. Crucially, the IIRC process and the accord provided a way ahead for committed public action by religious leaders to denounce violence, deny terrorism, demonstrate support for democratic principles and the constitution, and display national unity.

The accord was signed by representatives from twenty-two Sunni clerics, eleven Shia clerics, four Kurds, two Christians, two Council of Representative members, and the prime minister of Iraq. The signing ceremony was solemnly attested by the ambassadors from the United Kingdom, Italy, and Denmark and by the political ambassador to the U.S. Mission–Iraq. Major General W. Scott III (USAF), director of strategic effects, Multi-National Force–Iraq (MNF-I), represented General Petraeus; Mr. Robert Macfarlane, former U.S. National Security advisor; and Mr. Matthew Shoffling (of Middle East Policy in the U.S. Department of Defense).

Peace rarely moves forward without a price. The next day, after the delegates left, a rocket attack destroyed the area outside one of the hotel entrances—the very site where many of us had gathered in our small groups to take the ten minutes of "outside" 115-degree air. Tragically, three El Salvadorian guards died in the attack—the same men who had watched over us so diligently the previous three days. One week later, a ceiling bomb planted in a hotel lobby murdered seven of the IIRC delegates, along with twenty other clerics, as they met to discuss the accords and plan the way ahead.

The accords became the basis for further meetings and eventually an unprecedented joint Shia and Sunni fatwa in March 2008 calling for an end to all religious violence, to include persecution of non-Muslim minorities. Canon White, Peter, Samir, and I followed up the IIRC event with the senior religious leaders of Islam in a Cairo meeting at two venues on August 7.

The senior religious leaders attending the Cairo meeting validated the IIRC accords for all concerned. One month later the Mahdi Army—the Shia militia of Muqtada al-Sadr—declared a cease-fire, followed by the Sunni militia, and Iraq civil strife began to reform into lower levels of violence primary controlled by al-Qaeda in Iraq and marauding criminal elements. Religion began to bind up some wounds instead of making them. The IIRC never met again. Nothing on its scale has occurred since the June 2007 event. The event did, however, create a new entity called the High Council of Iraq Religious Leaders. This council represent the Shia Majeria (the four ruling grand ayatollahs) in Najaf as well as the Sunni Islamic leadership in the Middle East. The council meets regularly to sustain Shia and Sunni dialogue and advise the GOI on matters of religious and political significance.

CONCLUSION: A RELIGIOUS OPPORTUNITY SEIZED

Secretary Madeleine Albright writes that, "in the wrong hands, religion becomes a lever used to pry one group of people away from another, not because of some profound spiritual insight, but because it helps whoever is doing the prying."[9] Peace work is always dangerous, rarely clean, and very conflicted. It demands the best one has to bring to it and a commitment to a result that exceeds self-interest, and to some degree national interests. Peace work is about people. Religion is personal. Religious leaders who want to advance the cause of conflict resolution should follow the basic principles of intentionality, authenticity, and credibility.

The key to religious dialogue lies in safeguarding the discipline of religion as the focused domain of effort. Trivializing religion guarantees negative outcomes. Religious dialogue, achievements, or councils cannot become staff gimmicks. Religion managed out of its context makes the results irreverent and therefore irrelevant. In other words, one brings other planning consider-ations and intellectual constructs to religion to find the connecting points to advance the end state rather than to drag religion through some preconceived checklists or outcomes to stylize a religious result. This is intentionality.

A military force that respects the religious milieu of its affected population (both at home and abroad) significantly increases its perceived legitimacy. Authenticity is actualizing the dogma and the design in a religion that makes life flow for its adherents. The strategic religious planner harmonizes military outcomes compatible with the salient spiritual truths that manifest themselves in the cultural norms and expectations of the territories in which they find themselves. A population that can normalize activities (military, political, legal) within their authentic religious practice is much less vulner-able to extremism, insurgency, and antagonistic sentiments. Authenticity is keeping the main thing (religion) the main thing.

Sustained religious success will manifest in sustained religious credibil-ity. Credibility links to example (personal and corporate) and is the single-most required and overlooked trait. American adversaries (as well as allies and Coalition partners) evaluate the actions, behaviors, and intentions of America through a religious prism. Strategic religious-engagement planning considers the prospects of maintaining "religious" credibility in the conduct of operations in order to sustain momentum. Persons involved in religious engagements meet based on their assessments of credibility as measured by actions, truth, and respect. When intentionality, authenticity, and credibility reinforce each other, the conditions for actionable religious outcomes remains high.

The real art of religious engagement is like two tightrope walkers meeting in the middle of a high-wire routine to transfer the weight of one onto the other and continue the journey to the opposite platform. Religious leaders must possess the skill, maturity, and professional commitment (including patrons) to make the engagements survive the perils of imbalance, showmanship, and circumstance. This kind of work is for neither the novice nor the imposter. It requires a thoughtful approach and commitment to continuity and synchronization. We cannot change religion, but we can affect the way religion impacts our world.

NOTES

1. Madeleine Albright, *The Mighty and the Almighty: Reflections on America, God, and World Affairs* (New York: HarperCollins, 2006), 77.

2. Ibid., 78.

3. "Al Qaeda Leader in Iraq 'Killed by Insurgents,'" Australian Broadcasting Corporation, http://www.abc.net.au/news/2007-05-01/al-qaeda-leader-in-iraq-killed-by-insurgents/2537000, accessed May 31, 2013.

4. David Kilcullen, *The Accidental Guerrilla: Fighting Small Wars in the Midst of a Big One* (Oxford: Oxford University Press, 2009).

5. James A. Baker III and Lee H. Hamilton, *The Iraq Study Group Report* (New York: Vintage Books, 2006), 45.

6. Ibid., 46.

7. The tasks listed above now appear normally as *religious advisement*, a new term codified with the publication of "Joint Publication 1-05: Religious Affairs in Joint Operations," codified November 20, 2009. In 2006 these tasks were well in line with staff responsibilities but generally not practiced at a strategic level by chaplains.

8. Reuters, "Iraq War Cost to Hit $8.4 Billion a Month," *Los Angeles Times,* January 19, 2007, http://articles.latimes.com/2007/jan/19/world/fg-cost19.

9. Albright, *The Mighty and the Almighty*, xi.

6

✝

Military Chaplains as Whole-of-Government Partners

S. K. Moore

The complexities of contemporary conflict have summoned from the international community a response of ever-increasing sophistication and ongoing adaptation. The whole-of-government approach to operations has emerged from this examination, representing a more integrative process of "creat[ing] sustainable conditions for peace in security zones by employing multiple different resources capabilities and expertise in a concerted effort expanded to include issues of domestic security."[1] In 2010 President Obama embraced the whole-of-government approach within the new National Security Strategy,[2] a policy shift echoed by then–Secretary of State Hillary Clinton. At the Brookings Institution Clinton stated the imperative "to make the case that defense, diplomacy, and development were not separate entities, either in substance or process, but that indeed they had to be viewed as part of an integrated whole and that the whole of government then had to be enlisted in their pursuit."[3] Taking collaboration further still is the notion of the whole of society—cooperation between whole-of-government entities and civil-society organizations already engaged in building security from the ground up. Much potential exists in establishing strategic alliances with these indigenous actors.[4]

It is in such operational venues that an irenic impulse among military chaplains is leading to a peace-building role among religious leaders and their respective communities within indigenous populations. Under their commanders' authority and in their explicit intent, chaplains are advancing peaceful relations among fractured communities providing opportunities for encounters to occur—creating a safe and transformative space for dialogue where conflicts, or their residual effects, have left intercommunal relations either strained or nonexistent. In some instances, exchanges with those of *tolerant voice* have precipitated shared ritual events and collaborative activities resulting in engendered trust and renewed cooperation across ruptured ethnic divides. It is this reframing of relation that provides the impetus for beginning the journey of reconciliation—actual religious diplomacy in certain cases.[5] The question before the reader is this: Does this facilitative role of chaplains—known as *religious-leader engagement* (RLE)—hold strategic benefit for the broader mission?

This chapter will consider RLE as an aspect of the whole-of-government approach against the backdrop of a candid exploration of the efficacy of today's nascent governments to garner the allegiance of the citizenry as a whole. The concept of a more hybrid approach of governance inclusive of traditional identity and structures will be examined. As such, serious consideration must be given to the *strategic social space* that religion holds within traditional societies globally, juxtaposed with the more secular culture of the West. In this light, the *social space* that chaplains inhabit when engaging indigenous religious leaders will be considered. The *intellectual space* of religion within civil society offers occasion for those of tolerant voice to oppose injustice and violence, bringing forward a different vision of a new society.[6] It is the *institutional space* of religious organizations, working within a coalition of endeavours, where the intellectual challenges are enacted. As will be seen, such engagement raises concerns in terms of the *political space* that encounters of this nature may engender. Noted is the chaplain's role as facilitator, as a means of bringing to bear the expertise of whole-of-government personnel where opportunity affords. Two case studies will be consulted, citing a Canadian and a French chaplain, collaborating with their whole-of-government partners in Afghanistan and Kosovo, respectively. In each instance the trust established and social capital achieved created the conditions for helping religious leaders to *transcend* their differences in pursuit of a better future for their respective peoples.

THE CONTEXT: FRAGILE AND FAILED STATES

In order to properly situate a discussion regarding the potential role of operational chaplains working alongside their whole-of-government partners, one must, among other things, consider the context of international missions offered here: fragile and failed states. The open warfare that, until recent years, has preoccupied the more "elite" countries in North America and Europe, as well as centers of power among Third World countries, in many instances, has been eclipsed by nonstate organizations, extremely elusive in terms of their structure and activities. Such groups are unable to seriously challenge major state power. Nevertheless, the potential for them to inflict material damage and loss of life is impossible to disclaim. Their ability to strike at civil society in ways that are hard to foresee and still more difficult to combat, evoking fear and creating instability, is worrisome.[7] The movement from the more traditional interstate warfare to what may be described as intrastate conflict has ushered in hostilities that tend to be more asymmetric and intractable in nature.[8] The following provides a glimpse into the complexity and chaotic nature of today's more intractable conflict environment:

> That environment is ever more dynamic, uncertain, and challenging. Often it involves irregular and asymmetric conflict conducted by a range of foes, including highly adaptive "media-savvy" terrorist organizations, intent less upon defeating armed forces than in eroding their will to fight, warlords seeking to retain power and influence over local populations at any price, and transnational criminal organizations ready, willing, and able to buy, sell, and trade everything from drugs to armaments for personal gain. Frequently it involves failed and failing states whose tenuous existence and inability to meet popular demands offer ready breeding ground for rebellion and civil war, as well as a secure base from which adversaries can function. And it involves complex human and physical terrain—with large, densely populated cities and highly diverse populations (i.e., ethnically, religiously, economically, and culturally) often serving as the backdrop for military operations.[9]

State fragility, its destabilizing effect regionally, and the capacity to export terrorism to other parts of the world together create undoubtedly one of the major concerns confronting the international community today.

The above overview aptly delineates the complexity of contemporary conflict precipitating the ever-evolving multifaceted response of the international community. Increasingly, it draws attention to the principle of hybridity, especially as it relates to local, on-the-ground collaboration.

HYBRIDITY: IS THERE SPACE TO ENGAGE TRADITIONAL FORMS OF LEADERSHIP?

Volker Boege, Anne Brown, Kevin Clements, and Anna Nolan—whose research this opening section will draw on—recognize the challenges facing the international community. In addition, they pose probing questions while offering cogent suggestions to seeing fragile states revitalized. From a historical perspective, they contend that much of the instability known to the global south can, in great part, be traced back to the move toward "decolonization" following the Second World War. Many of today's new states came into being during that time. Boege et al. suggest that these independence movements were partially driven by the exhaustion of the colonial powers and some of the more specific international dynamics of the postwar period. Both the political elites and the international community at large welcomed the newly achieved statehood, often confusing the formal declaration of independence with the formation of a state, without taking into sufficient account the myriad of obstacles these newly formed states still faced.[10] Much emphasis has been placed on the benefits of statehood with a paucity of recognition of its social costs in terms of the sacrifice of existing identities and structures that appear to run counter to hierarchies and systems being put in place—nascent statehood.[11]

The authors raise reasonable concerns regarding state institutions claiming authority over large territories, which may only give evidence to distant outposts in regions that may, to a large extent, remain stateless. Federal governments often experience difficulty in extending sufficient, let alone consistent, influence beyond their national capital regions. In such instances, it is not uncommon to find the vestiges of customary (indigenous) nonstate institutions of governance functioning similarly to a time prior to colonial rule. It is in this expanse of territory, great distances from any central authority, "where state 'outposts' are mediated by 'informal' indigenous societal institutions that follow their own logic within the (incomplete) state structures."[12] Here the identity of "citizen" and the "notion of the state" find it difficult to take root. Overcoming this relative disconnectedness from the state is challenging for national leadership when expectations are low among the people in terms of receiving much from the central government, much less any sense of responsibility among the "citizenry" to fulfill obligations. Despite the best efforts of the international community, extending adequate security and other basic services to the more distant points of the state, in many cases, has been difficult to achieve.

Historically, for many former colonies, transitioning to statehood often meant a marginalization of more traditional forms of societal governance by elites in an effort to establish their authority. Where the representation of central government has been weak, a concomitant dearth of allegiance to the state by the people has followed. Compounding this further has been the relative ease with which other entities have moved into the vacuum—where the state has failed to provide adequate security and basic services, others have gained the support of the local populace due to their ability to address these needs.

It is often the case that the lack of depth to the subjective notion of statehood among the people lessens a sense of citizenship. People profess loyalty to their group—whatever that may be—instead of the state: "As members of traditional communities, people are tied into a network of social relations and a web of mutual obligations, and these obligations are much more powerful than obligations as a 'citizen.'"[13] Fragile statehood in many parts of the global south exhibits diverse and competing claims to power and logics of order that coexist, overlap, and intertwine. The result has frequently proven to be a layered and complex convergence of more formal structures of statehood, traditional informal societal order, and the effects of globalization, all of which may be compounded with the social fragmentation associated with ethnic, tribal, and religious forms.[14] Boege et al. define this as a hybridity of leadership.

Within fragile states, hybrid political orders of this nature are more the norm. In establishing governance and expanding development, whole-of-government personnel are frequently confronted with sustaining change within such hybrid systems, especially in regions where effective representation of central governments struggles to be a consistent presence. The danger lies in "trying to produce a state that people do not recognize as their own or from which they feel alienated in important ways."[15] The authors cite cases where the lack of understanding of hybrid political orders has undermined efforts to revitalize the state in comparison to instances when central governments have successfully incorporated more traditional forms of societal structures and leadership into governance. In their estimation, conflict has often resulted where political elites have resorted to a more top-down imposition of values as opposed to sustaining change in the recognition of more bottom-up formation of political communities committed to peace building and development. "Accordingly, it is important to stress the positive potential rather than the negative features of so-called fragile states, focusing on hybridity, generative processes, innovative adaptation, and ingenuity, perceiving community resilience and customary institutions not so much as spoilers and problems but as assets and sources that can be drawn upon in order to forge constructive relationships between communities and governments and between customary and introduced political and social institutions."[16]

All too often, warlords and militias capture media attention, some of whom espouse a religiosity of sorts. Nonviolent community-based groups also emerge focusing on local peace and security—though their lower profile often finds their voices drowned out by the rhetoric of more radical elements. These may take the form of market associations, local trade groups, youth groups, or intercommunal peace committees representative of a cross section of ethnicity. Local religious authorities committed to more peaceful approaches to resolving conflict and maintaining the peace fall within this category.[17]

RELIGION: CREATING SPACE IN CIVIL SOCIETY FOR REFRAMING CONFLICT

The purpose of the above brief discussion on the hybridity of political orders within fragile states is twofold: (1) to more clearly identify what often is the sociopolitical landscape for whole-of-government personnel endeavoring to establish governance and foster development in recovering states, and (2) to open the way for a more candid discussion with respect to the constructive role religion may play in collaborative efforts at peace building and development where more hybrid forms of leadership are in effect.

Some would argue that one of the more significant aspects of religion is the social capital it enjoys within civil society. If such privilege does exist, it is, of course, dependent on certain causal factors within a given culture that create such possibilities. John D. Brewer, Gareth I. Higgins, and Francis Teeny offer clarity to the murky waters of implicating religion in the resolution of conflict when, normally, the tendency is for many to give such consideration a wide berth.

They begin by drawing a distinction between negative and positive peace, the former representing the absence of violence, the later affirming an environment that is just, fair, and exhibiting social redistribution, thus contributing to the socioeconomic well-being of the *other*.[18] In this light, peace means more than an agreement to a negotiated settlement; rather, it carries with it the sense of a sweeping reordering of social relations. It is fair to say that variance exists in how peace is understood. Further to this understanding is the lucidity Brewer et al. bring to the subtleties that exist between *bonding social capital* and *bridging social capital* as they relate to religious groups.[19] It is the bonding social capital among more regressive religious groups that contributes to the hesitancy of many to consider including religious leaders/bodies in peace-building endeavors. It is true that groups can display a high degree of solidarity where trust, sociability, and bonding are evident, and yet hold to a strict antipeace stance. More than a few terrorist organizations profess religious intentions and yet are capable of extreme violence and lawlessness. Such groups may be held in high esteem by local populations for the "good work" they do in addressing welfare needs: housing, education, medical care, and so on. It is for this reason that religion is often perceived as having high bonding social capital value but weak bridging social capital in terms of offering any serious contribution to peace-building and development endeavors.[20]

Bridging social capital, on the other hand, aids in conceptualizing the role of religion in the peace processes by defining *strategic social spaces* in civil society, thus moving beyond a listing of accomplishments to identifying special locations where peace building may occur. As such, religious organizations have been known to carry weight well beyond that normally enjoyed by the adherents of a giving group. It is in strategic social spaces that mechanisms may be identified, allowing religion to align itself with positive peace, which, in turn, transforms it into becoming part of the solution.[21]

Brewer et al. categorize a number of strategic social spaces within civil society that potentially lend themselves to religious peace building. The intent here is to borrow from their research insights by adapting their concepts to the operational environment. In particular, the following three areas relating to strategic social spaces will be examined for their value of religious-leader engagement as an emerging construct in operations: social spaces, intellectual spaces, and institutional spaces. Vital to the hypothesis brought forward here—chaplains engaging local religious leaders in collaboration with their whole-of-government partners—are the distinct opportunities present with religious leaders of tolerant voice in conflict and postconflict environments.

Social Spaces

Chaplains are religious leaders and, as such, are recognized by their indigenous counterparts as sharing certain commonalities: belief, positions of leadership in faith communities, a spiritual bond. The resulting social capital enhances occasions where dialogue may begin. Relationships build and trust develops as a safe space is created where indigenous religious leaders gain confidence due to the chaplain's genuine concern for the well-being of the other.

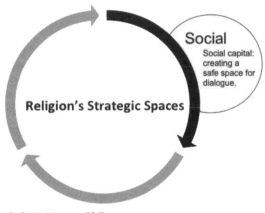

© S. K. Moore, PhD

As will be seen in the two instances below, Imam Suleyman Demiray (Canada) and Roman Catholic priest Father Michel de Peyret (France) each facilitated the emergence of bridging social capital between the religious leaders of faith communities experiencing strained relations due to the conflict of their respective identity groups. In such instances, positive peace is provided a chance to take root.

Chaplains must be cognizant of the political spaces they may potentially occupy in conflict's highly charged environment. Depending on the level of engagement—regional or national—this can be a concern, as it represents a space not normally entered by chaplains. By virtue of their ministry among the higher levels of religious leadership, both Imam Demiray and Chaplain de Peyret found themselves in that liminal space where the threshold of religion and politics begin to converge. This is precisely why such initiatives must be conducted with commanders' authorization and in collaboration with those who have expertise in such matters. This is not to suggest that chaplains should never cross the threshold of the political space. Rather, the point made here is that they should never proceed alone. Experienced whole-of-government personnel offer much by way of direction and support. Where opportunity presents, chaplains function as facilitators, introducing the appropriate personnel to the process. Remaining at the table as the trusted friend is a role more suited to chaplains. Political spaces may be broached in such a manner.

Intellectual Spaces

Perhaps one of the greatest contributions religion can make to facilitating societal change is its capacity to provide occasion to challenge the terms by which a given conflict is understood and to bring forward a different vision of a new society. Religious organizations within civil society may constitute intellectual spaces where societal injustice may be opposed.

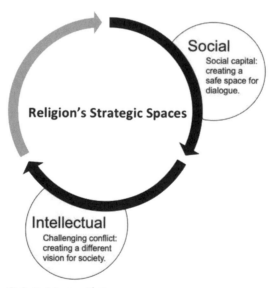

Social

Social capital: creating a safe space for dialogue.

Religion's Strategic Spaces

Intellectual

Challenging conflict: creating a different vision for society.

© S. K. Moore, PhD

Religious-leader engagement tends to function more on the individual plane of religious leaders. What's more, these leaders are linked to organizations having influence well beyond the individual—something to consider in operational environments where conflict, or its residual effects, continues to create division or overt hostilities between ethnic groups.

Documented case studies confirm that chaplains have successfully facilitated encounter between and among religious leaders from conflicting identity groups—sometimes from different faith expressions within the same faith tradition—bringing them together for dialogue where none existed. These may be local-, regional-, or, in some instances, national-level leaders. Not only are long-held stereotypes of the *other* challenged during such exchanges, leading to a gradual rehumanizing of the *other*, but encounters of this nature also provide the intellectual space for the reframing of present hostilities and structurally conceiving how life could improve for their respective peoples—such is positive peace. It is in the social strategic space of encounter that religious leaders of tolerant voice are able to envision together what others cannot at any particular moment. For many, it would be unthinkable to initiate dialogue with those of an opposing group in search of common ground, much less consider altering prevailing societal conditions that disadvantage another group.

Intellectual Space and the Kandahar PRT–Afghanistan

A cogent operational example of religion creating the intellectual space for engagement inclusive of other whole-of-government actors may be demonstrated in the work of Canadian Forces chaplain Imam Suleyman Demiray at the Kandahar Provincial Reconstruction Team (PRT) in Afghanistan (2006–2007). Posted to the PRT, Imam Demiray immediately began to collaborate with political advisor Gavin Buchan of Foreign Affairs Canada in engaging the local religious leadership, something that had been impossible up to that point. Initially Demiray chaired a *shura* in the PRT compound for the Ulema Council of Kandahar Province—a government-appointed body of Islamic scholars mandated to advise the provincial director of religious affairs on matters pertaining to koranic interpretation and public practice. This was the first contact that either the commandant of the PRT or the political adviser had with the religious leadership of Kandahar Province—a body that had remained inaccessible to PRT personnel since their arrival. Following this first meeting with the leading mullahs, the imam began attending local *shuras* with both Sunni and Shia faith groups. During these encounters he learned that 15 percent of the population of greater Kandahar City was Shia Muslim. A picture began to form as to the relations between the Kandahar Sunni and Shia religious leadership.

More than two years prior to Imam Demiray's arrival, the Taliban had assassinated the senior mullah of the Ulema Council. The demographics dictated that the majority of mullahs be Sunni with a Shia mullah serving as their representative on the council. Shia participation had not occurred since the loss of the former senior mullah. Communication at the highest religious levels between these two faith communities had ceased. Buchan readily recognized that the continued isolation of Shia leadership was ill advised. He and the imam began to strategize as to how the senior Shia mullah—the ayatollah—might be reunited with the Ulema Council, thus ending the alienation of his community from the majority Sunni population. The Sunni-Shia sectarian violence of Iraq held many lessons for International Security Assistance Forces leadership, a quagmire to be avoided at all costs for Afghanistan.

With continued consultation with Buchan and regular meetings with the local religious leadership of both the Sunni and Shia faith communities, a strategy began to emerge. Demiray learned that each faith group shared similar concerns: (1) numerous young males continued to stream to the territories in eastern Pakistan where they came under the influence of the radical teachings of the Taliban, and (2) both groups were desirous of help in building more madrassas in Kandahar Province, where their youth could be taught the more moderate teachings of Islam. Over a period of months and with much dialogue, Sunni and Shia leadership agreed that their interests were indeed similar, concurring that presenting their concerns as a united body would be the wisest move forward. In early 2007, at the governor's palace in Kandahar City, Shia representatives rejoined the Ulema Council to discuss how they might best present their shared concerns.

This documented case study underscores how Suleyman Demiray and Gavin Buchan succeeded in creating the necessary intellectual space whereby a different vision of relation between the Sunni and Shia religious leadership of Kandahar Province was brought forward.[22] Significant as well was the collaboration between he and Buchan, political advisor for the Kandahar PRT. This documented case study demonstrates more fully how religious leaders—a chaplain in this instance—are able to work effectively with their whole-of-government colleagues to aid the collective effort in creating a different reality for civil society where the influence of the religious sector cuts across all facets of society.

Institutional Spaces

It is in the institutional space of religious organizations where the intellectual challenges of change are enacted, often extending beyond the local to regional and sometimes international levels in terms of support.

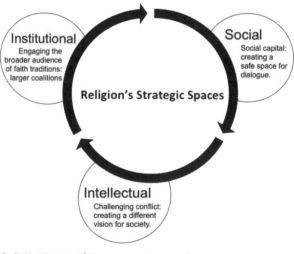

© S. K. Moore, PhD

Brewer, Higgins, and Teeney appropriately offer the cautionary note that religious groups are the most effective when they are part of a general coalition dedicated to future change. With such an integrated approach to whole-of-government initiatives, religious leaders and the groups they represent emerge as role models and drivers of the process of transformation. They are often among the first among the general citizenry to espouse nonracialism or nonsectarianism.

The Institutional Space and Facilitating Interreligious Dialogue in Kosovo

French Chaplain (LTC) Father Michel de Peyret served two consecutive tours of duty in Kosovo, once at the brigade level with the 2nd Armored Brigade of the French Army,[23] part of the larger Multinational Brigade North East,[24] and then as the theater chaplain for NATO forces under French Command in Kosovo (2005–2006). In light of the above discussion, de Peyret's experiences with religious-leader engagement take on additional significance in terms of social, intellectual, and institutional spaces with regard to his reconciling endeavors among the religious leaders of Kosovo.

Father de Peyret's initial deployment brought him to Kosovo just a few months after major rioting between the Kosovar Albanian Muslim and Kosovar Serbian populations, which, due to the level of targeted destruction, left the Serbian community devastated.[25] Trust among the Serbian population for the seemingly incapable or indifferent UN-deployed troops (Kosovo Forces, or KFOR) was at an all-time low, sentiments that were especially acute among the Serbian Orthodox religious community due to the many cultural and religious sites and symbols destroyed during the three days of uncontrolled rioting: churches, monasteries, and cemeteries. Repairing the discernible loss of confidence and frayed trust between the Serbian religious community and KFOR fell to Father de Peyret. Over a period of months, this French Roman Catholic priest adroitly and compassionately began the arduous task of binding up the wounds through the French-led restoration of the Serbian monastery at Devič. On designated days, as many as sixty troops would participate in the reconstruction, news of which soon reached the local Orthodox bishop, Monsignor Teodosije. The social capital that Chaplain de Peyret established led the bishop to become a prominent figure during the chaplain's second tour to Kosovo.

At the behest of the new KFOR commander, Lt. Gen. de Kermabon, Father de Peyret was extended for a second tour and elevated to the position of formation chaplain. In addition to his regular duties, he played the strategic role of establishing good relations with the senior religious leaders of all three religious traditions: Mufti Terrnava (Albanian Muslim), Monsignor Teodosije (Serbian Orthodox bishop), and Monsignor Sopi (Albanian Roman Catholic bishop). Having already established a good rapport with the Serbian Orthodox bishop, de Peyret then had to gain the confidence of the Muslim religious leader, Mufti Terrnava.

In due course it was discovered that no historical account existed in Kosovo of Muslim, Orthodox, and Roman Catholic religious leaders ever coming together for dialogue. It was deemed an opportune moment to seed reconciliation in the hopes of initiating a new narrative of cooperation and the beginning of the healing of memory. Through his continued overtures among these religious communities, de Peyret had garnered enough trust to bring them to KFOR headquarters for a shared meal with the KFOR commander. Monsignor Teodosije was late for the luncheon, and as those gathered waited, tension mounted—an inauspicious beginning. Unbeknown to all present, the monsignor was in fact en route from Belgrade, Serbia, where he had solicited and received authority from the Orthodox hierarchy the day prior to do what he was about to do. During a lull in what had become halted conversation, Bishop Teodosije stood in the midst of the assembled and offered a sincere apology for any wrong his people may have caused to the Albanian Muslim community. Before a speechless gathering, Mufti Terrnava took the bishop by the hand and pledged to him his support if it were ever needed. Encouraged by such progress, the following week all three religious leaders returned for an additional meal, which this time included the UN high representative and the prime minister of Kosovo.[26]

The above account represents the significance of the contribution of religion to peace building and reconciliation, most assuredly in a whole-of-government environment. Due to Chaplain de Peyret's social capital, sufficient strategic social space was created for three of the more prominent religious leaders of Kosovo to break bread together for the first time. In so doing, intellectual space was engendered for Orthodox and Muslim ethnoreligious communities caught in the vise of seemingly intractable sectarian violence to begin to envision a different future. The commander of KFOR and representatives from both the United Nations Mission in Kosovo and the Kosovo Provisional Institutions of Self-Government stood in for the institutional space of whole-of-government.

CONCLUSION

David Lee is a former career diplomat in Canada's Department of Foreign Affairs, Trade, and Development. In his estimation, where conflict or its residual effects persist, there may in certain cases be merit in engaging the religious sector. Religious leaders predisposed to peaceful resolution of tensions may benefit national-reconciliation endeavors. With respect to chaplains collaborating with their whole-of-government partners in RLE activities, Lee offered the following insights and suggestions:

1. Particularly in the global south, the significance of more traditional structures of governance has often been overlooked—religion being one such instance.

2. Experience has shown that religious-leader engagement can be effective within whole-of-government approaches.
3. Where religious engagement is deemed to contribute to the overall goal of reconciliation, the following principles apply:
   a. Religious-leader engagement belongs within whole-of-government formulations. It is essential that any such initiative be undertaken on the basis of a thorough and sound appreciation of the country history and context.
   b. One evident source for RLE is military chaplains—among other persons with similar capabilities. Care must be taken to select chaplains predisposed to such engagement, who exhibit the requisite knowledge and skills. In principle, chaplains conducting RLEs should not combine traditional duties with this new role.
   c. In collaboration with their whole-of-government partners and where opportunity is present, such initiatives should factor into national-reconciliation objectives, carrying maximum support within the country.[27]

As in the two case studies touched on here, establishing contact and meaningful dialogue with religious leadership—individuals revered by a large sector of society—may be challenging for whole-of-government personnel. Westerners are often perceived by the religious of more traditional societies to be secularists bent on changing traditional ways of life—individuals to be held at arm's length. But chaplains—religious leaders in their own right—can bring a degree of social capital to these strategic social spaces. Of course, this raises questions of instrumentalism, something chaplains should avoid at all costs. Care must be taken to ensure that such initiatives are not co-opted by others who might seek to reduce the encounters to just another tool in the toolbox for strategic advantage. Ongoing engagement with religious leaders in conflict and postconflict environments is established due to trusted relationships built over time and the benevolent intent of associated actions, all the while protecting the integrity of that process.[28]

The international response to today's protracted conflicts has given rise to a more integrated approach to international missions—collaboration of military and civilian entities as a means of enhancing stability and reconstruction efforts—whole-of-government. Religious-leader engagement at tactical and operational levels represents an added dimension of mission effectiveness now recognized by leadership at strategic levels. Some chaplains have already proved adept at such operational ministry. Mr. Lee alludes to the concept of specialist chaplains conducting RLE-type activities within religious communities in collaboration with their whole-of-government partners—a notion warranting consideration by chaplaincy senior leadership. A pool of chaplains trained in related fields could be of immeasurable assistance to the pursuit of peace and the resolution of conflict. As government departments and agencies move toward incorporating a religious element within their approach to peace-building and reconciliation efforts, serious reflection must be given to the unique contribution chaplains bring as an operational resource.

NOTES

1. Kim Richard Nossal, "Security Operations and the Comprehensive Approach," in *Security Operations in the 21st Century: Canadian Perspectives on the Comprehensive Approach*, ed. Michael Rostek and Peter Gizewski (Kingston, Ontario: Queen's Centre for International Relations, 2011).

2. "New National Security Takes Whole-of-Government Approach," *American Forces Press Service*, U.S. Department of Defense, May 10, 2010, http://www.defense.gov/news/newsarticle.aspx?id=59377, accessed 14 April 2013.

3. Ibid. See also U.S. Department of State, 2010 Agency Financial Report, "Smart Power in Action," available at http://www.state.gov/documents/organization/150505.pdf; *National Security Strategy*, http://www.whitehouse.gov/sites/default/files/rss_viewer/national_security_strategy.pdf.

4. 3P Human Security, "Civil Society, Government and Military Relations: 'Whole of Society' and the Comprehensive Approach," Policy Brief, 2011, 1, http://3phumansecurity.org/site/images/stories/PolicyBriefs/cs_government_military_relations.pdf, accessed 2 February 2013.

5. S. K. Moore, *Military Chaplains as Agents of Peace: Religious Leader Engagement in Conflict and Post-conflict Environments* (Lanham, MD: Lexington Books, 2013), 2.

6. Douglas Johnson, *Religion, Terror, and Error: U.S. Foreign Policy and the Challenge of Spiritual Engagement* (Santa Barbara: ABC-CLIO, 2011); R. Scott Appleby, *The Ambivalence of the Sacred: Religion, Violence, and Reconciliation* (Lanham, MD, and Oxford: Rowman & Littlefield, 2000); Daniel Philpott, *Just and Unjust Peace: An Ethic of Political Reconciliation* (Oxford: Oxford University Press, 2012).

7. Martin Ewans, *Conflict in Afghanistan: Studies in Asymmetric Warfare* (Oxon, UK, and New York: Routledge, 2005), 2, 173.

8. *Interstate* warfare refers to what historically has been the more traditional conflict of state against state, whereas *intrastate* conflict identifies conflict among groups within the borders of a sovereign nation inclusive of insurgencies.

9. Andrew Leslie, Peter Gizewski, and Michael Rostek, "Developing a Comprehensive Approach to Canadian Forces Operations," *Canadian Military Journal* 9, no. 1 (2008): 11–20.

10. Volker Boege, Anne Brown, Kevin Clements, and Anna Nolan, "Building Peace and Political Community in Hybrid Political Orders," *International Peacekeeping* 16, no. 5 (2009): 601.

11. Christopher Clapham, "The Global-Local Politics of State Decay," in *When States Fail: Causes and Consequences*, ed. Robert I. Rotberg (Princeton, NJ: Princeton University Press, 2004), 86, cited in Volker et al., "Building Peace," 602.

12. Boege et al., "Building Peace," 603. The authors offer the following word of caution in their notes (note 12), which bears repetition here:

"Traditional" or "customary" institutions are taken as ideal types. Obviously, traditional societies have not been left unchanged by the powers of—originally European—capitalist expansion, colonialism, imperialism, evangelism, and globalization. In practice, therefore, there are no clear-cut boundaries between the realm of the exogenous "modern" and the endogenous "traditional"; rather there are processes of assimilation, articulation, transformation, and/or adoption in the context of the global/exogenous–local/indigenous interface. An ideal type of "traditional" or "customary" institutions of governance is employed to elaborate as precisely as possible the specifics of phenomena that do not belong to the realm of conventional institutions originating in the West [that] were imposed in the South. It would be misleading, however, to think of this traditional realm as unchangeable and static. Custom is a constant flux and adapts to new circumstances, exposed to external influences, which allows traditional and introduced Western approaches to be combined so that something new—that is not strictly customary any longer but rooted in custom—might emerge.

13. Ibid., 606.
14. Ibid.
15. Ibid., 608.
16. Ibid., 611–12.
17. Ibid., 605. For a brief overview of more intercommunal approaches to peace building, see Moore, *Military Chaplains*, 111, 128. Note 36, page 128, reads:

Ashutosh Varshney's seminal research, published in *Ethnic Conflict and Civic Life: Hindus and Muslims in India*, contends that where communities in India were more integrated civically across ethnic lines, the propensity toward violence was less when *exogenous shocks* impacted the community—an ethnically/religiously induced crisis within a populace free of conflict, emanating from outside. Peace Councils were *inter-communal* groups of concerned individuals within neighborhoods who came together to address problems of prejudice, civic tensions, and religious rituals in order to foster communal harmony as a means of countering communal antagonism rooted in the sentiments of hatred. His examination of six cities—three more ethnically integrated compared with three more segregated—offers critical insight in terms of conflict transformation. He asserts where Hindu/Muslim tensions spilled over into violence elsewhere in the country, the more civically integrated urban centers were able to contain its spread—either outbursts were quelled in short order, or they didn't happen at all. The depth of civic engagement had much to do with maintaining the peace as it promoted more integrative structures, which held additional relational benefits, hence a peace dividend for the community when the contagion of violence originating externally threatened to metastasize locally. In communities where daily *inter*-communal activity and communication was less evident, ethnic segregation became the norm. During periods of internal strife elsewhere in India these localities were more susceptible to violence spreading to their communities, a *mimetic* phenomenon.

See Ashutosh Varshney, *Ethic Conflict and Civic Life: Hindus and Muslims in India* (New Haven: Yale University Press, 2002).

18. John B. Brewer, Garth I. Higgins, and Frances Teeney, "Religion and Peacemaking: A Conceptualization," *Sociology* 44, no. 6 (2010): 1023.
19. Ibid., 1023–24.
20. The following is a list of resources that speak to the domain of religious peace building and its importance:

Katrien Hertog, *The Complex Reality of Religious Peacebuilding: Conceptual Contributions and Critical Analysis* (Lanham, MD: Lexington Books, 2010)

Marc Gopin, *Between Eden and Armageddon: The Future of World Religions, Violence, and Peacemaking* (New York: Oxford University Press, 2000)

Marc Gopin, *To Make the Earth Whole: The Art of Citizen Diplomacy in an Age of Religious Militancy* (Lanham, MD: Rowman & Littlefield, 2009)

Daniel Philpot and Gerard Powers, *Strategies of Peace: Transforming Conflict in a Violent World* (New York: Oxford University Press, 2010)

David Little, *Peacemakers in Action: Profiles of Religion in Conflict Resolution* (New York: Cambridge University Press, 2007)

I. William Zartman and J. Lewis Rasmussen, *Peacemaking in International Conflict* (Washington, DC: United States Institute of Peace, 1997)

Howard Coward and Gordon S. Smith, *Religion and Peacebuilding* (Albany: State University of New York Press, 2004)

John Paul Lederach, Reina Neufeldt, and Hal Culbertson, *Reflective Peacebuilding: A Planning, Monitoring, and Learning Toolkit* (Notre Dame, IN, and Bangkok: Kroc Institute for Peace Studies and Catholic Relief Services, East Asia Regional Office, 2007)

Cynthia Sampson and John Paul Lederach, *From the Ground Up: Mennonite Contributions to International Peacebuilding* (New York: Oxford University Press, 2000)

Qamar-ul Huda, *Crescent and Dove: Peace and Conflict Resolution in Islam*, ed. Qamar-ul Huda (Washington, DC: United States Institute of Peace, 2010)

David Smock and Qamar-ul Huda, *Islamic Peacebuilding Since 9/11*, Special Report 218 (Washington, DC: United States Institute of Peace, 2009)

John A. McConnell, *Mindful Meditation: A Handbook for Buddhist Peacemakers* (Thailand: Buddhist Research Institute & Mahachula Buddhist University, 1995)

Yehezkel Landau, "Healing the Holy Land," *Peaceworks*, no. 51 (Washington, DC: United States Institute of Peace, 2003)

Louise Diamond and John MacDonald, *Multi-track Diplomacy: A Systems Approach to Peacebuilding* (West Hartford, CT: Kumarian Press, 1996)

John Paul Lederach and R. Scott Appleby, "Strategic Peacebuilding: An Overview," in *Strategies of Peace: Transforming Conflict in a Violent World*, ed. Daniel Philpot and Gerard Powers (New York: Oxford University Press, 2010)

21. Brewer et al., "Religion and Peacemaking," 1024.

22. See this case study in its entirety in Moore, *Military Chaplains as Agents of Peace*, 144–63.

23. An armored brigade is normally comprised of three battalions (four hundred to six hundred troops each, depending on the mission) of infantry supported by armored vehicles, such as tanks.

24. "Multinational Brigade Northeast: HEADQUARTERS: Nova Selo and Mitrovica—Responsible for: Northern Kosovo Lead Nation: France. Contributing Nations: Belgium, Denmark, Estonia, Greece, Luxembourg, and Morocco." See Paul Workman, "Kosovo: A Protectorate in Trouble," *CBC News*, May 25, 2004, http://www.cbc.ca/news/background/balkans/workman.html.

25. According to Human Rights Watch,

On March 17, [2004,] at least thirty-three riots broke out in Kosovo over a forty-eight-hour period, involving an estimated fifty-one thousand protesters. Nineteen people died during the violence. At least 550 homes and 27 Orthodox churches and monasteries were burned, and approximately 4,100 persons from minority communities were displaced from their homes. . . . The violence was sparked by a series of events, notably sensational and ultimately inaccurate reports that Serbs were responsible for the drowning of three ethnic Albanian boys. Other catalysts included anger among ethnic Albanians over the blocking of the main Pristina-Skopje road by Serb villagers to protest the shooting of a Serb teenager by unknown assailants and a March 16 demonstration organized by groups of veterans and others linked to the disbanded Kosovo Liberation Army who protested the arrest of former KLA leaders on war crimes charges.

See Human Rights Watch, "Kosovo: Faith of NATO, U.N. to Protect Minorities," http://www.hrw.org/news/2004/07/26/kosovo-failure-nato-un-protect-minorities, accessed April 1, 2012.

26. See this case study in its entirety in Moore, *Military Chaplains as Agents of Peace*, 169–84.

27. Discussions and e-mail exchanges between the author and David Lee, Ottawa, Canada, February 7–11, 2013.

28. For a discussion on *instrumentalism* and other related topics, see "Religious Leader Engagement in Implementation," in Moore, *Military Chaplains as Agents of Peace*, 235–64.

U.S. Navy Lt. Cmdr. Abuhena Saifulislam, a Muslim chaplain, conducts a key-leader engagement in the village of Habibabad, Afghanistan, March 10, 2010, in order to promote cultural and religious understanding between the International Security Assistance Force and local residents. (U.S. Marine Corps photo by Cpl. Mary E. Carlin/Released) (Courtesy of Cpl. Mary E. Carlin. Location: Habibabad Village)

U.S. Army Lt. Col. Avi S. Weiss, right, deputy chaplain, Installation Management Command Europe, speaks to soldiers during a Rosh Hashanah service at Freedom Chapel, Camp Mike Spann, Afghanistan, September 28, 2011. Weiss conducted services throughout the 170th Infantry Brigade Combat Team's area of responsibility in observance of the Jewish New Year. (U.S. Army photo by Sgt. Christopher Klutts/Released) (Courtesy of Sgt. Christopher Klutts. Location: Camp Mike Spann)

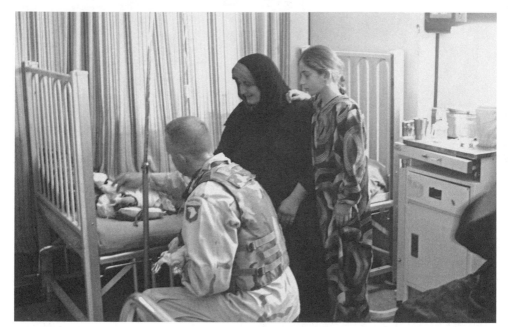

Chaplain Compton from 2nd Brigade, 101st Airborne Division, gives a Beanie Baby to an Iraqi child who is a patient at the Al Razzi general teaching hospital in Mosul, Iraq, August 21, 2003, during Operation Iraqi Freedom. (U.S. Army photo by Staff Sgt. Kevin Wastler/Released) (Courtesy of Staff Sgt. Kevin J. Wastler. Location: Mosul)

U.S. Navy Lt. Cmdr. Jose Pimentel, a Roman Catholic chaplain aboard the aircraft carrier USS George Washington (CVN 73), leads sailors in prayer during Mass while in the South China Sea, October 9, 2011. (U.S. Navy photo by Mass Communication Specialist 2nd Class William Pittman/ Released) (Courtesy of MC2 William Pittman. Location: USS George Washington (CVN 73))

U.S. Navy Lt. Cmdr. John Sears, right, a chaplain with Special-Purpose Marine Air-Ground Task Force Continuing Promise 2010 (CP10), creates balloon animals for Haitian children at the Northwest Haiti Christian Mission in Saint-Louis du Nord, Haiti, July 27, 2010. CP10 was a collaborative effort between military and civilian personnel that provided humanitarian assistance and disaster relief to residents of Caribbean and Central and South American countries. (U.S. Marine Corps photo by Sgt. Samuel R. Beyers/Released) (Courtesy of Sgt. Samuel R. Beyers. Location: Saint-Louis du Nord)

Pvt. 1st Class Katie Harwick, a chaplain assistant with Rear Detachment, 4th Brigade (Airborne) Combat Team, 25th Infantry Division, spins a prize wheel, offering food-assistance-program participants a chance to win a random gift on Joint Base Elmendorf–Richardson, Alaska, December 14, 2011. Possible winnings included buttons, pens, and a $50 commissary gift card. (U.S. Army photo by Staff Sgt. Matthew Winstead/Released) (Courtesy of Staff Sgt. Matthew Winstead. Location: Joint Base Elmendorf-Richardson)

U.S. Army Capt. Kevin Burton, a chaplain with the 47th Brigade Support Battalion (BSB) at Fort Bliss, Texas, helps unload food from a delivery truck at the Kelly Memorial Food Pantry, December 13, 2011, in El Paso, Texas. Soldiers with the 47th BSB began volunteering at the pantry in March 2011. (U.S. Army photo by Sgt. Sean Harriman/Released) (Courtesy of Sgt. Sean Harriman. Location: El Paso)

The chaplain of the Marine Corps, U.S. Navy Rear Admiral Margaret Kibben, left, speaks with female-engagement team members and a local Afghan national during a visit to Combat Outpost Dehli, Helmand Province, Afghanistan, September 22, 2011. Admiral Kibben, along with the 35th commandant of the Marine Corps, General James F. Amos, and the sergeant major of the Marine Corps, Sgt. Maj. Michael Barrett, traveled to Afghanistan to visit deployed service members throughout Regional Command (Southwest) and speak about recent events. (U.S. Marine Corps photo by Sgt. Mallory S. VanderSchans/Released) (Courtesy of Sgt. Mallory VanderSchans. Location: Camp Leatherneck)

7

Peace Building through Religious Engagement in East Africa

Jon Cutler

An African tribal chief once said to me, "To sit under the same tree and talk, that is the most important and most difficult step." I took these words to heart while collaborating on a peace-building project in Kampala, Uganda, on October 7, 2011. The brainchild of a meeting between an official from the U.S. embassy, President Jaffer Senganda (The Muslim Centre for Justice and Law), and me went on to become an event at which five thousand Christian and Muslim youths participated in a cleanup day in Uganda's capital. Because of recent tensions between Muslims and Christians due to the rise of religious extremism in both communities, this was the first-ever collaborative program between Muslims and Christians, and according to President Senganda the initiative was a great success. And because of the success there were now the potential for future projects and the beginnings of an interfaith youth organization, which continue to this day.

This project began as one of many efforts to engage African religious leaders in the pursuit of peace undertaken by U.S. military chaplains at Combined Joint Task Force–Horn of Africa (CJTF-HOA) in Djibouti and U.S. African Command (AFRICOM). These two agencies are the main U.S. government–employed religious representatives on the continent routinely engaging religious leaders. Many conflicts in Africa intertwine religious, cultural, racial, and socioeconomic issues; U.S. military chaplains are increasingly playing an important role in collaborating with African religious leaders to nurture working relationships and strengthen partnerships regarding conflict resolution and peace building. From January 2011 to January 2012, I was privileged to be part of this effort as director of religious affairs at CJTF-HOA, the first Jewish chaplain to hold this position. Africa (both Saharan and sub-Saharan) is a highly religious continent. Given that the mission of CJTF-HOA is to build partnerships with African governments, religion has to be brought into public discourse. Doing so in recent years has reaped significant rewards in fulfilling the CJFT-HOA mission. However, this approach is not without controversy. The chapter will discuss some of that controversy, including the underlying tension between the secular and sacred within national and international affairs and of the changing role of U.S. military chaplains over the past decade in the deployments abroad. These changing roles have resulted in sustaining achievements but not without its challenges, which I believe can be overcome as the U.S. military—and the U.S. government more generally—adapts for the future.

THE DEBATE BETWEEN THE SECULAR AND THE SACRED

One of the hallmarks of Western modernity is the demarcation between secular affairs in the public square and religious practices within the private sphere. By its very nature, secularism limits private expression of religious faith in public settings. This bifurcation has become institutionalized within many Western governments and in law, commerce, science and technology, foreign affairs, the military, and various dimensions of social life. Secular institutions are not by definition antireligious. They are a-religious. Secular institutions focus on matters for all citizens, regardless of faith. Western militaries, like other institutions of public life, often reflect and reinforce this.

In the United States, litigation over the past half-century has reinforced legal boundaries between government and religion; religion has increasingly been limited in the public sphere and remains individual and private for many people. The U.S. government as a whole and the Department of Defense and the State Department specifically have shied away from engaging with religious people, ideas, and communities abroad. Unlike the United States, however, in African societies religion is fully integrated into the public sphere, and it would be anathema for Africans to live otherwise.

As such, most Americans wear cultural and religious blinders as they engage the world. In his landmark book, *Religion: The Missing Dimension of Statecraft*, Douglas Johnston states that "the rigorous separation of church and state in the United States has desensitized many citizens to the fact that much of the rest of the world does not operate on a similar basis."[1]

Religion's narrative tells of the human condition, especially life and death. It is foundational to how people define themselves, and it shapes the culture, mores, and norms that drive decisions—as witnessed on 9/11. When President George W. Bush used the term *crusade* in reference to the 9/11 attacks, there was an immediate backlash from the Muslim world because of its historical religious reference.

In a post–9/11 world secular institutions need to adjust their understanding of how religious identity shapes human interactions and the global experience. As a society, we need to foster self-reflection and know our own religious sensibilities before we try to engage those of other societies. We need to comprehend the depth to which religion and politics interact in shaping the perceptions and motivations of individuals and societies.

Religion is a force in today's world. Religions structure meaning and purpose for billions of people. Religions can serve for both ill and good, catalysts of violent conflicts and potent forces for brokering reconciliation and sustaining peace. Religious-extremist violence may be a backdrop to life today, but it is the countless mundane ways in which people live their lives and demonstrate their religious faiths that are not noticed. For example, every day Africans demonstrate their religious practices and commitment in the public realm. In their culture, religion is not relegated to the margins of society. They live in a world that recognizes no clear distinction between private individual faith and secular, public life. For example, at civic and government events religious leaders offer prayers specific to their faith traditions. There, no concept exists of a civic prayer; a Christian prayer will be offered at a government or secular event, followed by a Muslim prayer.

We are beginning to understand that we cannot hold a sacred-secular divide and be effective in building bridges to other cultures. With U.S. military engagement in Iraq, Afghanistan, and Africa, Americans have witnessed that religion is one of the most potent forces that shape societies and individual attitudes and perceptions. "Sustainable security cannot be achieved without engaging societies' own internal ethics. This in turn requires a deep understanding of the local context—a context that is suffused with religion."[2] Without understanding the spiritual-religious dimension of a culture, the ability to "win the hearts and minds of a people" is lost. As U.S. government professionals, military chaplains are the only resources at the disposal of the command to engage religion and society in the areas critical to the U.S. military.

U.S. MILITARY CHAPLAINCY

The military needs to increase religious awareness to leverage its strategic value. Secular approaches to religion and the military relegate the responsibilities of the chaplain to personal and private dimensions of faith. A chaplain's essential focus is supposed to be on the spiritual life of and pastoral care for the individual warrior and their families.

But within the past ten years the military chaplain's role has evolved and expanded to include active engagement with religious leaders abroad to establish trust relationships. The end state and purpose for such engagements is to promote peace and regional stability and to advise military commanders on the religious implications of command decisions and the effects on conflict or peace in the region. The new role challenges the secular definitions and expectations of military policy.

While the chaplain's fundamental adherence is to the traditional responsibilities, the circumstances of a post–9/11 world mean evolution and expansion. Military chaplains are at the cutting edge of a significant new ministry that includes encouraging traditional religious leaders to stand up against violent extremism.

By the very nature of being religious, military chaplains understand the significance that religion plays in the life of an individual, society, or nation. As a person of deep faith, a chaplain has a gained legitimacy, public respect, and credibility with religious leaders that the combatant necessarily does not. Chaplains understand and respect religious teachings, rituals, and practices, which creates an affinity with religious leaders to bridge the cultural divide.

Working cooperatively in a multifaith and multicultural environment, chaplains understand that there can be respectful cooperation without compromising individual faith. With one foot in the religious world and the other in the military as a secular office, chaplains are well suited to act as intermediaries between military, civilian, and religious leaders in areas of conflict and instability. "Senior military chaplains bring to the table all these factors: high credibility joined to a wide range of professional expertise and experience in working across religious divisions."[3]

The presence of a U.S. government religious professional sends a positive message to those countries where religion has a significant role in policy and diplomacy and where religious leaders play an important role in governance. Chaplains, as well as other religious leaders, are potentially a valuable resource for preventing conflict and mediating differences because of the religious legitimacy they bring to the table.

Military chaplains have been engaging with religious leaders starting "from the Spanish-American War to Operation Iraqi Freedom and Operation Enduring Freedom. . . . There is significant precedent for chaplains to conduct religious-leader liaison, and they have unique qualifications to make it effective."[4] When I was deployed to Iraq in 2008 as 3rd Marine Aircraft Wing chaplain, I accompanied a navy chaplain on his visit to the local imam several times. This chaplain was tasked by his colonel to meet with the local imam weekly in order to find out what the needs of the locals were—such as Americans possibly providing basic necessities, like medicine, food, and so on. When the chaplain met with the imam, they would engage in study and discussion on the common elements between Islam and Christianity. It was through this process that a trusting relationship was built.

Consider the case of the recent conflict in Afghanistan. Interaction with religious leaders and institutions in Afghanistan had been inconsistently addressed by military, diplomatic, and development officials: "Beginning in October 2009, Lieutenant Colonel Patrick Carroll, USMC (Ret.) . . . began to develop a religious-leader-engagement program for II Marine Expeditionary Brigade that addressed the tendency for religious leaders to be ignored in military and diplomatic engagement. . . . In [the] wake of such prevalent dismissal of religious leaders, Carroll observed that even if mullahs served only a religious role, the primary argument of the Taliban is that they are pious individuals fighting foreign infidels and therefore 'the most credible voices to counter the Taliban's rhetoric were moderate mullahs themselves.'"[5] Carroll requested a Muslim U.S. Navy chaplain, reporting that "attention to subprovincial religious leaders was furthered strengthened with the arrival of a U.S. Navy Muslim chaplain in February 2010 . . . it was determined that Chaplain Salam would be the ideal person to extend the reach of the religious engagement program."[6]

This development makes it clear that a sustained, consistent, well-thought-out religious-leader-engagement program supports and advances the traditional component of counterinsurgency. Systematic engagement of religious leaders at provisional, district, village, and farm levels created additional lines of communication whereby the International Security Assistance Force promoted its mission of stability and Afghans voiced their needs and commitment to a stable future.[7]

However, not all chaplains are qualified to engage with religious leaders, due to their lack of maturity, personal beliefs (some chaplains expressed their dislike for Muslims), education, and interpersonal skills. Within the Chaplain Corps there is a debate about whether using chaplains for religious engagement beyond their pastoral duties, such as interfaith dialogue, is the most effective and productive use of a chaplain, especially considering the downsizing of the number of chaplains as the military faces significant budget shortfalls.

To address the issues of this debate, a joint document on religious affairs was published—"Joint Publication 1-05: Religious Affairs in Joint Operations." The purpose of JP 1-05, as it's known, is to give guidance and direction to the chaplain and the command to engage in bridge building between religious communities. Chaplains at CJTF-HOA, starting in 2006, engaged actively with not only partner-nation chaplains Kenya and Uganda but also prominent (nongovernment) religious leaders in East Africa.[8] JP 1-05 defines chaplain support of engagement as "any command-directed contact or interaction where the chaplain, as the command's religious representative, meets with a leader on matters of religion to ameliorate suffering and to promote peace and the benevolent expression of religion."[9]

STRENGTHENING PARTNERSHIPS

The mission of Combined Joint Task Force–Horn of Africa is to strengthen partnerships with area nations Djibouti, Ethiopia, Kenya, Uganda, Tanzania, Somalia, South Sudan, and Sudan, working through individual country teams, U.S. Agency for International Development, and U.S. embassy officials. This is a comprehensive whole-of-government approach to support African partner nations to build and maintain stable and effective governments and societies. Long-term stability in Africa is a vital interest to the United States. As a result, the Office of Religious Affairs CJTF-HOA created a new standard to the traditional role of a chaplain to meet the end goals of the mission.[10]

With a mission to bring stability and security to the region of East Africa, chaplains have become instrumental in meeting these objectives by engaging area civilian and military religious leaders. Conflicts have torn the social fabric of these societies, displaced millions of people, traumatized their communities, and drained the continent of material and human resources, resulting in destabilized governments and communities, and over the years it is religious leaders and organizations throughout Africa who have consistently shown the most promise for improving the quality of life of people, making positive changes in socioeconomic conditions. As such, religious leaders and organizations are highly influential and trusted in African society and are in key positions to play crucial roles in promoting peace and security.

The desired objective is simple, but achieving it is quite difficult. The common goal shared by the peoples of the two major African religions, Christianity and Islam, is for individuals to live in peace and security, to live a life that allows them to raise children who will become healthy, productive adults, heads of their own families.

With their resources, connections with U.S. diplomatic and development personnel, and other tools, the chaplains at CJTF-HOA and USAFRICOM (the only U.S. government–employed religious representatives on the continent) can support Africans in reaching this objective. By collaborating with African religious leaders, U.S. chaplains can nurture relationships and strengthen partnerships to working towards security, and peace.

CHALLENGES WITHIN THE CHANGING ROLES

Over a one-year period serving as director of religious affairs at CJTF-HOA I promoted this approach and policy actively on multiple levels. It was not without its challenges—one of the greatest originating from the CJFT-HOA command itself. The mission for our office had not been integrated into the broader mission of CJFT-HOA, which was operational and tactical —engaging with African military and civilian officials, training African militaries, and getting involved with humanitarian efforts, civil affairs, and engineering projects. CJFT-HOA had a definite objective for the religious affairs mission—that the chaplain take care of the spiritual and emotional well-being of military personnel, especially "down range" in Kenya, Ethiopia, Uganda, and Tanzania. When it came to the chaplain engaging with military and civilian religious leaders, the objective was to counter violent religious extremism without further instruction. Due to the traditional understanding of the role of the chaplain, it was difficult for the admiral, commanding officer for CJTF-HOA, to shift his thinking on how the chaplain might be utilized to engage with religious leaders, especially civilians.

Since the religious affairs mission was never integrated into the long- or short-term planning process, the previous chaplains who'd directed the office had been challenged to create their own directions and objectives, which had not necessarily always been in alignment with the CJTF-HOA mission and goal. With each new director, the program found a new direction, steered by personality style. The chaplain became a lone ranger, so to speak.

My lone-ranger style is to look at an issue and find ways to resolve the problem. The issue then before me was that Muslim and Christian communities sometimes work at cross purposes and in the end become antagonistic toward one another. My objective was to create an interdependent relationship between both communities by supporting joint projects and programs—such as cleanup day in Kampala, for example. The positive aspect was supporting Christian and Muslim communities in creating joint projects that could ultimately become self-sustaining. The challenge became trying to convince the command of the value of such nonmilitaristic efforts and then to make such objectives part of the strategic plan. It was essential, therefore, that the religious affairs mission be integrated into an overarching strategic plan. Unity of purpose and singleness of objective were essential to ensuring that the individual pieces contributed to a strategic whole.

In order to strengthen CJTF-HOA's mission, it was important to find a means to integrate the Office of Religious Affairs by creating an operational order. An OPORD, as it is known, is an executable plan that directs a command to conduct an operation. It describes the situation, the mission, and what activities will be conducted to achieve the mission goals. In December 2011, in conjunction with the command-operations division's short-term planning section, an operational order for religious affairs was generated and signed. The mission for our program had now become integrated and institutionalized into the overall mission of CJTF-HOA.[11]

My being a Jewish chaplain—a rabbi—gave me unique status and brought with it several challenges. Before my first engagement, CJTF-HOA's command leadership raised some concerns. As director of religious affairs, I would be representing both Combined Joint Task Force–Horn of Africa and U.S. African Command. And as a rabbi, my presence could elicit a negative, or even hostile, reaction from Muslim and Christian leaders. In short, leadership feared that my presence might compromise CJTF-HOA's mission. Another fear was that Muslim leaders might not be able to separate me, a Jewish-American military chaplain, from the politics of Israel. But even if there were no negative response, another concern remained that there would be no common ground between a Jewish cleric and his Muslim counterparts on which to further a relationship.

In my entire tenure, I found the opposite to be true. This challenge turned into a great opportunity because none of the religious leaders had ever met a rabbi before, much less a Jew. I took the opportunity to educate them on Judaism and the common ground that we share as adherents to the tradition of Abraham. I found the vast majority of religious leaders to be quite open and respectful. Over the long term, using Jewish clergy in the Office of Religious Affairs could have positive effects on shaping religious discourse between Muslims and Christians.

For example, several times I met with the supreme judge of the Islamic Council of Ethiopia, Sheikh Ahemedi Chello. Because of my relationship with him, I was able to help resolve an issue with a water project for a mosque which had been built by CJTF-HOA. The sheikh made me promise that on my next visit I would teach him about Judaism; he wanted to learn so that he could teach his own people.

Another interesting outcome of being a rabbi was that I found myself in a unique situation. Since I traveled throughout the Combined Joint Operational Area (East Africa), I was able to identify the religious atmospherics within the region. Being neither Christian nor Muslim, I was a "neutral party," and some Muslim leaders were able to talk to me about their issues with Christians, and some Christian leaders were able to express their concerns about Muslims. For example, Ugandan Evangelical Protestant ministers expressed their fear that the parliament of Uganda would enact Sharia (Islamic law) as part of the new constitution. With the fear came anxiety about their own security in Uganda and strong negative views toward Muslims. Muslims, on the other hand, were concerned about Protestant missions targeting Muslim villages. It became clear that my eventual goal was to address the concerns so as to lessen the tension points, which all led to the interfaith cleanup day mentioned previously. In sum, I was able to identify the fault lines between Christian and Muslims groups.

However, my ability to discern tensions by no means reduced the complexity of religious life in East Africa—another challenge for any U.S. chaplain. Within each nation are numerous tribes with their diverse cultures and languages. Then religion is added with its distinct set of difficulties. Even though Christians and Muslims are present within each nation, the percentage of Christians and Muslims varies from nation to nation. For example, Djibouti is 99 percent Muslim, and Ethiopia is 80 percent Christian. Christianity has its own internal dynamic, and it varies from nation to nation.

Consider, for example, Ethiopia, where the dominant form of Christianity is Ethiopian Orthodox with a growing Evangelical Protestant presence, or Kenya, where the dominant denomination is Anglican while Islam dominates the coast (at 80 percent).

Not only does mistrust exist between religious groups, but there are also fault lines within religious groups. Even though the majority of Muslims are Sunni in East Africa, there is a significant presence of Sufis (Ethiopia), Aga Khans (Uganda), and Salafists (Tanzanian coast and Zanzibar). Adding to the complexity are the extremist elements within Christianity and Islam. The Somali-based extremist Islamist group Al-Shabaab, for example, is a direct threat along the Swahili Coast of Kenya and Tanzania, as its members actively seek Muslim youths to fight in Mogadishu. And even within the small Jewish community in Uganda there are intragroup rivalries. It takes a significant amount of time to grasp the religious complexity within East Africa.

Another layer of complexity chaplains engaging with local religious leaders must grapple with is who to reach out to—the local imam or the mufti for all of Uganda, the parish priest or patriarch of the Ethiopian Orthodox Church, the local Assemblies of God pastor in a remote Tanzanian village or the secretary general for all Evangelical Independent Churches of Africa? Each encounter will have a different dynamic and agenda. Each stakeholder has a distinct personal style as well. And the chaplain may engage with religious organizations of small size or great numbers—councils, boards, elders, and so on. With each comes its own internal dynamic and politics. These organizations can be local, national, regional, continental, or international.

On several projects, for example, I engaged with the Kenyan Muslim Youth Alliance, a national organization, where I worked with fourteen board members to write grants to establish a newspaper that would foster interfaith cooperation. Another time I engaged with the All African Conference of Churches—an international organization representing 130 million people belonging to 173 different Christian denominations in over forty-seven African nations—to collaborate on a project with seven senior AACC members to coordinate an East Africa interreligious conference. And there was the time I met with a local county board of five Muslim leaders in Mbale, Uganda, to discuss plans for an interreligious medical clinic. My point is that a chaplain must be mindful of the level and scope of each interaction.

But my final challenge was trying to explain to religious leaders exactly what my role was as military chaplain and director of religious affairs for CJTF-HOA. Finding it difficult to locate a context they could relate to, I ended up explaining my job in terms of representing the U.S. military as a religious leader hoping to partner with them to help bring peace and stability to the region.

SUSTAINABLE ACHIEVEMENTS

It took five months of visiting East African religious leaders and religious organizations to establish a direction and put in place a plan with a clear program for sustainability and continuity. In the end, the CJTF-HOA chaplain was decided to be a facilitator, a bridge builder between U.S. military chaplains and African military chaplains, and an ambassador.

"Religion," as the CJTF-HOA OPORD states, "is an integral part of the lives of the people of East Africa. It has the potential to foster increased social tolerance and respect aiding to the suppression of instability and conflict. . . . The CJTF-HOA chaplain is often viewed by Key Religious Leaders as an ambassador that can facilitate engagements [that] unite populations in cooperative activities and aid the construction of counter–Violent Extreme Organization narratives. Aiding Key Religious Leaders and religious organizations that oppose Violent Extremist Organizations ideologies ultimately constricts the space in which Violent Extremist Organizations operate and renders VEO ideologies irrelevant."[12]

Religious violent extremism is a threat to American interests, to stability within East Africa, to East African nations, and to the entire continent. One of the more effective means of meeting the threat is by making religious violent-extremist organizations irrelevant through helping to build African capacity and capabilities.

The cause for instability and the lack of peace in East Africa is found at the grassroots level—in a lack of opportunities for African youth, in poverty, in HIV rates, and so on. Religious organizations are among the few institutions in Africa that have earned trust among the people. Power resides within these religious organizations to effect change, and the most effective change comes from a united front.

The CJTF-HOA chaplain can help further the process by bringing together Christian and Muslim organizations and leaders who share the values of peace and stability and a willingness to work together to resolve grassroots issues. Working cooperatively sends a clear message that collaboration transcends the negative differences and sets an example for others to work together. The role of the CJTF-HOA chaplain is often that of the "honest broker," if you will.

I facilitated the meetings of religious organizations, introducing them to each other and supporting them on working to find solutions. As a broker, I engaged in the "3-D process"—defense, diplomacy, and development. I worked with officials from the U.S. embassies who introduced me to the religious leaders and organizations. In turn, the embassy officials accompanied me on meetings with religious leaders and contacted U.S. funding sources.

It is the youths of East Africa who are the most vulnerable to being recruited by violent extremist organizations because of the lack of opportunity and the bleak prospects for the future. Because it is the youths who are at risk, they have an enormous stake in resolving the situation. Therefore, one of my objectives was to engage with religious youth organizations and to bring them together to start working on resolving the daunting problems facing them.

There were two objectives before me at the start of this task. The first was to identify youth organizations valued peace and security and to support them by connecting them to funding sources through the U.S. embassy. One such organization is the Kenyan Muslim Youth Alliance, which has an extensive and positive track record in combating Muslim extremism and the strong infrastructure to continue to do so. They have established a speaker's series to educate Muslim youths about the dangers of extremism and have educational and job-training programs.

The second task before me was to connect youth organizations with one other in order to build strength through cooperation. My agenda was to connect KMYA with other youth organizations—both Christian and Muslim—throughout East Africa. For example, in the end KMYA connected with the Muslim Centre for Justice and Law in Kampala, Uganda, and with the Christian organization Active Youth in Mombasa, Kenya. Active Youth, in turn, also connected with the Muslim Centre for Justice and Law. Because of these connections Christian and Muslim youth organizations in Mombasa, Kenya, went on to replicate what we had done in Kampala, where 2,500 Christian and Muslim youths participated in service projects.

Out of this process can come a greater understanding and appreciation for the other. Through this process of engagement Christian and Muslim leaders came together who value peace and stability. A goal is to bring these leaders together to address challenges to African peace and security and to form enduring partnerships with East African Muslim and Christian communities, developing educational programs and community projects to further promote the peace. The youths of Africa are the future, and if Africa is going to change, they must be involved. But such an alliance has even broader ramifications, as it demonstrates to the world that Muslims and Christians can live and work next to one other, thereby making religious violent extremism irrelevant.

Another CJTF-HOA objective was to build enduring relationships between East African partner-nation militaries and the U.S. military to share best practices. The only nation that has a military chaplaincy in East Africa is Kenya, and their military chaplaincy is directed by three principal chaplains. Each chaplain represents one of the three official religions of Kenya—Roman Catholicism, Islam, and Protestant Christianity. My job was to develop a supportive and cooperative relationship with them and to engage a sharing of best practices between U.S. military chaplains specifically at Camp Lemonier, Djibouti, and the Kenyan military chaplains. Approximately one hundred chaplains serve the Kenyan army, air force, and navy.

I met with the three principal chaplains in Nairobi and invited them to Camp Lemonier to engage with the U.S. military chaplains stationed on base and to learn about U.S. chaplaincy, and vice versa. These chaplains visited for three days in July 2011. They learned about the organizational structure of U.S. military chaplaincy and professional chaplaincy and met with counselors from our Fleet and Family Service Center to learn about family and military separation and deployment, posttraumatic-stress syndrome, alcohol abuse, and so on. American chaplains interacted with the senior chaplains and learned about the structure of Kenyan chaplaincy and the role of the chaplain within the Kenyan military.

In order to build stronger ties between our two organizations, I invited three junior-grade Kenyan chaplains to CJFT-HOA, Camp Lemonier, for a three-week U.S. military professional chaplaincy familiarization. The goal was to familiarize both U.S. and Kenyan chaplains with one other's chaplaincy programs, to increase Kenyan chaplains' knowledge and understanding of U.S. professional chaplaincy, to familiarize Kenyan chaplains with Fleet and Family Service Center programs, and to build a relationship between Kenyan chaplains and U.S. chaplains and military personnel on base. The idea was for the Kenyan chaplains to be fully integrated into such base activities as preaching, counseling, and space visitation and to learn.

The program covered twenty-six hours of familiarization lectures and ten hours of personnel visitation, with three participating U.S. chaplain mentors. The Kenyan chaplains preached at worship services, attended different worship services, received an orientation to the Chaplain Assistant program from army, navy, and air force enlisted personnel, and presented a Kenyan cultural briefing to the U.S. chaplains and their assistants.

One Kenyan chaplain was particularly appreciative of the training section on advisement and developing nonsectarian prayers. At first he did not see the value of a nonsectarian way of praying, since in his context it was unnecessary. However, discussion with an American chaplain gave him much to consider. This anecdote is particularly important in light of Kenya's contribution to multinational deployments.

Besides facilitator and relationship builder, the chaplain is an ambassador not only of the U.S. military but also of the U.S. government. In coordination with the U.S. embassies in Djibouti, Kenya, Uganda, and Ethiopia, in August 2011 CJTF-HOA and U.S. African Command's Office of Religious Affairs brought American imam Shakur Abdul Ali to visit those four nations during the observance of Ramadan. The purpose of the visit was for Imam Shakur to interact specifically with Muslim leaders and organizations and to develop positive relationships, putting a positive face on the U.S. government's respect and tolerance for all religions, especially Islam, worldwide, to counter any negative views toward America and Islam, and to demonstrate in action the cooperation and friendship among clergy from different faiths—myself, Shakur, and Protestant Chaplain Jerry Lewis (the senior chaplain for USAFRICOM). The three of us traveled together, talking to individual religious leaders and groups throughout the four nations.

Imam Shakur explained to Christian ministers and leaders about how Jesus is revered in the Koran, quoting passages from the Koran that refer to Issa (*Jesus* in Arabic). None of the Christian ministers whom we spoke to had previously known that Jesus is revered in Islam. One minister said he would have to study Islam and the Koran. Later Imam Shakur and I were hosted on two radio programs—one in Mombasa, Kenya, and the other in Mbale, Uganda. Over a million listeners tuned in for our discussion. Since it was a call-in program, we were able to hear the positive feedback firsthand, including listener appreciation that the U.S. government respects Islam.

One of our visits was with a Christian youth group in Mombasa, Kenya. The group's director was so motivated by our visit and program that he later wrote me, "I was a participant in a workshop on peace and conflict resolution, Mombasa, Kenya, organized by the U.S. embassy. I represented a local organization . . . as we strive to make ourselves and the youth at large more responsible part of the citizenry, if not the *most* responsible."

The general consensus was that the imam, rabbi, and Christian chaplain traveling together and speaking on panels and to individuals put a positive light on America's attempts to integrate Muslims into society and dispelled myths that the U.S. government is anti-Islam. This program also showed the cooperation among Jews, Christians, and Muslims and how American society can fully integrate all religions. The four U.S. embassies were positive about the program and the rewards that were gained, and officials requested that the same program be reprised over the next Ramadan. This story is another example of interagency cooperation between the U.S. embassies and the U.S. military.

THE WAY FORWARD

The complexities of the persistent present-day world conflicts have generated new interest in the role and work of chaplains. Military strategic planning has incorporated a new role for their chaplains, as evident by the publication of JP 1-05. However, there is continued debate within some military circles—especially with the chief of chaplains for the army, navy, and air force—as to how to mitigate obstacles that may be associated with an expanded chaplaincy mission. Challenges to the new mission abound. With the reduction of forces even within the Chaplain Corps, chaplains are stretched thin in providing even the traditional type of services. Can the Chaplain Corps, without jeopardizing its essential mission, afford to redirect a resource to engage with religious leaders? Can a chaplain perform both of these services, given the amount of time each takes? Are chaplains equipped—educated and trained—for this second role?

Even when chaplains liaise with civilian religious leaders there is consternation among some State Department officials that chaplains are overstepping the bounds into diplomacy. Nonetheless, military chaplains stand at the cusp of an exciting and immensely significant new era of ministry. Because military chaplains are the only U.S. government personnel trained to effectively communicate across religious boundaries, they are the choice to interact with indigenous religious leaders. And the presence of a U.S. government religious professional sends a strong message to these countries that the U.S. government recognizes, affirms, and values their public discourse and that religion has a legitimate place in the world of diplomacy and international relations. Religion cannot be ignored; it is a force in today's world.

We live in an interconnected and interdependent world in which human rights, political democracy, and particular religious loyalties matter profoundly. Winning the hearts and minds of local people by respecting their diverse religious beliefs and cultural orientations is more critical than ever. Thus it is important to understand that underlying religious dynamics can sometimes make the difference between mission failure and success.

Clearly, if one hopes to gain the full benefits of a broadened mandate to transform nations and societies, then U.S. government agencies—diplomatic, military, and development—must have a basic familiarity with the religious imperatives at play within their areas of responsibility.

Interaction with religious leaders and institutions, whether in Afghanistan, Iraq, or Africa, has been inconsistently addressed by military, diplomatic, and development officials. There is still inadequate interreligious education and training for officials who develop and implement U.S. foreign and military policy. The role of the military chaplain de facto as the only government religious professional is continuing to be redefined when it comes to key religious engagement. Because of this inconsistency, military and diplomatic interaction with indigenous religious leaders—and the chaplain's role in this activity—has basically been a function of instincts and judgment.

The U.S. government is starting to craft its foreign policy recognizing that religion is not separated from public life and that religious leaders in many countries play an important role in governance. Through the 1998 International Religious Freedom Act, the U.S. Congress established the U.S. Commission on International Religious Freedom and a State Department Office of International Religious Freedom, the latter headed by an ambassador-at-large for international religious freedom.

That said, the debate about the role of chaplains will continue within the military and even in diplomatic circles. Without boots on the ground—chaplains engaging with religious leaders and institutions—along with inconsistent policies for interreligious engagement, the U.S. government will find itself consistently at a deficit. It will constantly be trying to turn the tide in bringing peace and stability to the areas of the world where religion is interwoven in the fabric of society. Therefore, the U.S. government can do no worse by utilizing the resources at hand. If not military chaplains, then the State Department should explore the idea of developing a diplomatic chaplain corps whose purpose would be to engage with religious leaders to serve as peace builders across religions and cultures.

NOTES

1. Douglas Johnston, *Religion: The Missing Dimension of Statecraft* (Oxford: Oxford University Press, 1994), 4.

2. Chris Seiple, "Ready . . . Or Not? Equipping the U.S. Military Chaplain for Inter-religious Liaison," *Review of Faith and International Affairs* 7, no. 4 (2009): 43–49.

3. George Adams, CDR, CHC, USN, "Chaplains as Liaisons with Religious Leaders: Lessons from Iraq and Afghanistan," *Peaceworks*, no. 56 (March 2006): 1–56.

4. Alex Thompson, "Religious Leader Engagement in Southern Afghanistan," *Joint Force Quarterly* 63 (4th Quarter 2011): 95–101.

5. Thompson, "Religious Leader Engagement," 96.

6. Ibid.

7. Ibid., 98.

8. U.S. Department of Defense, "Joint Publication 1-05: Religious Affairs in Joint Operations," November 20, 2009, http://www.dtic.mil/doctrine/new_pubs/jp1_05.pdf. "This publication," declares the preface, "provides doctrine for religious affairs in joint operations . . . [and] provides information on the chaplain's roles as the principle advisor to the joint-force commander . . . on religious affairs and a key advisor on the impact of religion on military operations. . . . It sets forth joint doctrine to govern the activities . . . [and] provides the doctrinal basis for U.S. military coordination with other U.S. government departments and agencies during operations and for U.S. military involvement in multinational operations."

9. Ibid., x.

10. Combined Joint Task Force-Horn of Africa (CJTF-HOA), "Operation Order 12-008: Religious Engagement," December 16, 2011. The mission of strategic religious engagement was incorporated via Operations Order 12-008 into the overall mission of CJTF-HOA. This is one of the first religious affairs operation orders to be incorporated into a Combined Joint Task Force mission.

11. Ibid.

12. Ibid., 1.

8

Strategic Engagement and Advisement at the CENTCOM Center of Excellence

David West

In 2007 then–Secretary of Defense Robert Gates began to publicly acknowledge what many already knew: the United States poorly understood other cultures, including the highly religious contexts of places like Iraq and Afghanistan, and the United States was losing the war of ideas over its intentions and values. In one speech Gates admitted that "it is just plain embarrassing that al-Qaeda is better at communicating its message on the Internet than America. . . . Speed, agility, and cultural relevance are not terms that come readily to mind when discussing U.S. strategic communications."[1]

Of course, any form of "strategic" communication involves knowledge, messaging, and listening. In order to get at some of these issues, particularly in the context of Central Asia, the Afghanistan-Pakistan Center of Excellence was established in late 2009, headquartered in Tampa, Florida, as part of the Intelligence Group (J-2) of U.S. Central Command (CENTCOM). At the forefront was the idea of coordinating engagements with indigenous religious leaders within Afghanistan and Pakistan in pursuit of greater understanding and, ultimately, reconciliation and peace. This resulted in an invitation for a military chaplain to become a member of the center's Strategic Integrated Assessment Branch.

At about the same time, President Obama's Advisory Council on Faith-based and Neighborhood Partnerships was tasked with establishing the current state of outreach to and partnership with religious communities by all cabinet agencies, the most typical being charitable, development, and humanitarian work, whether at home or abroad. Because the majority of religious engagements within the Department of Defense were occurring in the CENTCOM area, it was decided that CENTCOM should send a chaplain to represent the Department of Defense to the advisory council. The decision was made to send the Center of Excellence's chaplain as the Department of Defense representative to the advisory council. It is noteworthy that the council's final major public document stipulated that "no government, nonprofit organization, or foundation can coordinate the assets of religious communities by itself."[2]

The director of the Center of Excellence encouraged and approved the initial blueprint for an initiative to explore the coordination of religious-leader outreach related to Afghanistan and Pakistan. These coordinated efforts included other government agencies outside the Department of Defense, academia, and nongovernmental organizations. General Petraeus, then-commander of CENTCOM, was presented with a brief that provided the initial concept for the development of a more robust engagement of religious leaders. This concept included a request for thirty-one analysts to develop an in-depth understanding of the influence of religions and religious leaders within the Afghanistan, Pakistan, and Central Asian states. Direct liaison authority to meet with nongovernmental organizations, other governmental agencies, and other military offices was requested to support the efforts of the newly formed Strategic Outreach Initiative. Additional authority for the initiative team members to directly engage religious leaders within the Afghanistan, Pakistan, and Central Asian states was requested from, and approved by, General Petraeus. This provided the initiative team with the impetus to greatly expand the aperture of direct religious-leader engagement throughout all government agencies, nongovernmental organizations, Afghanistan, and Pakistan. The additional authorities granted by the CENTCOM commander also greatly opened the avenues to reach out to other agencies within the U.S. government.

This chapter discusses the chaplains as a strategic U.S. government resource, as well as the limits on chaplains, within the context of the global war on terrorism, using the story of the CENTCOM's Afghanistan-Pakistan Center of Excellence Initiative. The strategic challenge was understanding Afghanistan's and Pakistan's religious landscape—or *human terrain*—in order to work for peace, but it required significant work at home before we could really move forward with our work in the Strategic Outreach Initiative. Consequently, this chapter first considers challenges of the initiative, then actual engagements during the initiative, and finally recommendations following the initiative that stem from the many challenges—most of them institutional—that the initiative encountered. The later sections of this chapter talk about a series of engagements made to universities, think tanks, other government agencies, and ultimately foreign religious leaders, concluding with recommendations for the future.

THE CHAPLAIN CHALLENGE

The assignment of a chaplain to CENTCOM's intelligence group presented some challenges among chaplains. All three services (army, navy, and air force) provide chaplains to the CENTCOM staff. Each service has a different perspective on the role of the chaplain. Throughout the career of most chaplains, regardless of service, most of their efforts are focused on direct religious ministry, such as counseling, preaching, and providing the sacraments. Indeed, chaplains are trained as pastors first and foremost before joining the military as religious professionals. Thus an assignment to a joint (multiservice) command staff like CENTCOM requires a shift of focus from direct ministry to more of a religious-advisement role. For most chaplains, this is challenging, since it is very different from the direct ministry they have been performing within their service.

The service-specific philosophies regarding the noncombatant status of chaplains also presented challenges to the Strategic Outreach Initiative. More specifically, the air force and the navy often voiced concerns about chaplains working within the staff groups to provide religious advisement—counsel and insight on the religious and cultural context of an area—specifically within the operations group (J3) and the intelligence group (J2). Much of this concern had to do with the chaplain being made a part of the decision process, which resulted in kinetic combat actions, where direct force was used. Within the intelligence group, decisions were made concerning who should be killed or captured, and then the operations group planned and oversaw operations that targeted the individuals identified by the intelligence group. From the perspective of the air force and navy, the involvement of a chaplain as an advisor within these two groups—even if the chaplain eschewed all kinetic operations—tended to place the chaplain in what could be interpreted as a combatant status, despite efforts to the contrary.

An informational meeting was held with representatives from the Army, Navy, and Air Force Chief of Chaplains' Offices to introduce them to the Strategic Outreach Initiative. The chiefs of chaplains are the senior-most chaplains in their respective services, typically wearing the rank of a two-star flag officer and supported by several senior chaplains. For this meeting, the Joint Chiefs of Staff chaplain coordinated between the initiative team and the representatives from the three services' Chief of Chaplains' Offices. This meeting provided the three services the opportunity to understand the initiative concept approved by the CENTCOM commander and afforded them the opportunity to voice their support or concerns.

While the approval of the three Chief of Chaplains' Offices was not required, their buy-in would provide additional impetus to the initiative. The three services' initial reaction to the initiative was very negative. The air force's representative voiced their opposition to chaplains participating in any form of religious-leader engagement abroad, such as U.S. military chaplains going "outside the wire" to meet with local imams and mullahs. Concerns about maintaining the noncombatant status of chaplains were strongly voiced by the air force and navy. All three services voiced a strong concern with religious-engagement efforts of any kind proceeding from the intelligence group; including chaplains made the scenario even more complicated. After lengthy discussions, most of the services' concerns relating to the inclusion of a chaplain on the initiative team were addressed with the understanding that continuous coordination should exist between the chaplain on the initiative team, the CENTCOM command chaplain, and the services' Chief of Chaplains' Offices. Each service provided additional guidance specifically related to any chaplain of their respective service who might be engaged in religious-leader engagement. For the navy and air force, this included specific restrictions on any chaplain assigned to CENT-COM, which included that they neither be assigned to nor participate in any efforts related to the intelligence group. A major outcome of this meeting was that the initiative team received a green light to coordinate with chaplains in all services who had participated, or would participate, in the future with religious-leader engagements throughout the CENTCOM area of responsibility, which included the greater Middle East and Central Asia.

THE RELIGIOUS CHALLENGE

Religion poses a unique challenge to the understanding of religious leaders and their impact within a specific country. For the most part, religious leaders tend to be nonstate actors with a transcendent ideology spanning transnational networks. Because of this, there is little expertise on religion among U.S. government agencies, other than among military chaplains, regarding understanding the dynamics and impact of religion and religious leaders. Within the Department of Defense, intelligence professionals narrowly focus on religiously inspired threats but little else. Prior to 9/11, chaplains provided the Defense Department with limited religious information, focusing on basic information about religion and religious practices of a particular area. Even after several years of operations within Afghanistan, little effort was made to understand the dynamic international role of religious leaders in the Afghanistan and Pakistan area.

The Strategic Outreach Initiative sought to address the lack of *religious-terrain analysis* in Afghanistan and its region. This phrase is borrowed from human-geography literature and has to do with developing an appreciation for the social, faith-based, and cultural currents of a given area. Such analysis could help the Defense Department narrow its focus to areas, leaders, groups, and institutions where engagement would be the most effective. Although engagement of religious leaders was taking place in Afghanistan, no one had established the leaders or groups who would provide the greatest influence within the country. There also had been no effort to determine the religious leaders in Pakistan who held great influence within Afghanistan because of tribal and religious affiliations. While there had been some engagement with religious leaders in Afghanistan by chaplains and some engagement with religious leaders in Pakistan by nongovernmental agencies, there had been no effort to coordinate or prioritize these efforts.

The initiative team, supported by General Petraeus, was established to specifically address the coordination and prioritization of religious engagements in the Afghanistan and Pakistan area. The team initially consisted of a sociologist, three human-terrain analysts, an Afghanistan expert, and a Pakistan expert. The assignment of a chaplain to the intelligence group was very unique. Even more unique was the fact that a chaplain had been assigned as the leader, or team chief. This type of assignment is atypical for chaplains working within the intelligence group. In fact, Joint Publication 1-05, "Religious Affairs in Joint Operations," clearly states that chaplains will not engage in intelligence-collection actions, which is usually the role of the intelligence group. However, the Afghanistan-Pakistan Center of Excellence expanded the role of the intelligence group with the direction from General Petraeus to widen the aperture of efforts relating to reducing violence, restoring peace, and achieving reconciliation within Afghanistan and Pakistan. The idea was to allow all staff sections to participate in the center, and what could be more central to the role of a chaplain than peace and reconciliation?

THE ESTABLISHMENT AND
DEVELOPMENT OF THE INITIATIVE

In late 2009 and early 2010 an initial effort was established to help several human-terrain analysts understand the role of religion and religious leaders within the Afghanistan and Pakistan area. This effort included meeting on a regular basis with the analysts to review and discuss various articles written by chaplains who had been involved with religious-leader engagements in Iraq and Afghanistan. The analysts also reviewed and discussed the doctrinal publications provided by the Department of Defense: JP 1-05 provided doctrine and authority to chaplains regarding advising the commander and the chaplains' role in religious-leader engagement. Department of Defense "Directive 1304.19: Appointment of Chaplains for the Military Departments" identified military chaplains as the principal advisors to the commander on the impact of religion within military operations. The knowledge from both documents provided the analysts with a framework for understanding past religious-leader engagements.

The role of the initiative team was to widen the aperture of traditional military analysis by working with nontraditional sources. This method brought together chaplains, nongovernmental organizations, think tanks, academia, other governmental agencies, and religious leaders. The initiative team worked with these organizations to identify the knowledge gaps that existed in understanding the religious dimensions in Afghanistan, Pakistan, and the Central Asian states. One result of this effort was coordination of, collaboration with, and expansion of relationships between religious leaders inside and outside Afghanistan and Pakistan. The idea had been to build consensus within the entire religious framework of Afghanistan and Pakistan to work toward peace—from the local through the national and international levels. Gathering and considering knowledge from all organizations—public, private, and governmental—working within the Afghanistan and Pakistan area would offer a more comprehensive understanding of the interactions of religious leaders within the religious dimension. This served as the initial framework for mapping the religious terrain in the area.

In order to accomplish the task that lay before me, I asked a simple question: Who are the strategic influential religious leaders within, and without, Afghanistan and Pakistan? To my amazement, no one at CENTCOM was able to provide this level of information. While some religious-leader engagements were then taking place at the local level, there was no apparent effort to gather this information and analyze it at the CENTCOM level to determine who the key religious leaders may have been within Afghanistan. Likewise, no one at the CENTCOM level had developed any understanding related to the religious leaders residing outside of Afghanistan who may have been influencing the religious dynamics within Afghanistan. The task ahead of me was daunting and one that I knew would require additional resources within CENTCOM together with resources that lay far beyond the grasp of the Department of Defense.[3]

During the early phase of the Strategic Outreach Initiative, coordination was undertaken between a variety of agencies in Washington, D.C., in an effort to understand their involvement in religious-leader engagement and religious-terrain mapping. Many of these organizations had seldom—if ever—interacted with chaplains. Among others, participating organizations included the National Security Agency, the Central Intelligence Agency, the Marine Corps Intelligence Agency, and the Defense Intelligence Agency. Much of the discussions with these agencies revealed the abundance of work required to continue gaining a complete understanding of the religious-dimension terrain within the Afghanistan and Pakistan area. These meetings proved to be invaluable.

Exchange of information between various organizations opened the door for future opportunities to understand and develop a comprehensive religious-terrain mapping within the Afghanistan and Pakistan area. Before the Strategic Outreach Initiative had been established, the U.S. government had made no focused efforts to appreciate the implications of religion within the makeup of a specific group of people, though numerous voices in the academic and NGO communities had been arguing for this for years. The initiative's focus, then, became to understand at all levels—from the local to the international—the influence of religion and religious leaders within the Afghanistan and Pakistan area. Gathering the data and entering it into an analytical framework might reveal a graphic and detailed understanding of the religious dimension within the area.

THINK TANKS AND ACADEMICS

In early 2010 the initiative team began communicating with various agencies and organizations throughout the United States and England. One of the earliest think-tank organizations that the team met with was the United Kingdom's Quilliam Foundation, which describes itself as the world's first antiradical think tank. Cofounded by Maajid Nawaz, a former Islamist extremist, and Ed Hussein, who currently serves on the Council on Foreign Relations, Quilliam seeks to counter extremism through grassroots events. Nawaz particularly focuses on Pakistan since he is a British-Pakistani. The initial meeting and ongoing dialogue between the initiative team and Quilliam established a relationship that created a better understanding of the challenges to religious-leader engagements within Pakistan.

Quilliam invited the initiative team to several dialogues and presentations to discuss thoughts on reducing radicalization within the Afghanistan and Pakistan area. As a result of these meetings, initiative team members attended presentations at Oxford University that were focused on Muslim religious-leader engagements.

Then, in a further effort to broaden their understanding of religious-leader roles throughout the Afghanistan and Pakistan area, the team followed the Quilliam model, visiting other academic institutions, such as the Kroc Institute for International Peace Studies at the University of Notre Dame; the Berkley Center for Religion, Peace & World Affairs at Georgetown University; the Center for World Religions, Diplomacy, and Conflict Resolution at the School for Conflict Analysis and Resolution, George Mason University; and Johns Hopkins University.[4] In every case, scholars like Scott Appleby, Dan Philpott, Eric Patterson, and Marc Gopin graciously gave their time and expertise, and we learned that a wealth of expertise was waiting to be tapped—much of it freely available online.

Most important, all of this brought new insights to our analytical perspective. No longer did the CENTCOM analysts view religious leaders as localized. Instead, a framework for understanding the influence of religious leaders in a strategic context began to emerge. This also reinforced the team's understanding that we needed a great deal of outside expertise in order to develop a religious-terrain map.

ENGAGING WITH NGOS AND MEETING THE ISLAMISTS

Over the first few months of 2010, several visits to Washington, D.C., afforded the initiative team an opportunity to meet with several influential NGOs, one of which was the World Organization for Resource Development and Education. WORDE's mission is to enhance communication and understanding between Muslim and non-Muslim communities and to strengthen moderate Muslim institutions worldwide to mitigate social and political conflict.[5] President and founder of WORDE, Dr. Hedieh Mirahmadi, centers much of her work on Barelvi Islam, which makes up an estimated 50–60 percent of Pakistan's Muslim population.[6] WORDE connects local religious leaders to Muslim leaders abroad, helps them find ways they can stay in touch, and publishes literature on the topic. WORDE also examines how groups and organizations can be more effective in messaging and reaching out to the media in an effort to influence religious leaders in Afghanistan.

Another organization the initiative met with early on was the International Center for Religion and Diplomacy (ICRD). Dr. Doug Johnston, president and founder, had begun a relationship with the CENTCOM Command Chaplain's Office back in 2003. Over the years, the relationship was maintained and eventually resulted in significant interactions with the initiative team. After learning of the initiative's development and the authorities provided by the CENTCOM commander, Dr. Johnston invited three initiative team members to attend a briefing at the Center for Strategic and International Studies in Washington, D.C., hosted by ICRD. The briefing was a presentation from five Islamist madrassa leaders who shared that they were now promoting nonradical Islam. The importance of these leaders' work was far-reaching, since their ideas were incorporated into Friday sermons that were then distributed to tens of thousands of individual religious leaders.

Because of our previous relationship with ICRD, the initiative team was able to meet privately with the five madrassa leaders. Four were Wahhabi extremists, and the fifth a Deobandi. This marked the first time a military chaplain had engaged with religious leaders from either group, and it was especially important that positive contact was made with leaders of madrassas where Taliban leaders and fighters had been trained. One madrassa leader admitted it was likely that he would have been fighting with the Taliban without the understanding he had gained over the past few years. Without the ICRD's interaction, these meetings would never have taken place. The relationship between the madrassa leaders and ICRD, coupled with the mutual relationship between ICRD and CENTCOM, allowed this historic event to occur. The leaders asked that we deliver specific messages to CENTCOM leadership, including requests that CENTCOM continue to reach out to religious leaders in Pakistan. The religious leaders also expressed their gratitude to the initiative team for being the first U.S. government representatives to reach out to them. The team was also specifically asked by the religious leaders to continue this engagement. As a result of this initial meeting, these religious leaders offered to help the initiative team engage with various Taliban leaders who would willingly discuss how to bring peace to the Afghanistan and Pakistan area. The potential to move forward on the invitation of peace discussions with these religious leaders and Taliban leaders rested with the leadership of CENTCOM.

Another meeting with a nongovernmental organization in greater Washington, D.C., occurred with the Institute for Global Engagement. Dr. Chris Seiple is president of IGE and has also worked with religious leaders in Pakistan. Specifically, IGE worked with the Jamiat Ulema-e-Islam (Fazlur Rehman) (JUI-F), a Deobandi organization that has established a very large number of madrassas throughout Pakistan. During this initial meeting with IGE, a specific request was made through Dr. Seiple from JUI-F representatives that the initiative team consider meeting with several JUI-F representatives. This was a very critical request, since it had come from one of the most senior leaders of the JUI-F. This request was taken back to CENTCOM for research, discussion, and a decision. The request was specific in that only three individuals of the initiative team were asked by IGE to participate in this meeting. The primary member of the team requested by the JUI-F was the chaplain. Without the chaplain as the initiative team leader, this meeting would not have occurred.

The decision was made by CENTCOM for three initiative team members to meet with the JUI-F leaders and Dr. Seiple. As the initiative team leader, I requested that the sociologist and the Pakistan expert accompany me to the meeting. One of the early decisions in coordinating the meeting was to select a country that the JUI-F members and the initiative team members could travel to without great difficulty. The city and country chosen in consultation with IGE was Dubai, United Arab Emirates.

Our initial meeting with the two JUI-F religious leaders began with a scheduled dinner shortly after their arrival. We met the individuals, together with Dr. Seiple, at their hotel. We immediately sat on the cushions on the floor and held our first impromptu meeting. This was a relationship-building time when we shared our "first cup of tea"—actually several cups of tea. The JUI-F leaders and the initiative team members shared their personal and professional backgrounds.

As the afternoon progressed, we discussed the importance of religious leaders within Pakistan. The JUI-F leaders expressed the importance of their organization and their religious leaders within Pakistan. They also discussed some of the roles they felt that Pakistan—and particularly the JUI-F—could play in relation to Afghanistan. The discussion of roles specifically related to reconciliation and peace building.

Much of the discussion from the two leaders involved their perception that Pakistan felt excluded from the reconciliation process. Specifically,

U.S. reluctance to engage religious leaders, like the leadership of the JUI-F, resulted in their feeling excluded. The JUI-F has specific ties to both Afghanistan and Pakistan: the founder of the JUI-F is considered a cofounder of the Taliban. Because of this, they stated that had they been consulted earlier, even before bombings had taken place in Afghanistan, they might have been able to resolve the major issue with less loss of life. Each JUI-F leader we met with seemed genuinely concerned over the loss of life, even American lives.

After several hours the leaders begin to open up more and voice some specific concerns. These were very broad in nature, and we listened with care and concern. We left the hotel and went to a local restaurant of their choosing for dinner. When we arrived at the restaurant, a specific table had been prepared for us. The JUI-F leaders decided the seating arrangement for dinner. During dinner we continued to develop the relationship. The dinner conversation took on a more personal tone. Traditions from their specific tribe and culture were discussed. The leaders were very interested in discussing the similarities and differences regarding family and marriage between their culture and those of the United States. One of the important takeaways from the dinner discussion was the importance of family and marriage within their culture. As we were leaving the table, a group sitting about two tables over spoke to the senior JUI-F leader with us. It was evident by the dress of the group that they were Taliban leadership. It seems as though members of various religious groups travel from Pakistan to the UAE on a regular basis for both business and pleasure.

The meeting on the second day was more detailed, building on the trust we had built during that first day of meetings. The leaders voiced several concerns throughout the day related to India, including concern over India's involvment in Pakistan. The question as to why India had seventeen consulates in Afghanistan was discussed. Even though these were not specific CENTCOM issues we had prepared to discuss, we lent a sympathetic ear to their concerns.

The JUI-F leaders were very interested in discussing why the United States did not consider the JUI-F a positive influence to work with in Pakistan. This opened the door to discussing the difference in the role of the religious leaders in Pakistan and the religious leaders in the United States. We also discussed the role of the chaplain within the military. There was a lengthy discussion on the differences between the relationships of the religious leaders in Pakistan and those within the United States, particularly the chaplains in the military. The JUI-F leaders also raised questions related to the issue of five hundred JUI-F members, mostly madrassa leaders, who had been arrested in Pakistan. This was the first we had heard of the arrests. We informed the JUI-F leaders that we could not take any action on this matter but might be able to relay our concern to other organizations within the U.S. government. However, in order to voice this concern with other government officials, we would need additional information—including the names and details of the five hundred arrested. The leaders agreed to send a detailed list through the Institute for Global Engagement.

A very interesting event took place on the second day. The discussions during lunch took on more of a personal tone. Throughout the conversation we continued to discuss our backgrounds and how we each had became involved in our present work. Near the end of the lunch, one of the religious leaders placed his hand on my shoulder and said, "I know you are a holy man. You are invited to visit our country and my home. I will guarantee your protection because you are a holy man." This is the impact of religious-leader engagement, even when the religious leaders are from different faiths.

The meeting concluded with the two leaders asking for an additional meeting in about a month's time to develop a framework to move ahead with engaging religious leaders in Pakistan. When asked specifically who they would be willing to meet with in the future, they stated that they would only meet with the people present in the room. Several conclusions can be drawn from this specific request. The religious leaders wanted to meet with U.S. religious leaders who were connected with senior military leadership and who were also connected with other governmental organizations. Since they were placing themselves in possible danger by meeting with members of the U.S. military, they wished to limit the number of individuals they might meet with. Limiting the attendees of the next meeting to only the three initiative team members present for this first meeting enabled us to gain the leaders' support and agreement for us to meet the founder and leader of the JUI-F after the next meeting. They also assured us that as these meetings progressed we could expect a reduction in the vitriolic rhetoric coming from their senior leader and additional support for our efforts in Pakistan and Afghanistan.

THE DEPARTMENT OF STATE CALLS

One of our first interagency calls was at the State Department. The initiative team was contacted by several State Department individuals who requested meetings, which were scheduled for the day after our return from UAE. The primary meeting was to take place with Ambassador Holbrooke, the Special Representative to Afghanistan and Pakistan, and his staff during their weekly meeting. The initiative team was invited to present a fifteen-minute brief on the concept of the Strategic Outreach Initiative. Since the invitation to present at the Holbrooke meeting came from the State Department, the initiative team did not know that other CENTCOM representatives would be involved. We soon found out that the plans, strategy, and policy group (J5) would be the Holbrooke meeting's senior-representative group from CENTCOM. While the initiative team members had been engaged with other religious leaders in the UAE, our office was contacted by a plans, strategy, and policy group representative for coordination of the Holbrooke meeting presentation. The required internal CENTCOM coordination—another of the seemingly endless bureaucratic maneuvers necessary in the Department of Defense—was finalized by other initiative team members during our return travel from the UAE. They joined me and our team's sociologist for the meeting in Washington, D.C.

Prior to presenting at the Holbrooke meeting, the initiative team was required to meet with the senior advisor to Ambassador Holbrooke and State Department attorney. The senior advisor was a British Foreign Service officer who had previously served in Pakistan. One of the primary purposes of this meeting was to discuss "the separation of church and state" issue, as "there are few issues that generate as much controversy as those surrounding the separation of church and state in the United States."[7] Within the U.S. government, care is taken to ensure there is no possibility that an agency will promote one religion over another so that there is no perception of the establishment of a state-sponsored religion. To some extent many governmental offices and individuals tend to go so far as to not allow for any religious consideration or discussion within meetings and decision-making processes.

The initial atmosphere of the Holbrooke meeting seemed to be a bit adversarial. But soon this changed, after enlightening the attorney about the role of the chaplain. After understanding that the chaplain was the only governmental officer specifically paid by government funds to discuss religion, both the senior advisor and the attorney were very engaging and seemed genuinely interested in the initiative. One important result of this meeting was that I received unfettered access to a variety of offices within the State Department for future strategic engagements. Additional meetings took place without any discussion of the separation of church and state.

When we entered the room for the Holbrooke meeting I was surprised to find my seat only one removed from the ambassador himself. Usually the more important an individual was considered, the closer they were placed to the leader. Other individuals seated around the table were assistant secretary of state–level individuals. Just before Ambassador Holbrooke entered the room we were reminded that we only had fifteen minutes for our briefing—if that. Ambassador Holbrooke opened the meeting and soon turned to our team for our presentation. He and his staff were very engaging during the presentation. The allotted fifteen minutes turned into about forty-five, and the initiative became the focus discussion of the meeting.

During our time, Ambassador Holbrooke and his staff voiced their concerns and provided insightful discussions and suggestions. One concern related to engaging religious leaders in the Afghanistan and Pakistan area was the guidance and training provided to chaplains prior to their engaging religious leaders. We discussed the concern that an engagement could go wrong and potentially cause an international incident. Ambassador Holbrooke also discussed the policy, guidance, and training currently in place for religious-leader engagement. While the current level of policy and guidance afforded chaplains the opportunity to conduct religious-leader engagement, it was suggested that additional policy related to religious-leader engagement be established that would reach beyond the Department of Defense and include other departments within the U.S. government. The meeting concluded with Ambassador Holbrooke stating that the initiative was "fantastic." This meeting served to raise State Department awareness about religious-leader engagements. Additional meetings were requested by other State Department offices as a result.

DISCUSSIONS WITH THE WHITE HOUSE

The day following the Holbrooke meeting the initiative team had three additional meetings with State Department representatives. The most productive meeting was with Rashad Hussain, the presidentially appointed Special Envoy to the Organization of Islamic Conference (OIC). Mr. Hussain stated that it was most important that the initiative concept be developed and that religious leaders within Afghanistan and Pakistan be engaged. The initiative team was asked to expand the relationship with Mr. Hussain to include an advisor role related to the Afghanistan and Pakistan area. The relationship continued to develop with additional meetings occurring on several subsequent visits to Washington, D.C.

Mr. Hussain requested assistance during his planned visit to Afghanistan. This visit took place at a time when Afghanistan was suffering from an ever-increasing crisis of legitimacy due to widespread corruption within government institutions and their inability to protect the population against insurgents' threats.[8] Mr. Hussain requested coordination assistance from the initiative team. In conjunction with the International Security Assistance Forces (ISAF) and the State Department, the initiative team provided its Afghanistan expert as an assistant to work and travel with Mr. Hussain.

During Mr. Hussain's visit to Afghanistan he met with numerous dignitaries, including President Hamid Karzai; Dr. Niazi, Afghanistan's minister of hajj and religious affairs; General David Petraeus, by then commander of ISAF; and U.S. ambassador Karl Eikenberry. President Karzai viewed Mr. Hussain's visit to Afghanistan as one of the most important visits due to his role within the Organization of Islamic Conference member states. He requested Mr. Hussain's support in convincing and encouraging further participation of the OIC member states in Afghanistan's stability and reconstruction programs. General Petraeus viewed Mr. Hussain's visit as a very positive multiplier in support of the ISAF mission in Afghanistan. He encouraged Mr. Hussain to further promote OIC's participation and support in peace and stability programs. General Petraeus also noted to Mr. Hussain the importance of CENTCOM's Afghanistan-Pakistan's Center of

Excellence. Particularly, he noted the importance of the Strategic Outreach Initiative—both the initiative's outreach to the White House's special representatives and its support of Mr. Hussain's Afghanistan visit. General Petraeus said that the ISAF mission would seriously benefit from further cooperation from Mr. Hussain and from broader participation of the OIC members in Afghanistan.[9]

CONCLUSION AND NEXT STEPS

The first-ever Strategic Outreach Initiative Working Group was convened in September 2010. This working group served as the culmination of twelve months of collective initiative team effort. The intended goal of this first-ever working group was to map U.S. government agencies, nongovernmental organizations, academia, and ISAF activities and efforts pertaining to key religious leaders, as well as discovering areas of cooperation across agencies. It was an attempt to understand the current religious dimension and the greater situation in Afghanistan. The working group was designed to enhance the understanding of who among the government, nongovernmental organizations, and academic organizations was working on strategic outreach to Afghan religious leaders through open dialogue and debate regarding opportunities and options for the way forward. Participants offered a variety of perspectives grounded in both recent field research and long-standing experience in the region. Specific goals of the working group that were met included:

- updating current religious-leader-engagement efforts by an initiative-team member via video teleconference from Kabul,
- gaining an understanding of how and where the organizations represented were engaging in the Afghanistan and Pakistan region,
- developing an expanded "brain trust" and network for CENTCOM and the center,
- addressing how we enhance interagency understanding of the religious dimension to support the ISAF commander, and
- discussing practical mechanisms to coordinate efforts in reaching out to key religious leaders, institutions, and networks to support the ISAF mission.

The working group consisted of twenty-one participants from nine governmental agencies, four nongovernmental organizations, and one academic institution. The first session highlighted the difficulties in coordinating the religious-terrain-mapping effort and nongovernmental organizations' sensitivities about sharing information and sources with intelligence, defense, and other governmental agencies. Information was collected regarding organizational efforts in Afghanistan. The afternoon session discussed enhancing understanding and cooperation in the religious dimension to support the ISAF commander.

The working group consensus was that since religion is part of the problem then we must make it part of the solution. The Taliban has established an extremist religious narrative aimed at the clerics that must be countered. The United States can never counter this narrative if we refuse to engage within the religious dimension. Several group members mentioned the need to establish a counternarrative with appropriate religious leaders. Members also discussed the difficulty involved in engaging with some of these religious leaders who might be critical of U.S. policy. The working group recommended that the U.S. government not be publicly out in front of this type of effort, but rather work with nongovernmental organizations and academic institutions in developing a counternarrative and in developing a strategy for supporting engagements. Members also commented that the United States must develop a long-term strategy to speak to, train, and engage with the Afghan community, something that the United States was not equipped for at the time. The group members commented that the United States is better off than it was in 2001, yet nowhere near where it should be. One group member commented that "religious engagement must be as unpoliticized as possible; there must be depoliticized analysis."[10] Another member remarked that "the Taliban are effective in setting up the narrative in saying that we are fighting a war against Islam. In the minds of Muslims that's what we're doing. The only way we can defeat them is to face them on the religious level."[11]

The involvement of a chaplain as the initiative team leader was the first-ever of its kind. While this was the first effort to determine who the religious leaders and organizations are within the area that we can work with, it certainly should not be the last. A new approach must be considered in performing religious-factors analysis and religious-terrain mapping. While a broad approach is discussed in this chapter, a detailed global approach would provide a more succinct mapping and understanding of the religious terrain. Each geographical combatant command must plan and conduct detailed religious-factors analysis for each country.

Chaplains are a theological asset and may participate in the development of the analysis of the religious terrain consistent with their noncombatant status. They have the ability to engage with religious leaders in order to gain additional insight into the theology of specific religions in the area. Because of their clerical and noncombatant status, chaplains are best utilized as members of the plans, strategy, and policy group (J5) or the Religious Affairs Offices, in close coordination with the intelligence group (J2). The required coordination with the intelligence group, and other staffs, necessitates the appropriate level of security clearance. In addition to the clearance, chaplains assigned as religious-factors analysts or planners must have direct access to all other analysts and planners in order to provide the theological view of the analysis early in the religious assessment and intelligence preparation of the battlefield process. The religious-factors analysis—or religious-terrain mapping—provided by the intelligence group should be complete with the theological considerations included before it is delivered to the other staff sections. Within the plans, strategy, and policy and operations groups, chaplain involvement should continue throughout the planning process.

Throughout all of this, the ultimate goal was and is peace. Currently most military and other governmental analysts consider religion through anthropological and sociological lenses. Triangulating the interpretation of religious factors through the additional study of theology and religious practice yields a more accurate picture of how religion affects the military mission and allows commanders to properly understand their enemies and potential allies on the ground. Currently there is little, or no, theological and ecclesiastical consideration during the analysis of the religious terrain. This identified theological gap in religious analysis could be bridged in several ways. The first option is to use military chaplains as an integral member of the analysis team. All chaplains must receive at least seventy-two hours of theological training at the master's level. Some chaplains have had at least one year of specific world-religions training at the master's level, while a few have studied at the doctoral level. The ideal chaplain to participate as a member of an analytical team would be one who has received some training in world religions.

A second way to bridge this gap is to establish permanent civilian positions within each graphical combatant command that requires that participating individuals have theological training at the master's level. The third option, which may be more immediately applicable, is to contract individuals with theological training to bridge the gap until one of the other options has been enacted. The geographical combatant commands could tailor their civilian or contractor positions to focus on the specific major religious figures within the combatant-command area. Having civilians filling these positions would also provide the much-needed continuity to the combatant command.

NOTES

1. Robert M. Gates, Landon Lecture, remarks delivered in Manhattan, Kansas, November 26, 2007, text available online at http://www.defense.gov/speeches/speech.aspx?speechid=1199.

2. President's Advisory Council an Faith-based and Neighborhood Partnerships, *A New Era of Partnerships: Report of New Recommendations to the President* (Washington, DC: White House Office of Faith-Based and Neighborhood Partnerships, March 2010), 74.

3. Two other combatant commands (COCOMs) shared the interest of religious-leader engagements and the mapping of the religious terrain within the Afghanistan

and Pakistan area: Special Operations Command (SOCOM) and Strategic Command (STRATCOM). Unlike CENTCOM, which is a geographical combatant command, SOCOM and STRATCOM are functional combatant commands and have global responsibilities. STRATCOM "conducts global operations in coordination with other Combatant Commands, Services, and appropriate U.S. Government agencies to deter and detect strategic attacks against the U.S. and its allies" (see http://www.stratcom.mil/mission/). Some of the STRATCOM operations involve understanding how to counter perceived threats, which may include a religious dimension. Several meetings between the command chaplains of these two functional combatant commands and the initiative team were conducted to enlist their support and ensure there was no duplication of efforts. Continual interaction between the initiative team and the two command chaplains reinforced the great working relationship between all three combatant commands. SOCOM's command chaplain introduced additional SOCOM staff members who participated in several aspects of the initiative.

4. Other institutions include, in part, the Catholic University of America, National Defense University, West Point, Liberty Baptist Theological Seminary and Graduate School, University of South Florida, and University of Central Florida.

5. Hedieh Mirahmadi, *The Other Muslims: Moderate and Secular*, ed. Zeyno Baran (New York: Palgrave Macmillan, 2012).

6. See https://csis.org/event/global-security-forum-2011-perilous-course-future-us-pakistan-partnership.

7. Douglas M. Johnston Jr., *Religion, Terror, and Error: U.S. Foreign Policy and the Challenge of Spiritual Engagement* (Santa Barbara: ABC-CLIO, 2011), 96.

8. Thomas Barfield and Neamatollah Nojumi, "Bringing More Effective Governance to Afghanistan: 10 Pathways to Stability," *Middle East Policy* 17, no. 4 (2010).

9. Ibid.

10. Personal note by the author following the conversation, September 2010.

11. Ibid.

9

✝

Military Chaplaincy: Religious Leadership and Character Development

Eric Wester

In the wake of the Abu Ghraib scandal, a medical team informed senior leaders on the staff of General David Petraeus, then–commander of Multi-National Force–Iraq, that only about half of U.S. military personnel would report a colleague for mistreating a noncombatant. More specifically, 40 percent of Marines and 55 percent of soldiers agreed with this survey question: "I would report a unit member for intentionally injuring or killing an innocent noncombatant." The deployed medical team, established by the Office of the Surgeon General of the Army, was made up of a small team of psychologists and behavioral-health researchers who presented the findings of their fourth annual survey in Baghdad in November 2006. Imagine the reaction of the senior leaders in the room to this jarring finding! How could we only have a fifty-fifty chance that our military members would recognize and respond to the very definition of a war crime? This led to a series of other questions, most notably about how to improve the moral strength and ethical conduct of our armed forces. What resources are immediately available to deploy against this dilemma?

Even before the idea of a "holistic approach" took root in the wider national culture, General George C. Marshall spoke of the duty of commanding officers to develop conditions and influences "to promote health, morals, and spiritual values," all for the sake of the national interest. "It is in the national interest that personnel serving in the armed forces be protected in the realization and development of moral, spiritual, and religious values consistent with the religious beliefs of the individuals concerned. To this end, it is the duty of commanding officers in every echelon to develop to the highest degree the conditions and influences calculated to promote health, morals, and spiritual values of the personnel under their command."[1]

Effective commanders model the integration of these dimensions in their personal and professional lives. Effective commanders also rely on subordinate leaders to both uphold standards of conduct in military personnel and foster the aspirations of others to grow in physical, ethical, and spiritual well-being.

The "religious values" and "spiritual values" of which Marshall speaks are at the center of the practice of military chaplaincy, and they are elements of character. Marshall serializes these in discussing the lives of personnel serving in the armed forces; this chapter aims to address the interplay of spirituality, ethics, and resilience—physical as well as psychological—through survey measurements of soldiers in a combat zone. The chapter does so in a way complementary to, yet different from, the other chapters in this volume, describing the efforts of religious, medical, and mental-health professionals in the armed forces to define that amorphous area of values, morality, and individual resilience as it relates to the military profession in conditions of combat stress. The chapter does this, in part, by analyzing a unique set of survey data as well as by discussing the context within which these results were developed.

In short the issues of conscience, belief, and morality are not simply something for the base chapel but are critical facets that help determine how soldiers react on the battlefield. True, the religious and spiritual facets of the work of military chaplaincy remain central to the roles and responsibilities of this profession. Yet chaplains have the chance to engage members of the military where spirituality, ethics, and resilience intersect. The focus here is on soldiers in combat facing the terrible stresses of warfare in Iraq and Afghanistan, where the enemy challenged the basic principles of the laws of armed conflict by using the cloak of noncombatant immunity as a shield from which to strike. This chapter presents research describing correlations between individual-soldier spirituality with ethics and psychological and physical resilience under such conditions. Among the findings presented are strong statistical correlations between spirituality and emotional and physical resilience. Thus a strong spirit in soldiers may be viewed as instrumental in fostering ethical conduct and personal resilience. This is an important finding as the military draws its lessons from Iraq and Afghanistan, cares for its veterans, assigns responsibilities to its chaplains, and plans for the future. Chaplains can both provide for the religious requirements of military members' and families' personnel and engage the interplay of spirituality with character development and resilience.

A CHANGING CHAPLAINCY FOR A CHANGING MILITARY

Historically military chaplains have provided religious rites, ordinances, ceremonies, or sacraments according to the faith group or denomination that endorses and sends them as clergy in uniform. Chaplains lead the activities of religious practitioners with whom they share a faith tradition, accommodate others whose practices are similar, and provide for religious activities beyond their own traditions. But religious activities no longer convey the full range of chaplains' duties.

There are some parallel developments both inside and beyond the military that stretch the traditional practice of chaplaincy ministry. Demographic shifts indicate that chaplains may have a smaller proportion of the military seeking traditional religious ministrations. But functionally chaplains seem to have increasing opportunities to engage in the holistic well-being of personnel as the armed forces develop initiatives fostering resilience as well as intentionally address the moral and ethical aspects of military service.

Regarding the demographics mentioned above, over the last decade there has been a detectable increase in military members declaring they have no religious preference. This parallels a measurable shift in the general population with diminished denominational preference. Further, in addition to viewing chaplains as religious leaders, the institution includes chaplains in other endeavors such as fostering the resilience of military members and developing character.

Resilience is the contemporary term of art for holistic health, well-being, health and welfare, fitness—constructs that describe the physical, emotional, and spiritual endurance of individual members of the military. The concept of resilience in the context of twenty-first-century military chaplaincy opens a pathway into the lives of soldiers and also offers chaplains a place in the institutional life of the military. A resilient member of the armed forces is one whose physical, mental, and moral stamina withstands the rigors and ambiguities of complex war. Institutionally chaplains conduct programs of personal and family care—what some traditions call *pastoral care*—educational activities, retreats, and unit-sponsored training to prevent suicide or sexual assault. Such chaplain efforts parallel traditional functions of clergy in uniform and are aimed at reducing misconduct and bolstering the inner strength to what is both needed and right.

Rod Dreher, senior editor at the *American Conservative*, describes blockbuster growth in American religion among a category dubbed *Nones*—people claiming no religious affiliation, most of whom believe in God. He calls this the "spiritual but not religious" crowd, which encompasses 17 percent of America, three percentage points higher than the 14 percent who identify as mainline Protestants. For a younger cohort, the Nones number is actually even higher, signaling a generational wave breaking on the U.S. religious landscape. Among adults aged eighteen to twenty-nine, 30 percent are Nones.[2] This age cohort makes up more than 75 percent of people in the military.

If No Religious Preference (as expressed in the military) or Nones (in civilian jargon) make up a growing share of young adults in the military, what then can be made of the religious leadership of chaplains? Are there points of connection between the work of chaplains and military personnel who do not automatically identify with a religious faith group or denomination? Can the professional practice of chaplains meaningfully engage members of the military in addressing spirituality, resilience, and character?

EXAMINING SPIRITUALITY AND CHARACTER

In order to get at the state of spirituality and ethics in the military, not only as the context within which chaplains work but also as a critical area of focus for senior leaders, this chapter examines results from the army's Excellence in Character, Ethics, and Leadership (EXCEL) survey about spirituality and how it affects ethics and the resilience of soldiers.[3] Curiosity is a guiding principle of this study: curiosity about the how soldiers in combat might report their spiritual beliefs and behaviors and curiosity of how spirituality might correlate to ethical awareness and actions. Does the spiritual life of soldiers—the domain of chaplaincy activity—make a difference in the moral thinking and activity of people in uniform?

But curiosity alone did not sponsor years of this research by the military. Rising suicide rates, post-traumatic stress disorder, and the raw challenges faced by young soldiers and Marines in places like Fallujah and Anbar demanded careful inspection of the mental, emotional, and spiritual health of the military. These findings are based on a sample of more than 1,250 soldiers in a combat zone. This chapter discusses findings about spirituality using a three-factor construct of spirituality. The three-factor model emerged from the survey data by calculating fit indexes of scores on fifteen items, which will be described in the methods section below. Higher-mean scores of spirituality surfaced among certain demographic groups. Soldier responses indicate correlations between spirituality, ethics, and resilience in their lives. These findings point to areas for further research, and the chapter concludes with recommendations to commanders and chaplains.

Influential leaders in the U.S. military have advanced concepts and programs to engage spirituality as an element of character. For example, spirituality—or the domain of the human spirit—is one of the three domains in the character-development model for cadets at the U.S. Military Academy—along with the ethical and social domains.[4] Across the army and the Department of Defense, holistic-fitness programs include spiritual fitness.[5] In the areas of training, education, and development, leaders aspire to inculcate character development—including spirituality—to complement the military training soldiers receive.[6]

The EXCEL survey presents an honest and thought-provoking perspective from soldiers in a combat zone. The interdisciplinary survey addresses more than twenty constructs, including ethical attitudes, values and behavior, leadership, physical and emotional health, and spirituality. Items about spirituality were included within the larger, interdisciplinary, research instrument. Spirituality, ethics, and resilience converge to give some contours of the interactions of these factors as elements of character in soldiers.

U.S. ARMY CHAPLAINCY AND DEPARTMENT OF DEFENSE TERMS OF REFERENCE ON SPIRITUALITY

The EXCEL model identified three factors of spirituality: connection to others, religious identification, and hopeful outlook. This three-factor model of spirituality parallels and complements the definition for spirituality that the army chief of chaplains employs, which is "a process transcending self and society that empowers the human spirit with purpose, identity, and meaning."[7]

Another definition comes from the Chairman of the Joint Chiefs of Staff's instruction on the Total Force Fitness framework. TFF, as it is called, defines spirituality as "the expression of the human spirit in thoughts, practices, and relationships of connection to self, and connections outside the self, such as other people, groups, nature, and concepts of a higher order."[8]

Although these definitions use different words about spirituality, they overlap and incorporate common ideas. The three factors that fit the data from the EXCEL survey cluster along three identifiable constructs: connection to others, religious identification, and hopeful outlook. These factors, when present, correlate in the lives of soldiers to positive attributes and may act as a buffer against some psychological and physical risk factors. It is also clear that when these factors are not present the individual may be in an unhealthy situation. For instance, individuals who feel "disconnected" or experience anomie have a high likelihood of behaving in a personally destructive fashion, including addictions and suicide. It also puts the individual at higher risk for being a threat to the well-being of others. In short, each of the three factors is considered further and then examined in light of correlations between spirituality and subscales addressing ethics and resilience.

Definitions of spirituality have evolved over the past decades and vary across diverse faith groups and cultures. The word suggests a journey or process tied to spirit, defined in this research project as a multidimensional, cohesive core of the individual expressed in beliefs, ideas, practices, and connections.[9] Going into this survey of soldiers, the working hypothesis was that spirituality could be assessed using three subscales.

Spirituality as Part of the Army's EXCEL Study

In 2008, the U.S. Army initiated designs and plans for the Multi-National Force–Iraq (MNFI) Survey—2009. The study was requested by General Petraeus as he relinquished command of the MNFI in September 2008. The study had the backing of the chief of Staff of the Army and was implemented by the Center for the Army Profession and Ethic (CAPE) in collaboration with the Institute for National Security Ethics and Leadership at National Defense University, the U.S. Army Chaplains Corps, and a wide range of military and civilian academic partners. The study tests a wide range of constructs about the ethical attitudes and behaviors of U.S. land forces, with the intent to aid leaders in self-assessment, reflection, and continuous learning.

The survey was developed to examine findings from earlier reports conducted by the Mental Health Assessment Team. In these reports, significant percentages of soldiers and Marines stated that they would not report a fellow member of the military for "killing or wounding an innocent noncombatant."[10] The army set a high priority on ethics and ethical decision making in the face of sustained operational demands. In a combat zone ethical dilemmas abound, and soldiers are constantly faced with demanding challenges. Lapses like Abu Ghraib and other severe ethical failures make it evident that ethics training is an ongoing necessity.[11] Survey results reveal correlations between an individual's level of spirituality and two other constructs: ethics and resilience. The EXCEL-research findings indicate spirituality measurably correlates with five factors of ethics, such as moral courage and moral confidence, as well as increased psychological and physical resilience.

The term *resilience* gained usage in recent years, while military personnel have long been known for their endurance. For soldiers, resiliency includes not only sustaining themselves physically and emotionally while in combat but also coming home fit: "The final step in the long road home for the veteran is completing this initiation as a warrior. A veteran does not become a warrior merely for having gone to war. A veteran becomes a warrior when he learns to carry his war skills and his vision in mature ways. He becomes a warrior when he has been set right with life again."[12]

Spirituality, like other constructs such as stress, social support, or self-worth, cannot be observed directly. Spirituality for the EXCEL survey was measured using fifteen items that formed three subscales. The items used for the three subscales or factors were clustered by calculating fit indexes using five items per subscale. These spirituality items clustered around these three factors: connection to others, religious identification, and hopeful outlook. These three factors do not cover all dimensions of spirituality, but they do reveal a workable model of spirituality for the soldiers surveyed. Using this three-factor substructure provides extremely strong fit indexes and a unifying construct of spirituality.

Calculating a fit index is one statistical method used to assess how well specific items measure a particular factor. By statistically analyzing patterns of responses on several items, it is possible to calculate the relative "fit" of items around conceptual models. Two calculations of fit indexes are shown. A fit index above .90 is considered extremely strong. Fit indices at .75 are acceptable. As shown, the fit of the three-factor model is much better than a one-factor model. Table 9.1 presents the fit indexes of the items' structure into three factors.

Table 9.1.   Comparison of Factor Models for Spirituality

Factor Structure	χ^{2}*	Normed-Fit Index	Comparative-Fit Index
3 factors	335.12	.952	.958
1 factor	1662.12	.759	.764

*χ^2, chi-square, also called the *discrepancy function*, expresses the likelihood or goodness of fit. The lower the number, the closer the fit.

NFI (or *normed-fit index*) expresses the covariance among items. Zero indicates *no covariance* and 1.0 is *exact covariance*. *This calculates an adjustment to the nonnormed index accounting for sample size and degrees of freedom.*

CFI (or *comparative-fit index*) expresses the fit of items to form a factor and is used to avoid underestimation of fit noted in small samples. This is a rather large sample, so the fit index here is strong.

METHODS IN THE EXCEL STUDY

Survey Design

The EXCEL survey is a paper-and-pencil instrument survey that collects demographic and survey data primarily using Likert scales. EXCEL addresses topics ranging from ethical attitudes, actions, and observed behaviors in others to leadership, attitudes about the army, general physical concerns, attitudes, and well-being. Surveys were collected from 2,572 soldiers and leaders deployed in Iraq between June 20, 2009, and July 24, 2009.[13] To protect the anonymity of participants, data was collected from randomly selected units.

Survey Items

Fifteen items relating to spirituality were included in the EXCEL survey at the request of the Institute for National Security Ethics and Leadership at National Defense University and the U.S. Army Chaplain Corps. Items were selected from established surveys. All items were formatted using a five-point Likert scale in line with the layout of the larger survey.

Thirteen of the fifteen items included in EXCEL were based on the "Dimensions of Religion/Spirituality and Relevance to Health Research" by Haber et al. from the VA Palo Alto Health Care System. The purpose of the Haber study was to "identify unique religion/spirituality (R/S) factors that account for variation in R/S measures of interest to health research."[14] That research focused on identifying religious and spiritual items relevant in health-care research through meta-analysis of personality and medical instruments. Haber et al. took many of their questions from other well-established studies, including the *Brief Multidimensional Measure of Religion and Spirituality* by the Fetzer Institute/National Institution of Aging and R. L. Piedmont's *Development and Validation of the Spiritual Transcendence Scale: A Measure of Spiritual Experience*. In addition, Haber et al. used what they called two "classic measures with exceptional histories of use."[15] The first is C. W. Ellison's Spiritual Well-Being Scale, which measures well-being associated with God and existentialism. The second is the Age-Universal version of Allport and Ross's Religious Orientation Scale. These sources, combined with one of Haber's "Religion/Spirituality Motivation, Devotion, and Coping" questions and two MNFI-specific questions, make up the fifteen items.

In the design, the fifteen spirituality items were proposed to measure three dimensions of spirituality in individuals: spiritual worldview, prayer/personal piety, and connection to a faith community. These address private and personal spirituality, as well as the public aspects of spirituality, paralleling the approach in a study by Greenfield, Vaillant and Marks.[16] Also, by matching leader scores with scores of followers in their units, future analysis can examine spirituality within units and interactions between leaders and followers in multifactorial analysis.

Survey Participants

Of the 2,572 soldiers surveyed, just over half—1,366—completed version B and version B Leader, which included the spirituality items. Of the 1,366 version B surveys, there were 1,263 valid responses, meaning surveys were sufficiently complete to be tabulated and analyzed. Table 9.2 presents a summary of demographics of version respondents. Note that 61 percent of respondents were under age twenty-seven and that 76 percent were grade E5 (sergeant) and below.

Based on a literature review, this is the largest sample of soldiers assessing spirituality in a combat zone. The army does collect annual data on religious preference for soldiers but not qualitative survey data. The closest comparable sample probing aspects of spirituality numbered eight hundred in an unpublished thesis written after World War II, which probed the effect of combat on religious belief and personal morality.[17]

From a review of relevant literature, surveys addressing spirituality and well-being most often sample populations in hospitals or other treatment

Table 9.2. Demographics of Version Respondents

Gender	Male	Female	Unknown
	1123	130	13

Age	Number	Percentage	
18–22	378	27.7	
23–27	457	33.5	
28–32	219	16.0	
33–37	130	9.5	
38–42	77	5.6	
43–47	43	3.1	
48+	13	1.0	
Unknown	49	3.6	

Marital Status	Unmarried	Married	Unknown
	736	611	19

Army Component	Active Component	Reserve Component	
	909	428	29

facilities, college students, or congregational members. No comparable data was previously available about military personnel in a combat zone.

Procedures

To obtain a representative sample, the Multi-National Force–Iraq inspector general (MNFI-IG) randomly selected platoons from two brigade-sized units from each of the four army divisions then serving in Iraq. In addition to these surveying platoon members, key leaders at the platoon, company, and battalion levels also completed surveys. This enabled the survey to assess the culture and climate leaders had developed in their units. Battalion chaplains and chaplain assistants carried surveys to forward operating bases. They implemented survey administration protocols, distributing and collecting surveys in platoon-sized elements (twenty to forty individuals). Chaplains and chaplain assistants were chosen to administer the surveys because of their formal obligations for confidentiality and their roles as trusted agents.

To protect privacy and ensure anonymity, respondents filled out the survey and returned them to the unit chaplains who served as survey administrators. Data collectors placed surveys in sealed folders immediately upon collecting them from participants. Chaplains used a coding scheme with each unit. This scheme randomly assigned a code to each unit, and the code was written on the outside of each sealed envelope. Using these precautions, it was not possible to associate an individual's recorded data with that individual or their military unit unless the individual failed to follow instructions and put his or her name on the survey. Chaplains were the only people to have access to both the unit designation and their data, and each chaplain had access to approximately one-twentieth of the full sample's data. The paper surveys were transported from chaplains to the MNFI staff and shipped to the Center for the Army Profession and Ethic at West Point, New York. From the time the chaplain turned in the sealed envelopes for shipping, neither the staff nor the CAPE knew the unit designations and thus were unable to determine the unit from which any survey set came. Data was entered, analyzed, and reported by code only.

All leaders surveyed were also asked to rate certain effects of leadership at the platoon, company, and battalion levels. Further, leaders were asked to evaluate the leadership and unit performance of subordinate leaders at the next level down from them. All soldiers completing the survey reported on their individual ethical behavior and beliefs, rated the ethical behavior of their immediate leaders and their peers, and evaluated the culture and climate in their respective units and their psychological and somatic conditions. All respondents receiving version B (leaders and followers) rated themselves on three factors of spirituality.

When the survey respondents completed their surveys, the chaplains and chaplain assistants collected the surveys and sent them to the MNFI-IG. The surveys were shipped to CAPE for further analysis by staff and colleagues at the University of Washington, Michigan State University, University of Akron, and Pennsylvania State University. The draft technical report of the data was prepared by Dr. John Schaubroeck and Colonel Sean Hannah with assistance from doctoral students at Michigan State University.[18]

THREE FACTORS OF SPIRITUALITY

Connection to Others

McMillan and Chavis, writing about inclusion with others, defined *sense of community* as "a feeling that members have of belonging, a feeling that members matter to one another and to the group, and a shared faith that members' needs will be met through their commitment to be together."[19] Spirituality is often expressed through community activities, such as worship and service to others. Spirituality acknowledges realities beyond the self. Soldiers report a connection to others as a dimension of spirituality. This factor correlates with intentions for ethical actions, moral attitudes, and a general increased ability to withstand the rigors of combat. Members of the military are familiar with feeling a common bond with each other, just as Shakespeare coined the famous phrase, "we happy few, we band of brothers." But this sense of connection to others goes far beyond camaraderie or esprit de corps.

While esprit de corps is important, it is vital for a soldier to feel like he or she belongs not just to the unit but also to the rest of the human race. Soldiers who integrate this perception at a deep level of their humanity recognize that even their enemies are still part of humanity and deserve certain rights and protections. A connection to others may mitigate enemy abuses, POW mistreatment, and civilian casualties.

The following items comprise the subscale for the factor *connection to others*:

Q.151 I feel that on a higher level all of us share a common bond.

Q.152 Although there is good and bad in people, I believe that humanity as a whole is basically good.

Q.154 Although individual people may be difficult, I feel a bond with all of humanity.

Religious Identification

Spirituality is not experienced in a vacuum. Soldiers who recorded a higher level of spirituality tended to connect that spirituality to some level of participation in recognized religious activity—prayer, prayer by others, and worship. Though definitions of spirituality are sometimes vague, the spiritual practices of soldiers can be quite clear and specific. For soldiers, practice is important, and practice is a prominent factor in their expression of spirituality. In correlating scores for total spirituality, the two items most closely related to this score are those that express beliefs about prayer:

Q.160 I believe my personal prayers help me during this deployment. (.794)

Q.161 I believe the prayers of my family and friends back home help me. (.786)

The EXCEL study data indicates that when soldiers were surveyed concerning spirituality, their spirituality was most typically described with recognizable religious identifiers such as prayer, chapel attendance, and corporate worship, which are common to organized religion. In addition to the two items about prayer, three other items were used to measure this factor:

Q.155 My spiritual life is an important part of who I am as a person.

Q.159 I go to my place of worship (chapel, church, synagogue, temple) because it helps me connect with friends.

Q.162 I believe the presence and ministry of my unit chaplain brings value to the unit.

Religion and spirituality are sometimes complicated to discuss. As the instruction issued by the Chairman of the Joint Chiefs of Staff points out, "defining *spirituality* in the armed forces is difficult because of the diversity of service members and their preferred spiritual practices and the confusion, ambiguity, and blurred lines that exist between understanding and defining *spirituality* and religion."[20] The EXCEL study shows that spirituality is experienced through religious identification. This underscores the need to ensure that individual soldiers have the opportunity to practice their respective beliefs with freedom and respect. Soldiers who make use of these opportunities have a higher level of spirituality, and, as considered below, this translates into increased resiliency and a strengthened personal ethic.

Hopeful Outlook

A third factor of spirituality that emerged from the survey was termed *hopeful outlook*. Hope, optimism, and positive outlook are notable given the conditions under which these surveys were collected—living in a combat zone.

This hopeful outlook was revealed through soldiers' responses to the following questions:

Q.157   I feel a sense of well-being about the direction in which my life is heading.
Q.163   I feel good about my future.
Q.164   I have forgiven myself for things that I have done wrong.

This last item acknowledges the issue of guilt, which combat veterans face. Guilt can often become a debilitating symptom if not properly processed and dealt with. This will be discussed as an aspect of resilience.

CORRELATIONS OF SPIRITUALITY TO AGE, RANK, AND OTHER VARIABLES

Regarding spirituality, a literature review identified no longitudinal studies spanning the adult life cycle from early adulthood to senior adulthood that could provide conceptual descriptions of spiritual development. Most evidence of spiritual development comes from the study of individual lives[21] or is generalized from other fields like analytic psychology,[22] moral development,[23] or faith development tied to a quest for meaning apart from transcendence.[24]

In table 9.3 the three factors using subscales for spirituality and the spirituality-total scores are listed with means from the Likert scale.

Table 9.3.   Correlation of Demographics to Spiritual Factors

Factor/Demographics	Connection to Others	Religious Identification	Hopeful Outlook	Total-Spirituality Score
Mean (R = 1–5)	3.0347	3.0343	3.4717	3.1517
Gender	.114**	.100**	.088**	.121**
Age	.242**	.232**	.181**	.268**
Education	.155**	.127**	.128**	.162**
Component	−.079**	−0.054	−0.023	−.064*
Married	.026	.063*	.093**	.073**
Children	.090**	.137**	.118**	.145**
Rank	.205**	.161**	.179**	.213**

* Correlation is significant at the 0.05 level (2-tailed).
** Correlation is significant at the 0.01 level (2-tailed).

Notes: Range of Likert scale = 1–5 and N = 1,223–1,263

Strong = > .350
Moderate = .300 to .349
Modest = .200 to .299
Slight = 100 to .199

The strongest correlations (at the 0.01 level, 2-tailed) indicate that

- Higher spirituality scores correlated modestly with older respondents (.268)
- Higher spirituality scores correlated modestly with increased rank (.213)
- Higher spirituality scores correlated slightly with women (.121)
- Higher spirituality scores correlated slightly with higher education (.168)
- Higher spirituality scores correlated slightly with marriage (.073)
- Higher spirituality scores correlated slightly with having children (.145)

The cross-sectional data in this study indicate that variables of age and rank produce the strongest statistically significant differences in all measures of spirituality but leave open the reasons for these differences.

In the EXCEL data, there are two additional items of note in the correlations. First, there was no statistically significant correlation between the number of deployments and any reported higher or lower total-spirituality scores or scores on any of the three subscales. Second, an interesting and very strong correlation emerged in using single items about spirituality and the total-spirituality score. The item that best correlates (.794) with the total-spirituality score is belief in the benefits of personal prayers. This is nearly identical to and closely followed (.786) by the item regarding belief in the benefits of prayers by family members and friends. The convergence of belief *about* prayer and the practice of prayer may be of particular interest. These responses on the belief in the effectiveness of prayer provide justification for chaplains and leaders to encourage soldiers' spiritual practice and growth.

FIVE FACTORS OF ETHICS CORRELATING WITH SPIRITUALITY

In addition to describing spirituality, this chapter examines correlations between spirituality and two constructs: ethics and resiliency. Correlations between spirituality and five factors of ethics are reported. In table 9.4, resiliency is analyzed, describing correlations between spirituality and two factors, emotional and physical resiliency. In ethics, measuring individual responses indicates a positive correlation between spirituality and the following factors of ethics. These five factors taken together could frame a useful approach to the ethical dimension of character.

- Moral courage/ownership (.408, strong)
- Moral efficacy (.391, strong)
- Embracing army values (.387, strong)
- Intent to report unethical conduct (.335, moderate)
- Soldier identification (.295, modest)

Table 9.4.   Correlations between Spirituality Scales and Ethics Variables

Factor\Spirituality Scale	Connection to Others	Religious Identification	Hopeful Outlook	Total-Spirituality Score
Moral courage/ownership	.355**	.277**	.380**	.408**
Moral efficacy	.331**	.257**	.380**	.391**
Embracing army values	.318**	.286**	.345**	.387**
Report intentions	.309**	.232**	.283**	.335**
Soldier identification	.274**	.219**	.234**	.295**

* p < .05.
** p < .01.

Notes: N = 1107–1220.

Data taken from the Center for the Army Profession and Ethic, "Correlational Analyses of Spirituality Scales Report," unpublished, as prepared by Dr. John Schaubroeck (April 2010), 1.

These correlations above indicate probabilities less than 0.01 and that there are notably strong correlations between total-spirituality scores and moral courage/ownership, moral efficacy, and embracing army values. These correlations are all between .387 and .408, indicating a notable interaction in the character of individuals who identify with the army values and believe and intend to act on those moral ideas with those who report beliefs and practices of spirituality.

Moral Courage/Ownership (.408)

The EXCEL study used seven items to assess personal moral courage and beliefs about ownership of moral responsibility. These items asked whether a soldier would address unethical acts. Each item was anchored on a five-point Likert scale ranging from *strongly disagree* to *strongly agree*.[25]

According to the report, "a majority (56 percent to 72 percent, depending on the ethical issue) of soldiers reported that they would confront others for unethical acts and would stand in the way of ethical misconduct as shown in table 26 [table 9.5 below]. Soldiers were most likely to agree that they would confront a peer, rather than a leader, if they observed that person committing an ethical act. Soldiers were least likely to agree that they would not accept anyone in the unit behaving unethically, but even in this case the majority of soldiers agreed."[26]

Table 9.5. Soldier Self-Reports on Personal Moral Courage/Ownership

	Percent (disagree or strongly disagree)	Percent (agree or fully agree)
I will confront my peers if they commit an unethical act	9.6	71.8
I will confront a leader if he/she commits an unethical act	10.8	69.1
I will always state my views about an ethical issue to my leaders	11.5	63.4
I will go against the group's decision whenever it violates my ethical standards	12.5	58.1
I will assume responsibility to take action when I see an unethical act	10.4	62.9
I will not accept anyone in my unit behaving unethically	12.9	55.7
I feel it is my job to address ethical issues when I know someone has done something wrong	13.2	56.0

Notes: N = 2572 individual soldiers. Effective sample size ranges from 2,434 to 2,468 (includes versions A and B).

This table was reproduced from Hannah et al., *ACPME Technical Report*, 37.

Hannah and Avolio propose a psychological concept of moral potency comprised of moral courage/ownership and moral efficacy.[27] Moral potency is framed as the link between moral cognition (built out of awareness and understanding) with moral action.[28] Moral potency is proposed as the key valence in understanding an answer to the question: Why do leaders who recognize the right ethical decision or action to take still fail to act when action is clearly warranted? Moral action is preceded by moral awareness and understanding, and perhaps it is in the area of moral potency where spirituality activates one's sense of identity, courage, and responsibility.

Moral Efficacy (.391)

Moral efficacy is essentially "one's confidence in his or her capabilities to organize and mobilize the motivation and cognitive resources needed to attain
desired moral ends while persisting in the face of moral adversity."[29] Moral
efficacy is important for individual soldiers who are facing complex moral
dilemmas in the contemporary operating environment on a regular basis.
Moral efficacy is developed over time in an individual's life and, indeed, is
never completely developed. An integrated approach involving cognitive,
affective, and social domains would likely enhance moral confidence.

Embracing Army Values (.387)

The American military is a values-based organization. These values are
uniquely expressed in *Army Values: The Soldier's Creed* and *The Warrior Ethos*
as outlined by the Department of Defense; its ideals are established within the
Constitution of the United States of America. The army values are presented
as those attributes by which a soldier must live. The expectation is mandated
for active and reserve component soldiers and applies regardless of the individual's military occupation specialty (MOS) or rank. The army stipulates
seven values vital to the success of the warrior: loyalty, duty, respect, selfless
service, honor, integrity, and personal courage. Soldiers reporting they internalized the seven army values to a great extent reported lower levels of misconduct. They also reported higher levels of moral courage—that is, higher
levels of intention to confront others for misconduct.

Intentions to Report Unethical Conduct (.335)

Six items assessed whether the respondent would report unit members if he
or she observed unethical behavior directed toward a noncombatant. Each
item was anchored on a five-point Likert scale with responses ranging from
strongly disagree to *strongly agree*. Soldiers reported an intention to report a
fellow unit member if that member was observed mistreating noncombatants, as shown table 9.5. In particular, 70 percent would report a unit member for injuring or killing a noncombatant, while 57 percent would report
"a buddy" for "abusing" a noncombatant. A minority of 15 percent stated
they would not report a fellow unit member for these unethical behaviors.[30]
Note that higher spirituality scores correlated with higher likelihoods that
soldiers would respond with their intention to report such misconduct.

Soldier Identification (.295)

Soldier identification means, in a word, internalization—the soldier internal-
izes the army's values and identifies with the roles and responsibilities of

being a soldier. These are the aims of character development as the army furthers initiatives in the tiered learning model: training, educating, and development. The pamphlet *U.S. Army Concept of the Human Dimension in Full Spectrum Operations* discusses how the army aims to have soldiers internalize army values as part of their identity by linking physical, moral, and cognitive components.

FOUR FACTORS OF RESILIENCE
CORRELATING WITH SPIRITUALITY

Army medical-research psychologists who investigate resilience (or *hardiness*) define resilience as "the ability of adults in otherwise normal circumstances who are exposed to an isolated and potentially highly disruptive event such as the death of a close relation or a violent or life-threatening situation to maintain relatively stable, healthy levels of psychological and social functioning."[31]

The effect of combat and the need to adapt upon returning home is reiterated by a university professor of philosophy who observes the effects of combat on veterans as students. She writes how war involves a "shifting of habit and attitude. The point is that in putting on a uniform and going to war, a soldier grows skin that does not shed lightly. And even when it is time to slough that skin, after years of service, it does not come off easily."[32] Because combat affects soldiers on many levels, the need for resiliency is amplified—before, during, and after deployment.[33]

Emotional Resilience

Regarding emotional resiliency, soldiers displayed the following correlations between their levels of spirituality and emotional resilience:

- Higher spirituality scores correlated strongly with positive affectivity (.442, strong)
- Higher spirituality scores inversely correlated with negative affectivity (−.185, slight)

Positive affectivity reflects the extent to which a person feels enthusiastic, active, and alert. In table 9.6, positive affectivity correlated with spirituality and is similar to results from previous studies. These indicate a potentially notable and strong linkage between spiritual perceptions and psychological well-being. Positive affectivity is generally viewed as a buffer against risks for depression, a serious variable in suicide risk. Also, the inverse correlation between spirituality and negative affectivity indicates some interaction between these constructs.

Table 9.6. Correlation of Affectivity with Spiritual Factors

Variable\Spirituality Scale	Connection to Others	Religious Identification	Hopeful Outlook	Total-Spirituality Score
Positive Affectivity	.339**	.321**	.424**	.442**
Negative Affectivity	−.157**	−.084**	−.215**	−.185**

* p < .05.
** p < .01.

Notes: N = 1107–1220.

Given that the soldiers surveyed were in a combat zone, the EXCEL survey found a surprisingly high level of hopeful outlook as well as other items reflecting positive views of the future regarding the soldier's situation in Iraq. Among the items describing hopeful outlook is one item assessing the perspective of soldiers who forgave themselves for actions that had occurred during combat. This capacity to forgive oneself is related to emotional health in the period following combat deployment.

Resilience and Dealing with Guilt

Absolution from guilt is a core dynamic for combat veterans reentering life after war.[34] Encountering veterans as college students, one professor writes of how many combat veterans struggle with guilt. While researching for a recent book, Sherman found that "in virtually all of my interviews, guilt was the elephant in the room." She categorized the guilt soldiers experience into three forms: accident guilt, luck guilt, and collateral-damage guilt. The first of these, *accident guilt*, is rather straightforward, referring to the type of guilt veterans experience for mishaps that occurred in combat resulting in the loss of fellow soldiers or the lives of innocents. Although no one person can be found responsible in these types of situations, veterans still may blame themselves and experience accident guilt. *Luck guilt* is a form of guilt Sherman describes as a generalized form of "survivor guilt." Sherman interviewed Marines who had recently returned from Iraq and were touring Annapolis. They felt genuine guilt about relaxing on a sailboat while their brothers were still in combat. The most troubling kind of guilt Sherman studied is what she calls *collateral-damage guilt*, associated with the unintended killing of innocents by the actions of someone in combat.[35]

Physical Resiliency

A soldier's physical health is a large part of resiliency. During deployment, soldiers may endure a wide array of physical hardships. When they return home, it is essential that they receive treatment for injuries and ailments incurred during deployment in order to prepare for future deployment. Since the ongoing process of deployment, redeployment, training, and subsequent additional deployments is a reality, resiliency is important. The correlation between a soldier's level of spirituality and his or her physical health is a vital link. The EXCEL study revealed an inverse relationship between a soldier's spirituality and somatic complaints and fatigue (see table 9.7).

- Spirituality inversely correlated with physical and psychological fatigue (–.183)
- Spirituality inversely correlated with somatic complaints (–.146)

Table 9.7. Correlation of Somatic Factors/Fatigue with Spiritual Factors

Variable\Spirituality Scale	Connection to Others	Religious Identification	Hopeful Outlook	Total-Spirituality Score
Somatic Complaints	–.140**	–.064*	–.154**	–.146**
Fatigue	–.162**	–.124**	–.160**	–.183**

* $p < .05$.
** $p < .01$.

Notes: N = 1107–1220.

This study is consistent with other investigations that link spirituality with physical health. Among military populations, Frederick M. Dini, LCDR, SC, USN, wrote an unpublished master's thesis on a strategy for a military spiritual self-development tool and physical well-being.[36] Dini reports that these studies show positive correlations between spiritual development and health in the following areas: lower blood pressure, improved physical health, healthier lifestyles and less risky behavior, improved coping ability, less depression, faster healing, lower levels of bereavement after the death of a loved one, decrease in fear of death, and higher school achievement.[37] These studies describe civilian populations. For military populations, physical health is a potentially a life-and-death issue. A soldier's health and personal resiliency can very well mean the difference between coming home alive and well and coming home injured (or not at all).

CONCLUSION AND IMPLICATION

This chapter describes three factors that express aspects of spirituality and reports measurable correlations between spirituality, ethical attitudes and action, and personal resilience. While spirituality is not identical to religious practice, the survey findings about soldiers in combat indicate beliefs about the benefits of prayer and participation in worship most strongly correlate with overall spirituality scores. The convergence of belief *about* prayer and the practice of prayer may offer a primary means for engaging soldiers regarding spirituality, from a variety of religious perspectives. Also regarding spirituality, survey scores correlate moderately with age and rank, while spirituality scores correlate slightly with gender (higher in women), education, having children, and marriage.

Spirituality positively correlates with both ethical attitudes and intentions. Spirituality strongly correlates with moral courage/ownership, moral efficacy, and embracing army values. Spirituality moderately correlates with intention to report ethical violations observed in others and with soldier identification. These attitudes and intentions may be understood as an expression of character, with spirituality as one dimension of character. From a leadership perspective, fostering moral potency may be a direct benefit of deepening spirituality as a dimension of character.

Spirituality correlates with indications of emotional and physical well-being. As reported in other research, there are apparent connections between spirituality and measures of emotional and physical health. These findings about soldiers provide data that support the army's efforts to strengthen physical and emotional well-being.

The EXCEL study helps bring spirituality and its effects into the realm of legitimate study and is worth scientific inquiry and further analysis. Though often categorized as the domain of anthropologists, psychologists, sociologists, and religious leaders, the topic of spirituality deserves to be brought into a wider, interdisciplinary line of study. In efforts to develop ethics, resilience, and character, benefits of including spiritual growth could be an area for continued research. Data from the EXCEL study could be analyzed to measure whether the amount of combat exposure, length of deployment, or frequency of deployments affects spirituality. A longitudinal study measuring spirituality during intervals of military service may indicate increases or decreases in factors of spirituality. Additionally, research could examine whether leadership styles, as measured in the EXCEL survey, correlate with spirituality scores among leaders, or if the spirituality of leaders has effects on scores of spirituality among followers.

RECOMMENDATIONS FOR LEADERS AND CHAPLAINS

It is hard to imagine a study of this type taking place during World War II or Vietnam, although undoubtedly it would have helped the nation and its veterans in many ways. Just as the role of contemporary military chaplains is evolving to take into account this wider set of individual and service needs, the military has also become more sophisticated in evaluating and responding to the mental, emotional, and spiritual needs of its members.

Leaders in military service can apply findings from the EXCEL study by acknowledging the value and positive impact of religious and spiritual activities on ethical behavior and resilience. In speaking about ethical attitudes and behavior, leaders of all ranks can include spiritual values in reinforcing moral courage, responsibility, and reporting unethical conduct. Leaders can ensure military members have the opportunity to practice their faith, in line with both the individual's expression of spirituality and fostering resilience and character. For those who do not identify with a religious label, leaders can make it clear that religious values and military values affirm respect for individual conviction and conscience. Leaders should provide adequate resources (funding, time in the training schedule) to unit chaplains to offer spiritual-fitness training and activities. And although this research was not structured to demonstrate a clear causal relationship between spirituality and ethics or resilience, there are correlations that indicate measurable interactions.

Chaplains can contribute to the moral, emotional, and physical strength of the force by assisting military members in strengthening their spirituality according to the faith tenants of those individual military members. Chaplains can foster relationships in faith communities as a means of reinforcing ethical behavior. In their religious training, chaplains can incorporate moral dilemmas and address what scriptures say about moral decision making. Since beliefs about prayer were prominent in the measures of spirituality in this study, chaplains can pray. Chaplains can provide instruction on prayer and conduct prayer services. In interacting with military members, chaplains can emphasize prayer as a means of resilience, as an item of personal protective gear. Effective chaplains will encourage connections "back home" with those who will offer prayers on behalf of military members. In their daily work, chaplains can provide scripture studies and instruction on the meaning and purpose of life and God working in spite of evil situations. Further, chaplains can respectfully reach out to those who do not identify with a religious label. They can make it clear that religious values and military values affirm respect for individual conviction and conscience. Finally, chaplains can emphasize the practical application of love. Love is about selfless service—treating others with respect and dignity, both others within the ranks and even adversaries.

NOTES

1. S. W. Husted, *George C. Marshall: The Rubrics of Leadership* (Carlisle, PA: U.S. Army War College Foundation Press, 2006).

2. Rod Dreher, "Why Is Faith Falling in the US?" *BBC News Magazine*, accessed 29 August 2012, http://www.bbc.co.uk/news/magazine-19262884.

3. Rightly and by design, individual religious beliefs and practices have been protected in the military with attention to the twin principles of avoiding the "establishment" of religion for soldiers and urging "free exercise" through a pluralistic military chaplaincy.

4. Don M. Snider, *Forging the Warrior's Character: Moral Precepts from the Cadet Prayer*, ed. Lloyd J. Matthew (New York: McGraw Learning Solutions, 2008).

5. See the Comprehensive Soldier Fitness and CJCS Total Force Fitness models. Because this is a dynamic enterprise, it is best to see updates at the army program website, http://csf2.army.mil/.

6. Joe Doty and Walter Sowden, "Competency vs. Character? It Must Be Both!" *Military Review* (November–December 2009): 72, available online at http://www.dtic.mil/dtic/tr/fulltext/u2/a532524.pdf; and Training and Doctrine Command, Fort Monroe, VA 23651-1047, "The U.S. Army Concept for the Human Dimension in Full Spectrum Operations 2015–2024," *TRADOC Pamphlet 525-3-7* (June 11, 2008): 15.

7. E-mail from the staff at the Center for Spiritual Leadership at the U.S. Army Chaplain Center and School, Fort Jackson, South Carolina, May 14, 2010.

8. Chairman of the Joint Chiefs of Staff, "Instruction 3405.1: Chairman's Total Force Fitness Framework," September 1, 2011, updated September 23, 2013, available online at http://www.dtic.mil/cjcs_directives/cdata/unlimit/3405_01.pdf. See also Chairman of the Joint Chiefs of Staff, "Instruction: Total Force Fitness Framework; Spiritual Fitness Domain," enclosure B5, March 23, 2010.

9. K. I. Pargament and P. J. Sweeney, "Building Spiritual Fitness in the Army: An Innovative Approach to a Vital Aspect of Human Development," *American Psychologist* 66, no. 1 (2011): 58–64. Also see P. J. Sweeney, S. T. Hannah, and D. M. Snider, "The Domain of the Human Spirit," in *Forging the Warrior's Character: Moral Precepts from the Cadet Prayer*, ed. L. J. Matthews (Sisters, OR: Jericho, 2007), 23–50; and W. Teasdale, *The Mystic Heart* (Novato, CA: New World Library, 1999).

10. Survey results indicated that 45 percent of soldiers would not report a unit member for killing or wounding an innocent noncombatant.

11. Charles J. Dunlap Jr., "The Joint Force Commander and Force Discipline," *U.S. Naval Institute Proceedings* (September 2005): 34–38, reprinted in U.S. Army Command and General Staff College, *A534 Syllabus/Book of Readings* (Fort Leavenworth, KS: USACGSC, September 2008), L11-5-1. Brigadier General Charles J. Dunlap wrote of the effects that the Abu Ghraib prison abuse had on the military: "The highly publicized reports of the Abu Ghraib prison-abuse scandal energized the Iraqi insurgency and eroded vital domestic and coalition support. Most damaging was the negative reaction of ordinary Iraqis, a constituency whose backing is essential to strategic success. A 2004 poll found that 54 percent of them believed all Americans behave like those alleged to have taken part in the abuse. So adverse were the strategic consequences that it is no overstatement to say that Americans died—and will continue to die—as an indirect result of this disciplinary catastrophe."

12. Edward Tick, *War and the Soul: Healing Our Nation's Veterans from Post-Traumatic Stress Disorder*, 1st Quest ed. (Wheaton, IL: Quest Books, 2005), 251.

13. S. Hannah, J. Schaubroeck, B. Avolio, S. Kozlowski, R. Lord, and L. Trevino, *ACPME Technical Report 2010-01 MNF-1, Excellence in Character and Ethical Leadership (EXCEL) Study* (West Point, NY: Army Center of Excellence for the Professional Military Ethic, U.S. Army Combined Arms Center, TRADOC, June 24, 2010).

14. Jon Randolph Haber, Theodore Jacob, and David J. C. Spangler, "Dimensions of Religion/Spirituality and Relevance to Health Research," *International Journal for the Psychology of Religion* 77 (2007): 271.

15. Ibid.

16. E. Greenfield, G. Vaillant, and N. Marks, "Do Formal Religious Participation and Spiritual Perceptions Have Independent Linkages with Diverse Dimensions of Psychological Well-Being?" *Journal of Health and Social Behavior* 50 (June 2009): 196. The authors examined a two-factor model of spirituality distinguishing "spiritual perceptions" as the inner perspectives of individuals and "religious participation" as public practice.

17. Mahlon W. Pomeroy, "The Effect of Military Service and Combat Experience on Religious Beliefs and Personal Morality" (master's thesis, Syracuse University, August 1946). Pomeroy and a colleague collected data about the meaning and importance of faith in God and attitudes about prayer from eight hundred soldiers on hospital wards at Camp Kilmer, New Jersey, during January–March 1946. He reports that sixty-five thousand soldiers passed through Camp Kilmer over the course of some weeks. His major findings are that "men felt their religion meant more to them now than before the war," that "God evidently seemed more personal to the men now," and that "34 percent indicate that they pray more now than before the war, and only 9 percent pray less."

18. Hannah et al., *ACPME Technical Report*, 1.

19. D. W. McMillan and D. M. Chavis, "Sense of Others: A Definition and Theory," *Journal of Others Psychology*, 14 (1986): 6–23.

20. CJCSI Total Force Fitness Framework.

21. E. Bianchi, *Aging as a Spiritual Journey*, 2nd ed. (New York: Crossroad, 1987); and L. Tornstam, "Late-Life Transcendence: A New Developmental Perspective on Aging," in *Religion, Belief, and Spirituality in Late Life*, ed. L. E. Thomas and S. Eisenhandler (New York: Springer, 1999), 178–202.

22. C. G. Jung, *Man and His Symbols* (New York: Laurel, 1964).

23. Lawrence Kohlberg, *Essays on Moral Development, Vol. 1: The Philosophy of Moral Development* (San Francisco: Harper & Row, 1981).

24. James Fowler, *Stages of Faith* (New York: Harper and Row, 1981).

25. Hannah et al., *ACPME Technical Report*, 37.

26. Ibid.

27. Sean Hannah and Bruce Avolio, "Moral Potency: Building the Capacity for Character-Based Leadership," *Consulting Psychology Journal: Practice and Research* 62, no. 4 (December 2010).

28. James Rest, *Development in Judging Moral Issues* (Minneapolis: University of Minnesota Press, 1979).

29. Snider, *Forging the Warrior's Character*, 82.

30. Hannah et al., *ACPME Technical Report*, 36.

31. Paul T. Bartone, Mark A. Vaitkus, and Robert C. Williams, "Psychosocial Stress and Mental Health in a Forward-Deployed Military Community," paper presented at the sixth annual convention of the American Psychological Society, Washington, D.C., July 1994, available for download at www.dtic.mil/cgi-bin/GetTRDoc?Location=U2&doc=GetTRDoc.pdf&AD=ADA285940. Cf. George A. Bonanno, "Loss, Trauma, and Human Resilience: Have We Underestimated the Human Capacity to Thrive after Extremely Aversive Events?" *American Psychologist* 59, no. 1 (January 2004): 20.

32. Nancy Sherman, "Soldiers' Moral Wounds," *Chronicle of Higher Education* (April 11, 2010): 1–8.

33. The U.S. Army Medical Department first called their resilience program Battle-Mind Training; now it is called, simply, Resilience Training. For more information on the program, see https://www.resilience.army.mil/.

34. Larry Dewey, *War and Redemption: Treatment and Recovery in Combat-Related Post Traumatic Stress Disorder* (Burlington, VT: Ashgate, 2004), 201.

35. Sherman, "Soldiers' Moral Wounds," 1–8. See also Nancy Sherman, *The Untold War: Inside the Hearts, Minds, and Souls of Our Soldiers* (New York: Norton, 2010).

36. Peter C. Hill and Kenneth I. Pargament, "Advances in the Conceptualization and Measurement of Religion and Spirituality: Implications for Physical and Mental Health Research," *American Psychologist* 58, no. 1 (January 2003): 64–74; Doug Oman and Carl E. Thoresen, "Do Religion and Spirituality Influence Health?" 435–59, along with Lis Miller and Brien S. Kelley, "Relationships or Religiosity and Spirituality with Mental Health and Psychopathology," 460–78, both found in *Handbook of the Psychology of Religion and Spirituality*, ed. Raymond F. Paloutzian and Crystal L. Park (New York: Guilford Press, 2005).

37. William G. Huitt and Jennifer L. Robbins, "An Introduction to Spiritual Development," paper presented at the eleventh annual conference of Applied Psychology in Education, Mental Health, and Business, Valdosta, Georgia, October 2003.

10

Occupational-Stress Coping Skills of Military Chaplains: The Role of Spiritual Intelligence

Gary Roberts and L. Diane Hess-Hernandez

During the American Revolution, George Washington recognized the valuable service of military chaplains.[1] From those humble beginnings until today, the functions of military chaplains have evolved with the changing roles and needs of those they serve. The subject of much conflict, stress, and controversy, U.S. military chaplains receive commissions as military staff officers in the chaplain corps. Military chaplains are foundational emotional and spiritual sources of support for armed-forces personnel and their families. However, as with any care-giving role, military chaplains experience high levels of stress given the inherent demands of the job.[2] As with pastors who experience elevated levels of burnout, emotional exhaustion, depersonalization, and low personal accomplishment,[3] military chaplains face a multiplicity of demands that strain coping and adapting abilities.[4] This chapter is divided into two sections. The first portion provides a summary of the chaplain occupational-stress literature with an occupational stress-diagnostic inventory for military chaplains, which includes conventional stress risk factors, such as role conflict and ambiguity,[5] along with elements of spirituality, specifically servant-leadership workplace spiritual intelligence (WSI) linked with enhanced stress-coping skills.[6] Servant leadership is an approach embracing stewardship through mission achievement while meeting the needs of others in an altruistic fashion.[7] We support the empirical findings with quotations from our interviews with military chaplains. The second section of this chapter provides a more detailed elaboration of the principles and attributes of WSI using a formal framework supplemented by military chaplain interviews.

CHAPLAIN WORKPLACE STRESS

Former chief of chaplains Rear Admiral Barry Black illustrates many of the challenges faced by military chaplains in his book, *From the Hood to the Hill*.[8] His years as a military chaplain were evident through his disciplined speech and clarity of thought. A career chaplain who rose through the ranks of the armed forces to become a rear admiral and the chief of chaplains, he was the first African American to hold this esteemed post. He entered the navy with a heart to serve based on his commitment to his faith and ended up serving in the highest places of power in the nation's capital. However, the challenges surrounding the role of chaplains, the politics of the armed forces, and the environment of Washington, D.C., can be powerful stressors.

As a senior-level chaplain, Rear Admiral Black was often called upon to provide support and counsel on ethical issues in a nonpartisan and non-sectarian way. In an incident described in his book, Black, living in D.C. at the time, was left in charge as acting chief of chaplains. One of the most important calls came on a Monday morning from Senator Edward Kennedy, asking for help given the disappearance of the plane that John Kennedy Jr. had been piloting. As the deaths of John Kennedy Jr., his wife, and her sister were confirmed, Black says he became an "action officer," arranging all of the logistics for a military sea burial while providing spiritual support to the family. Black says that serving the Kennedy family was a great honor and privilege. It was also incredibly stressful, due to the prominence of the family. Black notes that this is just one example of the many stressors faced by chaplains serving others, whether on or off the battlefield. This raises an important issue of how military chaplains handle stress in the face of such political and personal pressure. What impact does their own spiritual state have on their performance and coping mechanisms?

Exhibit 1, the first portion of the interview (below), presents a framework for a military chaplain occupational-stress audit based on the work of Jex and expanded by Roberts.[9] This framework can be used as a foundation for the development of a variety of qualitative and quantitative diagnostic methods (surveys, focus groups, and interviews) to identify the sources of chaplain stress, on both an aggregate and an individual basis. Based on the data generated, and in combination with existing archive data (performance, mental and physical health, etc.), individual or group-stress risk profiles are developed. From these profiles, chaplains and their supervisors can develop individual stress-reduction (ISR) plans. The system can become part of an integrated workplace hazard-monitoring and audit process identifying the source and cause of accidents, illness, disease, and negative job stress. It empowers chaplains to jointly identify, diagnose, and develop solutions for the identified hazards and develop means for maintaining and enhancing chaplain well-being.

At the foundation of the stress-reduction plan is the ability of chaplains to identify the presence of dysfunctional job stress through self-monitoring, awareness, and identification of mental and physical cues and symptoms, such as elevated heart rate, difficulty in concentrating, and being easily distracted, among others.[10] To supplement the stress-reduction plan, chaplains should undergo continuing education and training on stress reduction.[11] The need for such training was illustrated by a chaplain who noted that, "as a military instructor, the military training chaplains receive is military specific, not how to cope with stress or trauma initially. They are taught the functions of a chaplain, not how to be a chaplain." An example of this training might be a four-day small-group workshop that addresses post-traumatic stress disorder (PTSD), secondary traumatization disorder, relevant coping techniques, the role of spirituality, self-care issues, and family support.[12]

STRESS RISK FACTORS

Returning to exhibit 1, chaplains experience many sources of frustration while working in a military bureaucratic environment.[13] Role ambiguity and role conflict are both powerful stress sources common to military and other bureaucratic systems in which the demand for services outstrips service capacity. Chaplains face long hours and serve large numbers of soldiers and their families, thereby creating potential role conflicts between the numbers of clients and the breadth and depth of the counseling and support issues and needs.[14] Chaplains in Iraq and Afghanistan have been responsible for up to fifteen hundred soldiers of different faith traditions.[15] Large caseloads attenuate a chaplain's capacity to provide the desired quality of service, generating high levels of frustration, anxiety, and dissonance. Several quotations from interviewed chaplains further indicate the existence of various types of role conflict. "How does a chaplain serve all military members without violating the tenants of his personal faith?" asks one chaplain. "This creates an internal level of stress all on its own. Often we violate our boundaries for the sake of serving." Another noted the role conflict associated with serving those of other faiths: "One of the greatest challenges that military chaplains face is the internal dilemma to serve all people regardless of religious tradition, whether Jewish rabbis, Christians, or Muslim imams. We are often called on to perform tasks outside of our own religious traditions, and this is challenging." Another form of role conflict and ambiguity relates to differentiating their role as chaplain from that of a military officer. An interviewee noted that, "as a senior chaplain in the Marine Corps, I must keep in mind that I am not a line officer in the Marines. Marines and officers lead by task.

Chaplains are there to serve and minister, not to be a taskmaster. I have access to the nations of the world, and I must remember my purpose."

Another key stressor is working conditions. Chaplains work with all types of personnel, including those with serious conduct issues. One chaplain noted, "I was assigned as the military chaplain for the military at the base brig. As the deputy base chaplain, I had to minister to military members facing life for murder while serving abroad or those charged with rape. I often led military members to Christ in the midst of their adversity." Obviously combat-duty stations present an array of physical, mental, and spiritual stressors that adversely influence physical stamina and emotional well-being.[16] Given the nature of the military chaplaincy, there will be significant diversity in the stressors faced. Chaplains deployed to combat arenas with multiple tours will obviously face higher levels of traumatic stress than will those posted at noncombat-duty stations.[17] Higher number of deployments and greater years of service are also associated with higher burnout and compassion fatigue.[18] The stress from combat situations—from both direct exposure and the challenges of serving military personnel in combat—creates the most demanding situation. Another closely related occupation, the clergy, demonstrates similar effects. Burnout rates for pastors are high across a range of denominations and countries.[19] A study of clergy reported higher levels of emotional exhaustion and depersonalization with dysfunctional coping behaviors including venting, disengagement, and self-blame.[20]

Another key risk factor is trauma from combat and other stressful life events increasing the risk of post-traumatic stress disorder and secondary traumatic stress (STS) problems. Research indicates that PTSD-risk levels increase significantly with preexisting trauma for chaplains as well as the general population.[21] Hence it is important to screen chaplains for preexisting primary and secondary traumatic stress, and vital to develop individualized chaplain-support interventions, given that research demonstrates the absence of social support in conjunction with additional life stress attenuates the severity of primary PTSD.[22] In addition, there is a positive correlation between time spent counseling traumatized clients under conditions of little or no social and supervisory support and elevated STS and burnout rates.[23] Further research demonstrates that high levels of client advocacy in conjunction with repression of traumatic events increased the effects of stress in the forms of compassion fatigue, burnout, and distress.[24] A study by Levy et al. of air force chaplains found that operational-stress exposure predicted PTSD-symptom severity.[25]

Compassion fatigue and burnout rates are higher with women chaplains and those that are divorced.[26] That same study found that compassion fatigue increased with number of hours worked with trauma victims.[27] Another factor related to burnout is workplace-fairness perceptions, with incongruities in fairness perceptions predicting higher levels of burnout.[28]

POSITIVE COPING STRATEGIES

Research demonstrates the chaplains with higher levels of self-differentiation experience less burnout and manifest a more collaborative conflict-management approach, thereby reducing stress levels.[29] With higher levels of differentiation and self-integration, chaplains and pastors are better able to set healthy boundaries and are less influenced by "people pleasing" and "affirmation addiction" personality attributes.[30] A quotation from an interviewed chaplain illustrates the value of boundary setting: "Managing negative emotions in the military is a challenge when dealing with others. Finding a balance between being tough and showing kindness and mercy is often a struggle. Being curt and direct is the norm." Another chaplain reinforced the importance of boundary setting by stating that, "as chaplains in the field with commanders and military members we serve, we often face social rejection. Chaplains must learn to deal with and know why they are called." Other key elements include proactive self-care strategies, including ongoing social support and involvement, strong family relationships, peer support, and strong levels of spirituality.[31]

Recent research provides insights into the importance of a healthy spirituality. Higher levels of neuroticism and lower extraversion scores correlate with greater emotional exhaustion,[32] depersonalization,[33] and depression and anxiety.[34] Conversely, higher extraversion levels correlate with greater personal accomplishment.[35] A study by Miner of first-year pastors found that those with an internal locus of control in which spirituality and competence are used to cope with the demands of the job (ministry and relational issues) manifested lower rates of burnout and exit from the ministry.[36] Conversely, a study of national guard chaplains found that a high percentage of chaplains with elevated stress and burnout levels engaged in negative religious coping strategies and thinking patterns, including anxiety and fear related to abandonment by God and the church.[37]

Conversely, burnout was lower with positive-thinking patterns of acceptance, active coping, planning, and positive reframing.[38] Other studies demonstrate that a close relationship with God and high levels of prayer fulfillment are associated with lower burnout levels.[39] Another study demonstrated that positive attitudes toward prayer were associated with lower levels of emotional exhaustion and depersonalization and with higher levels of personal accomplishment.[40] A interviewed chaplain reinforced this point by stating that "the military environment teaches you how to handle stress, but as a chaplain prayer helps me relieve that stress."

An interesting finding was that emotional exhaustion did not always indicate burnout.[41] The passion, love, and engagement that pastors and chaplains experience in their work contribute to unsustainable work-effort levels but concurrently serve as a protective effect from the discouragement and hopelessness associated with burnout. However, it remains important for chaplains and pastors to maintain healthy self-care boundaries to lower the risk of emotional and physical exhaustion. This paradoxical effect is illustrated in a study with Catholic priests in which a high percentage (36 percent) reported being "used up" at the end of the work day, with 14 percent burned out.[42] However, love for the job generated strong positive affect in terms of satisfaction rates (90 percent), a willingness to enter the ministry again (81 percent), exhilaration when working with parishioners (76 percent), and accomplishing worthwhile things (75 percent).[43] However, emotional exhaustion did correlate with consideration to leave the ministry for a sample of Anglican priests.[44] A study of air force chaplains further reinforced these paradoxical findings.[45] Overall only a small percentage of chaplains reported compassion fatigue, with the main risk factor being higher exposure to stressful counseling situations, which concurrently contributed to positive psychological growth.[46] Another study of army chaplains found similar results with a low incidence of compassion fatigue and burnout.[47] However, for those reporting high compassion-fatigue levels, there was a positive association with the amount of client-contact hours with wounded soldiers and their families.[48] An interview quotation illustrates the beneficial role of family contact: "The greatest influence I can have is often on a single person. I see military families come and go. An example of this was a military wife who was new to the Christian faith. During her time on base, she came to weekly classes and learned the scriptures and the Christian way of living. When her husband deployed, she started a class for other military wives in a new community." Factors that reduced compassion fatigue include collaboration with other mental-health providers, peer support, and education.

ORGANIZATIONAL PRACTICES TO REDUCE JOB STRESS

Given the set of risk factors, what are some of the recommended elements to reduce stress? In exhibit 2 (below) is a summary of practices to reduce chaplain occupational stress. In the final section, we will focus on the workplace-spiritual-intelligence area. Reducing workplace stress is a collective effort between employees and management. The military must manifest a sustained commitment to protecting the well-being of chaplains. The next section summarizes a set of recommended strategies.

Model and Practice Servant Leadership

When chaplains are secure in the knowledge that their superiors support them, encourage them, hold them accountable, and forgive their mistakes, they possess the security to resist dysfunctional stress-coping strategies and impeding organizational mission achievement.

Make an Authentic and Passionate Commitment to Chaplain Well-Being

To reduce dysfunctional stress, a genuine commitment to chaplain health is essential. This investment is not a slogan or a superficial marketing claim; rather, it becomes a deeply internalized value. In essence, the commitment to work-life balance is as natural as breathing and embedded in all decision making. Chaplains will very quickly identify a superficial and manipulative campaign leading to even greater levels of hypocrisy, cynicism, bitterness, apathy, and disengagement. It is better to be honest and promote more instrumental values than to superficially embrace work-life balance.

It is vitally important that military leadership embrace chaplain global health from a 360-degree perspective, with integration into the mission, vision, and values. It begins with an ironclad commitment to chaplain well-being by military leadership through policy and practice and a sustained and integrated communications campaign. This entails multiple means and methods (speeches, meetings, policies, procedures, hiring, and promotional materials) for communicating both symbolically and through concrete decisions and policies the importance of chaplain holistic health.

Another key aspect is a comprehensive set of SMART (specific, measurable, achievable, relevant, and timely) well-being performance goals, metrics, and standards linked to a balanced scorecard. For example, develop a longitudinal database through a chaplain-attitude survey and set high-level goals for chaplain satisfaction and balance rates. All key stakeholders should contribute to and be held responsible for reducing dysfunctional stress. Another general principle is to link supervisor evaluations with metrics on a healthy work environment and chaplain well-being through the performance-management system.

The gold standard is to engage in a comprehensive chaplain health and wellness program that promotes well-being and eustress (beneficial stress) and not simply work for the absence of negative outcomes (disease, injury, accidents, illness, stress). The former entails encouraging a healthy and sustainable lifestyle (rest, sleep, eating habits, and exercise) while utilizing knowledge-sharing systems on best practices for coping with job stress. Another key element is requiring that experienced and skilled senior officers mentor new chaplains along with chaplain peer support groups.

Model Healthy Behaviors and Attitudes

Military leaders and managers must model healthy workplace behaviors, or else chaplains will discount the message. This entails reasonable levels of work effort and hours, sensible performance standards, and adequate self-care. One chaplain noted, "In my early career as a chaplain, I was worried about position, education, and climbing the ranks. I was self-driven and liked to see the outcome of my work. Now I want to be faithful in whatever God has called me to do." Another noted, "The greatest temptation is to believe you are the answer to people's tragedies and to play God." This type of boundary setting reduces unreasonable expectations that lead to chronic stress.

Promote a Sustainable Work Pace

Given the nature of chaplaincy, it is important to recognize that "seasons" of high work demand are inevitable, but commit to proactive planning and employee empowerment to reduce the number and intensity of such episodes. There will be times when extra work effort and hours are necessary to meeting unanticipated challenges, problems, threats, or unusual opportunities. Once the crisis is addressed, chaplains should return to normal hours, demands, and balanced work hours as quickly as possible.

THE ROLE OF WORKPLACE SPIRITUAL INTELLIGENCE (WSI)

Research demonstrates that a healthy spirituality is an essential element in reducing workplace stress and that chaplains need to develop healthy spiritual coping strategies.[49] Workplace spiritual intelligence, or WSI, is the systematic integration of religious principles and values into human reasoning, decision making, and behavior. It is a derivative of the larger construct of spiritual intelligence and is a major factor in promoting individual life balance (work, family, and personal time). Several researchers propose adding spiritual intelligence to Gardner's eight-factor theory of multiple intelligences (linguistic, logical-mathematical, spatial, musical, bodily-kinesthetic, interpersonal, intrapersonal, and naturalist).[50]

Research in the area of spiritual intelligence is in its formative stages and receiving considerable attention in psychology literature. The seminal work in the field is from a 2000 special issue of the *International Journal for the Psychology of Religion*, which presented a variety of theoretical and conceptual views on the validity of spiritual intelligence.[51] There is considerable variability in the definition, scope, validity, and reliability of spiritual intelligence as a measurable and distinct construct. Empirical research is largely limited to a variety of educational and psychotherapeutic applications.[52] There is a great need to extend spiritual-intelligence research to the workplace. There is a growing popular press literature with some twenty-four books written on the subject, with only two addressing the workplace perspective.[53] There is no empirical research in secular academic journals, with almost all of the empirical data coming from unpublished dissertations. Research on workplace spiritual intelligence is interdisciplinary by definition, incorporating psychology, medicine, business, leadership, organizational behavior, and human-resource management, largely from prescriptive and secondary research sources.[54] Spiritual intelligence consists of five global components: a capacity for transcendence, the ability to enter higher states of consciousness, the facility to interject the sacred into everyday events, the capability to utilize religious principles and values to solve problems, and the ability to engage in ethical and virtuous behavior such as forgiveness, love, transparency, and humility.[55]

The conceptual definition of WSI consists of (1) a harmonious and integrated life orientation directed by prayer and the will of God, (2) a love-based, altruistic work motivational system balancing stewardship (achieving mission) and servanthood (helping others meet legitimate needs), (3) the application of moral/ethical reasoning to assess the integrity of motives, means (decisions and behavior), and outcomes (goals), and (4) "Golden Rule" work behaviors. There are sixteen global spiritual intelligence dimensions as noted in exhibit 3 (below).[56] Preliminary research indicates that WSI positively influences a range of desirable employee attitudes and behaviors, including more effective stress-coping and adaptation strategies, among others.[57] A high level of WSI entails a holistic integration overcoming the traditional barriers that contribute to the compartmentalization of faith, even among pastors and chaplains. To further elaborate on the definition and integration of key WSI attributes, exhibit 4 (below) illustrates the application of key WSI dimensions such as love, humility, and transparency.

WSI entails deontological and teleological ethical integration and integrity, producing cognitive and affective reasoning harmony of knowledge, belief systems, practice/behavior, and motives. Hence, decision-making and reasoning skills are nuanced and highly developed. One of the marks of WSI is identifying the higher-order principle in value-conflict situations. For example, when there is a conflict between a legalistic interpretation of attendance policies and the need for scheduling flexibility to care for a sick family member, the supervisor crafts a mutually satisfactory agreement preserving both mission readiness and empathy for the employee.

WSI INTERVIEWS: EXAMPLE OF INTEGRATION–LIMITED

To further explore the integration of WSI principles, we utilized a convenience sample of 101 respondents. As part of this group, a subset of seven interviews was conducted with senior chaplains in the armed forces to assess how their level of WSI influenced their own work and of those they led. The sample included all major services, and the respondents were career military officers with an average of over twenty years of military service, primarily in a leadership capacity supervising other chaplains.

The post–9/11 environment and the increased deployments in Iraq and Afghanistan, in conjunction with the increased moral and spiritual needs of service members, contribute to an increasingly stressful military workplace. In addition, mounting challenges regarding constitutional issues surrounding the U.S. Armed Forces chaplaincy have created speculation that the chaplain corps may itself face elimination.

Major stressors often include role ambiguity, organizational policies, and ethical leadership challenges. For example, military chaplains require confirmation by a religious organization in order to serve on active duty in any branch of the service. Hence chaplains will face conflict between denomination theological beliefs and military organizational policies, such as the recently overturned military policy "Don't Ask, Don't Tell." Role ambiguity is another source of tension, given the dual roles of military staff officer and chaplain. The chaplain contributes to mission accomplishment by serving their commander while being an advisor and counselor to service members. Senior chaplains also have the responsibility of overseeing a unit of chaplains assigned to military commanders. Senior leaders often are charged with dealing with politically sensitive and ethical issues in a diplomatic manner, supporting the mission of the military while also remaining observant of their religious traditions.

Table 10.1 presents a summary of the sample demographics presenting a balanced sample in terms of gender, with 58 percent males and 42 percent females. In terms of age, 9 percent are in the eighteen to twenty-five age category, 21 percent in the twenty-six to thirty-five bracket, 36.6 percent between thirty-six and fifty, 25.7 percent between fifty-one and sixty-five, and 4.9 percent at sixty-five years of age or older. A high percentage (40 percent) of the sample is minority, including 25.7 percent African American. In regard to education, the sample is more highly educated than the general population, with approximately 92 percent possessing some college (25.7 percent possess a bachelor's, 21.8 percent a master's degree, 13.9 percent a law degree, and 15.8 percent a PhD). The respondents were highly experienced, with a mean of 22.8 years in the workplace and 90 percent with ten or more years on the job. The majority of respondents were at the executive (36.6 percent) or managerial levels (24.75 percent), and the remaining (38 percent) occupied various types of staff positions. The interviews clustered into a variety of occupational areas, including law enforcement (21.8 percent), law (15.8 percent), the military (13.86 percent), education (9.9 percent), business (7.9 percent), finance (7.9 percent), government (5.9 percent), and health care (3.9 percent).

The section below provides summaries of three of the main interview questions illustrating the application of WSI principles based on conversations with military chaplains.

Table 10.1. Sample Demographics

Interview Type			Education (cont.)		
Category	N	%	Category	N	%
In-person	53	52.48%	Law	14	13.86%
Phone	15	14.85%	PhD	16	15.84%
E-mail	15	14.85%	Medical doctor	1	1%
E-mail/phone	15	14.85%	Job experience		
In-person/fax	2	1.9%			
E-mail/phone/person	1	.09%	Less than 10 years	8	7.9%
Gender			10–19	27	26.73%
			20–29	27	26.73%
Male	58	57.42%	20–39	20	19.8%
Female	42	41.58%	40+	15	14.85%
Age Category			Job level		
18–25	9	8.9%	Executive	37	36.63%
26–35	21	20.79%	Managerial	25	24.75%
36–50	37	36.63%	Staff	38	37.62%
51–65	26	25.74%	Industry		
65+	5	4.9%			
Race			Business	8	7.9%
			Education	10	9.9%
African American	26	25.74%	Finance	8	7.9%
White	60	59.40%	Government	6	5.9%
Hispanic	7	6.9%	Health	4	3.9%
Other	7	6.9%	Law enforcement	6	5.9%
Education			Law	16	15.84%
			Media	1	.9%
High school	5	4.9%	Medicine	1	.9%
Some college	3	2.9%	Military	14	13.86%
Associate's degree	10	9.9%	Nonprofit	3	2.9%
Bachelor's	26	25.74%	Missing	5	4.9%
Master's	22	21.78%			

WSI SUMMARY OF INTERVIEW RESULTS

The first question asked was "What are your greatest character strengths?" Interviewees seemed to believe that their honesty and integrity in the workplace was essential to everything else. Respondents mentioned this attribute in almost 40 percent of interviews. Humility seemed to be a perceived necessary trait for those in positions of authority. This was the second-most mentioned strength. Transparency was mentioned by interviewees numerically the most after humility. The examples given appeared to be a self-perceived strength, or the interviewees appeared to value this trait.

The key foundational WSI attribute in this instance is love. Respondents introduced love only five times in the 101 interviews. This attribute, which is the highest order of spiritual intelligence, was not a recognized or expressed strength for most of the interviewees. The interviewees who did mention this attribute tied it to a willingness to believe and please God. This may reflect that respondents view love as a foundational factor embedded in all character strengths, or it may also reflect complacency related to assuming a high level of love.

Although the language did not specifically use the word *love*, the characteristics of compassion and encouragement were equated with this virtue. One senior chaplain indicated that he instructed his junior chaplains to provide support to military wives with young children when they are separated from their husbands due to long deployments.

In the seductive environment in Washington, D.C., money answers all things, power is very tangible, and there is a strong temptation to compromise one's integrity. A respondent likened his personal struggle to Daniel's position in which "he made the decision not to be defiled" and to reject moral compromise.

A respondent recounted a situation that demonstrated the power of transparency. The respondent was counseling a married couple in the midst of a difficult three-hour session. There was a state of impasse and with divorce on the horizon. To break the stalemate, the respondent described his own marriage troubles twelve years earlier and how he and his wife had worked through their "feelings of not wanting to be married." He struggled with revealing his own personal discrepancies as a leader, but the transparency caused a turn in the conversation and allowed him to share his own testimony.

The second question the interview asked was "What is your greatest character weakness, and how are you trying to remedy it?" Pride/arrogance was described as a lack of "humility," especially by those in positions of authority. Another form of weakness noted among respondents was the tendency to be a people pleaser in order to be recognized, praised, and applauded. Being judgmental and "knowing it all as a Christian" can be another source of pride when dealing with nonbelievers. Focusing on circumstances instead of focusing on God and his promises was also a common response. Many respondents identified worrying, lack of trust in themselves and God, and their challenging circumstances. Many respondents also replied that they set high standards that are unattainable and then procrastinate to avoid failure. Doing lower-quality work is a huge barrier for most.

Again, many failed to mention their lack of love as a weakness. Many have an accurate awareness of their weakness but assume a "treat the symptom" or "Band Aid" approach that impedes effective problem solving. Few were able to articulate that they had or were in the process of using WSI to make a permanent change in their area of weakness. Others also struggled with being task oriented versus people oriented and finding a balance. One of the key spiritual-intelligence attributes is humility, in which we recognize our weaknesses and submit them to the Lord. The mature believer uses the Holy Spirit to identify the character weaknesses and the associated distorted thinking patterns that camouflage and disguise the cause and consequences of our strongholds. For example, we can exhibit ethical behavior motivated by self-serving factors (performing the correct action for the wrong reason). Another key element is that respondents did not mention that strengths could become weaknesses through the intersection of pride and using their gifts in appropriate and "unauthorized" ways that are not according to the will of God.

At the inception of the conversations, the senior chaplain demonstrated an authoritative position as a senior military officer interacting with a civilian or a junior service member. The inherent position of authority and ranking of the military officer often can be a conflict between humility and pride. Many had visible physical discomfort in answering questions regarding weakness. One respondent responded with silence and tears, and then requested that "he be allowed to not answer this question." The same respondent, at the end of the conservation, expressed gratitude that it was the first time he had been asked the question and didn't know how to answer.

Another respondent answered that humility is the enemy of pride in the military. The respondent indicated it is often challenging to transition from the military environment that demands respect and obedience to his personal life where such rank of authority may be lacking. Such stressors between environments can often be difficult to manage.

Many respondents really did not have an effective long-term strategy for dealing with the root of negative emotion. Many of the options are temporary-relief strategies that treat the symptoms. A major component of WSI is not suppressing or denying the emotion, but instead responding to the negative emotion with action and confronting it with timeless truths. One of the most powerful cognitive distortions is emotional reasoning, in which our emotions control our reasoning and decision-making abilities. One of the most basic WSI attributes is to recognize that we will all experience negative emotions (depression, fear, anxiety, worry, etc.), but that as Christ followers we do not rely on our senses or circumstances to predict outcomes but on our agreement with the word of God. As the great evangelist Smith Wigglesworth stated, "It is not what we feel or think that matters; it is what we believe." Negative emotions can possess both logical and rationale roots (loss of a job) or be generated by cognitive distortions and mental illness. Irrespective of their sources, the solution is the same—to "walk by faith and not by sight" and rely on the promises of God for protection and good from evil.[58] Many senior chaplains often described experiencing negative emotions but explained that in military culture expressing negative emotions is considered a weakness, a poor display of leadership, and contrary to the standard rule of "military bearing," which led them to repress their negative emotions.

Another respondent reported attempting to remove all emotion and be led by the Holy Spirit. There were many days and times that he just closed his office door to pray alone or with someone over the phone. He has his Bible on his credenza and picked it up often to help deal with putting out the fires in his daily business.

Another respondent described a time when he was compelled to testify against a fellow chaplain who had engaged in immoral conduct and was subsequently court-martialed. His testimony caused the removal of the chaplain but also brought embarrassing scrutiny related to his own actions. Therefore, although in a state of conflict, he ultimately had peace and a clear conscience as he did what was necessary for the greater good. He decided to tell the truth when under pressure and temptation to conceal it.

A military chaplain second in command at the Chaplain Base at the time of the interview indicated he was somewhat agitated and greatly distressed regarding the issues we discussed. After the formal interview was over, he took the interviewer to his office and dialogued regarding his personal experiences as a chaplain.

Another respondent indicated that chaplains must deal with social rejection and may be rejected by their peers. The pervasive attitude is that chaplains "are welcome always but not accepted always. Nobody wants chaplain to go the strip bar or drinking with them."

One of the key "signature" elements of WSI is the ability to place workplace trials and tribulations within a biblical context. The foundational element is the faith and hope that God is protecting workplace believers in all situations and that ultimately good is produced.[59] WSI provides the coping and adaptation skills to weather the storms. One essential WSI character attribute is hope, and another is the presence of a strong support network or community. All interviewee answers to questions about hope demonstrated heavy reliance on WSI and biblical tools for endurance, perspective, and identifying the standards for conduct and processing. Many answers demonstrated knowledge of the correct WSI principle but lacked concrete application examples.

During his last year in the military after twenty-six years as a chaplain, one interviewee's superior informed him that he was to retire after having denied his promotion request. The pain was intensified given that the chaplain had been informed two days before Easter and everyone knew, which further exacerbated his depression and resulted in his staying in the barracks for two days. When Easter Sunday came, he had prepared no message. Walking into the service a young sailor said, "Thank you for coming to bring us the presence of God." The chaplain had to work through anger and disappointment. He did what God required and made his peace.

ANALYSIS OF THE WSI DATA

This preliminary analysis of the WSI interview data provided examples of how military chaplains integrate spiritual intelligence into the workplace. The results demonstrate, not surprisingly, an ad hoc and unsystematic integration of WSI principles. This is partially explained by the absence of formal training and emphasis in workplace ministry by churches.

Several of the key themes illustrated by the analysis include the following: The interview process itself was powerfully moving at the spiritual level, with many respondents being moved to tears. The factors that contribute to this include that the interview forced the respondent to confront areas of spiritual strength and weakness and reduced defensive and rationalization mechanisms, increased the saliency of the need to improve, produced a safe environment for confession, and provided a means for exercising voice and input.

Interviewers benefited greatly from the process. It reinforced their faith and understanding of WSI. Respondents demonstrated a basic knowledge and belief in biblical truths. To solve workplace problems, Spirit-led integration of cognitive, affective, and behavioral attributes with biblical principles is essential for proper balance. Those with high levels of WSI demonstrated a high degree of intentionality in applying and committing to biblical principles in the workplace. Most interviewees did not manifest high levels of WSI. A few were mature enough to practice more heart-integrated spiritual intelligence and possessed the ability to use wisdom at a higher-level order of thinking. An increased awareness and commitment to integrating the Golden Rule love principle is needed to fully utilize WSI in the workplace.

In conclusion, one of the key recommendations is to develop a systematic education and training program in the area of WSI for chaplains. This would include a diversity of training and education methods that incorporate a variety of learning styles and methods. This entails a combination of critically reflective learning processes including the completion of WSI self-diagnostic inventory, journaling, 360-degree peer assessments, mentor programs, and group accountability and support programs. The more effective integration of spiritual intelligence will generate a host of benefits, including higher levels of workplace effectiveness and elevated mental and physical health outcomes.

CONCLUSION

Workplace stress is a ubiquitous element of the military chaplaincy. As with any care-giving occupation, "caring for the caregivers" should be a systematic and sustained policy and practice. If the chaplaincy is to maintain its effectiveness in meeting its mission to support and serve our men and women in uniform, a systematic occupational-stress audit embedded within an overall wellness program supported by training and education provides important support. In addition, cultivating the chaplain's own dynamic and authentic spiritually is essential for their growth and well-being. Chaplains cannot effectively "give away" what they lack; they cannot bolster the spirits of service members if they themselves possess a weak spiritual foundation. The goal is to further equip and support chaplains for the vitally important job with our nation's finest.

EXHIBIT 1: MILITARY CHAPLAIN EXAMPLE OCCUPATIONAL-STRESS AUDIT MASTER LIST OF STRESS CATEGORIES[60]

a. Role Ambiguity

___ Lack of clarity over job goals, duties, and responsibilities
___ Lack of clarity over the job goals, duties, and responsibilities of other military personnel

b. Role Conflict

___ Conflict between job duties, responsibilities, or goals: quality versus quantity
___ Job duties not matched with interests and passions
___ Job duties not tailored to gifts and strengths
___ Greater emphasis on improving weaknesses than on developing and improving strengths
___ Excessive emphasis on workplace "face time" versus flexible means for completing work

c. Quantitative and Qualitative Role Overload

___ Quantitative workload: can't meet high standards in all work areas
___ Qualitative overload: lack the knowledge, skills, and abilities to complete job
___ Excessive quantity of work
___ Lack of adequate rest breaks
___ Absence or inadequate time for creative thought
___ Absence or inadequate time for recreation and self-care
___ Absence of unstructured time

d. Role Responsibility

___ Pressures from the responsibility of supervising employees
___ Pressures from meeting budget guidelines
___ Pressures from meeting performance standards

e. Working Conditions
   ___ Physical setting: heat/cold/lighting
   ___ Ergonomics: work structure and design
   ___ Physical demands of work repetitive stress
   ___ Excessive levels of sitting: more than five hours total or four hours consecutively
   ___ Isolated work environment
   ___ Shift work
   ___ Long hours
   ___ Frequent travel
   ___ Technology pressure to remain current

f. Compensation and Performance-Appraisal Measurement
   ___ Unfair compensation practices: lack of internal and external equity
   ___ Biased performance-appraisal systems
   ___ Being held accountable for performance factors beyond the chaplain's control
   ___ Absence of encouragement and support

g. Interpersonal Conflict
   ___ Office politics
   ___ Unfair treatment
   ___ Lack of support and help from colleagues
   ___ Excessive competition
   ___ Peer pressure to conform to excessive effort, performance, or work levels

h. Poor-Quality Supervision
   ___ Supervisor provides little or no clear, specific, timely, and actionable performance feedback
   ___ Supervisor models workaholic behavior and job attitude
   ___ Supervisor fails to model being content with reasonable efforts and trusting God for the increase
   ___ Supervisor provides little job structure
   ___ Supervisor provides little job support and encouragement
   ___ Biased treatment: in-groups and out-groups

i. Situational Constraints
   ___ Inadequate job information
   ___ Inadequate resources: money/supplies/equipment
   ___ Inadequate authority

___ Time: interruptions/tight deadlines/unanticipated projects/ poor planning or procrastination

j. Perceived Control

___ Lack of job autonomy: how job is done
___ Lack of control over pace of work
___ Lack of input
___ Lack of participation in decision making

k. Career Development

___ Inadequate training
___ Plateau syndrome: no advancement opportunities

l. Lack of Organizational Covenant

___ Absence of job security
___ Absence of work forgiveness
___ Absence of managerial transparency
___ Short-term performance emphasis

m. Work-Home Pressures

___ Long commutes
___ Lack of adequate childcare
___ Eldercare problems
___ Lack of support in domestic chores
___ Lengthy and frequent deployments

n. Traumatic Job Stress

___ Stress from combat exposure
___ Combat trauma: self-experienced
___ Secondary trauma from counseling others
___ Workplace violence
___ Workplace bullying
___ Workplace sexual harassment
___ Workplace discrimination: religion, race, gender, age, etc.

o. Low Levels of Spirituality and Workplace Spiritual Intelligence (WSI) and Absence of Character Elements

___ Hopelessness and discouragement
___ Unbelief and doubt
___ Lack of forgiveness and bitterness
___ Jealousy and envy
___ Inappropriate comparison to others
___ Perfectionism

___ Absence of humility
___ Absence of humor
___ Absence of play and recreation
___ Absence of emphasis on character growth and development, including addressing areas of weakness, sin, and strongholds
___ Inability to be content with doing our best and permitting God to be responsible for outcome: increase
___ Culture that condones or rationalizes ethical improprieties: theft, sloth, corruption, etc.

EXHIBIT 2: SUMMARY OF PRACTICES TO REDUCE CHAPLAIN OCCUPATIONAL STRESS

Job Selection

- Valid and reliable chaplain staffing from entry level to executive (recruitment and selection practices)
- Realistic job previews

Job Characteristics

- Aligning chaplain job duties and workloads with employee passions, capabilities, strengths, gifts, and interests
- Majority of developmental emphasis on strengths and gifts versus addressing weaknesses and deficiencies
- Adequate chaplain-staffing levels
- Clearly define chaplain roles and responsibilities
- Provide ample time for rest, recreation, fun, and humor
- Provide unstructured blocks of times for quiet reflection

Servant Leadership

- Covenantal work relationship that develops trust
- Set good personal example for work-life balance, including reasonable levels of work effort and hours
- High levels of consideration and empathy for chaplain needs and problems
- Military leadership sets clear mission, vision, and direction
- Military-leadership transparency
- Reward creativity, and don't penalize chaplains for good-faith mistakes
- Fair chaplain treatment in operational and personnel decision making
- Embrace and promote diversity
- Long-term goal focus

- Long-term career development of chaplains is a prime focus
- No in-group and out-group management

Chaplain Resource Support

- Adequate chaplain training
- Adequate tools, equipment, and supplies
- Safe working environment
- Ergonomically sound work process

Compensation and Performance Appraisal

- Internal and external pay equity
- 360-degree performance-based performance-appraisal system with employee input

Employee Input

- Give chaplains opportunities to participate in decisions and actions affecting their jobs
- Chaplains should have key input about work design and quality improvement rather than having decisions made solely by leaders who are, in the hierarchy, three or four levels removed from the level of service provision

Workplace Spiritual Intelligence (WSI) Character and Employee Support

- Instill hope, and cultivate faith
- Encouraging networks of social support
- Provide opportunities for social interaction among workers
- Develop a culture of faith, hope, and encouragement
- Generous grace and forgiveness policies

Work-Life Benefits

- Flexible schedules
- Flexible workplace
- Readily available, high-quality childcare
- Eldercare support

Chaplain-Wellness Programs

- Employee-assistance programs
- Employee wellness: physical fitness, nutrition, rest

Chaplain Servant-Followership Responsibilities

- Develop and apply spiritual-intelligence practices
- Select a job that fits with skills/abilities/interests
- Learn coping/stress-reduction techniques
- Invest in training and development, embrace lifelong learning
- Practice stress prevention by embracing and practicing healthy life-styles: health/nutrition/physical fitness/balance between work, family, and leisure
- Practice organizational citizenship behaviors: support, team player, sacrifice for others
- Honest/consistent and reliable work effort
- Honest effort at correcting, remedying performance problems

EXHIBIT 3: WORKPLACE SPIRITUAL INTELLIGENCE (WSI) ATTRIBUTES

1. Spiritual Foundations:
   - Embraces an integrated religious worldview
   - Active practice of the spiritual disciplines: Bible reading, prayer, fasting, and fellowship

2. Golden Rule Workplace Love Expression:
   - Primary motive of action is to obey and honor God and promote the best interests of others

3. Seeking and Following God's Will:
   - Work priorities and godly life balance based on active prayer guidance

4. Practice Forgiveness:
   - Patience in working with difficult coworkers, superiors, and clients
   - Provide forgiveness generously

5. Accountability:
   - Provides relationship accountability in terms of setting appropriate boundaries
   - Assumes personal accountability and teachability: assumes responsibility for errors, mistakes, and growth

6. Support and Encouragement:
   - Providing ample support to others

7. WSI Personality Attributes:
   - Transparency and humility
   - Gratitude and thanksgiving

- Embracing hope, faith, and perseverance
- Patience
- Emotional awareness and empathy

8. Identifying and Correcting Distorted Thinking and Reasoning Patterns:
   - Overcoming emotional reasoning and labeling
   - Overcoming fears

9. Identifying and Overcoming Character Flaws:
   - Rejecting perfectionism and promoting the healthy pursuit of excellence
   - Overcoming "people pleasing" and affirmation anxiety / addiction

10. WSI Communication Skills:
    - Promote empathy and active listening

11. WSI Lifestyle-Stewardship Elements:
    - Relationship stewardship with a balanced and fair allocation of household duties
    - Healthy interpersonal relationships
    - Live simple lifestyle with lower debt
    - Generous giving
    - Volunteering and civic engagement

12. Physical Health Self-Care:
    - Nutrition: healthy diet and portion control
    - Engages in preventive health care
    - Recognizes and addresses health risks
    - Adequate exercise
    - Adequate rest and sleep
    - Ample recreation

13. Life Margin and Simplicity:
    - Simple-lifestyle emphasis
    - Embraces work margin and rest

14. Gifts, Abilities, and Career Management:
    - Aware of strengths, weaknesses, passions, and interests

15. Servant Followership:
    - Works with excellence in all job situations

16. Servant Leadership:
    - Effectively develops and empowers others
    - Effectively provides corrective feedback
    - Healthy conflict-resolution abilities

- Stewardship and integrity
- Balanced decision making
- Managing change effectively
- Leadership humility

EXHIBIT 4: KEY WSI CHARACTER ELEMENTS ESSENTIAL FOR SUCCESS[61]

Table 10.2. WSI Attitudes with Corresponding Workplace Outcomes

WSI Attribute	Workplace Behavioral Examples	Workplace Outcomes
Love: The desire to promote the best interests of others, regardless of the personal cost. Love, from a WSI worldview statement, is not an emotional-state "feeling" but a decision and an action to obey and love God and others through mission achievement and helping others grow and develop.	Help and encourage all organizational members irrespective of our personal affective feelings. We must love all organizational members, even those who dislike us and are openly hostile. Examples include training a subordinate to replace you on your present position; ensuring that employees receive full credit for their accomplishments; promoting the best interests of your enemies (washing the feet of the office Judas); sacrificing personal interests for the benefit of subordinate organizational members (protecting subordinates from unethical higher-management behavior).	Increases organizational-member trust, commitment, and reduces individual and collective organizational member stress.
Humility: (1) Recognizing that God is the source of all our strengths, accomplishments, and successes and that he is responsible for the outcomes in our lives; (2) recognizing that love is the only motive that honors God in our actions	Recognize and reward excellent performance of subordinates publicly; commit to mentoring and discipling others through succession planning—in effect, training your replacement; admitting weaknesses and	Increases organizational-member trust, level of two-way communication, and transparency levels.

Table 10.2. (*continued*)

WSI Attribute	Workplace Behavioral Examples	Workplace Outcomes
and decision making (1 Corinthians 13); (3) possessing a confidence that God will use all of our weaknesses, sins, and failures to promote our long-term benefit and good (Romans 8:28); (4) recognizing that personal gifts, abilities, and high performance can only be realized in conjunction with others (a body of Christ perspective); (5) acknowledging personal limits and weaknesses; and (6) taking joy in the accomplishments of others, even when they exceed our accomplishments and abilities, and experiencing sadness when others fail.	failures and placing others in positions of authority and visibility to supplement personal weaknesses.	
Transparency: A commitment to open and honest communication of personal strengths, weaknesses, attributes, life experiences, motives, and beliefs. This is the "doing" aspect of humility and communicates trust of others through increasing our vulnerability. Transparency provides a window to the soul.	Providing an honest assessment of strengths and weaknesses, thereby promoting improved staffing, training, teamwork, and problem solving. When managers model transparency, it encourages others to share their weaknesses, thereby enhancing organizational learning and reducing organizational-member stress. One of the greatest sources of personal job stress is the burden of image management in which we hide our weaknesses and fears from others.	Reduced job stress, increased quality and quantity of communication, and reductions in suppression of adverse information, thus increasing problem-solving effectiveness.
Forgiveness: The ability to overlook the offenses, failures, mistakes, and sins	Develop a learning organization culture in which good-faith	Higher levels of innovation and creativity, reduction in organizational fear.

WSI Attribute	Workplace Behavioral Examples	Workplace Outcomes
of others. The practice of 360-degree forgiveness (self, others, and God).	mistakes are expected and encouraged, thereby facilitating growth and overcoming perfectionism.	
Hope and Perseverance: The ability to believe and trust God for protection and mission completion irrespective of the circumstances and our associated reasoning and logic regarding the situation. This enables us to maintain our mission focus in the face of the pain and suffering caused by trials and tribulations. Hope provides the foundation for perseverance. We can endure horrific circumstances if hope remains alive.	The ability to inspire organizational members to maintain efforts in the face of adversity by clearly articulating an inspiring future vision that articulates the reason and benefits of sacrifice.	Higher levels of performance, lower levels of turnover.
Compassion and Empathy: The desire and ability to understand and empathize with the life experiences of others at the intellect and heart level. This includes their life experiences, values, beliefs, emotions, motives, problems, and needs.	Effective Christian servant leaders pursue multiple avenues of communication to develop enduring and meaningful relationships. They embrace the practice of active listening to demonstrate their desire to understand and love their employees. For example, servant-leader human-resource organizations conduct stress audits to uncover workplace areas that contribute to burnout and overwork. The Christian servant leader protects his or her "flock" from overwork and excessive stress.	Enhances organizational member trust, commitment, and loyalty. Impedes the development of compassion fatigue— a condition in which organizational members are too tired and stressed to help coworkers or clients in need, creating an accelerating cycle of isolation and despair in the workplace, and engendering a Darwinian survival-of-the-fittest culture. Managerial compassion enhances Golden Rule behavior by modeling and reinforcing organizational member teamwork, support, and mentoring, thereby creating a supportive

(*continued*)

Table 10.2. (*continued*)

WSI Attribute	Workplace Behavioral Examples	Workplace Outcomes
	Even though the leader may be able to marshal the will, effort, and strength to support "superhuman" work efforts, unreasonable demands result in many organizational members perishing on the long march. The virtuous ends do not justify the employment of means that skew organizational-member priorities, placing work over family, personal self-care of our health and well-being, and time for spiritual growth in our relationship with God.	and loving work environment. This enhances organizational member motivation to engage in extra efforts to solve problems and help coworkers in need.

NOTES

1. Kenneth Lasson, "Religious Liberty in the Military: The First Amendment under 'Friendly Fire,'" *Journal of Law and Religion* 9, no. 2 (1992): 471–99, 493.

2. K. J. Flannelly, S. B. Roberts, and A. J. Weaver, "Correlates of Compassion Fatigue and Burnout in Chaplains and Other Clergy Who Responded to the September 11th Attacks in New York City," *Journal of Pastoral Care & Counseling* 59, no. 3 (2005): 213–24; Hannah C. Levy, Lauren M. Conoscenti, John F. Tillery, Benjamin D. Dickstein, and Brett T. Litz, "Deployment Stressors and Outcomes among Air Force Chaplains," *Military Journal of Traumatic Stress* 24, no. 3 (June 2011): 342–46; K. Besterman-Dahan, S. D. Barnett, E. J. Hickling, S. Gibbons, and D. Watts, "Military Chaplains and the Mental Health of the Deployed Service Member," *Military Medicine* 177, no. 9 (2012): 1028–33.

3. B. R. Doolittle, "Burnout and Coping among Parish-Based Clergy," *Mental Health, Religions & Culture* 10, no. 1 (2007): 31–38.

4. Vance P. Theodore, "Care Work: Factors Affecting Post–9/11 United States Army Chaplains; Compassion Fatigue, Burnout, Compassion Satisfaction, and Spiritual Resiliency" (PhD dissertation, Kansas State University, 2011).

5. Waldo W. Burchard, "Role Conflicts of Military Chaplains," *American Sociological Review* 19 (October 1954): 528–35; J. Beder and G. W. Yan, "VHA Chaplains: Challenges, Roles, Rewards, and Frustrations of the Work," *Journal of Health Care Chaplaincy* 19, no. 2 (2013): 54–65.

6. G. Roberts, "Leadership Coping Skills: Servant Leader Workplace Spiritual Intelligence," *Journal of Strategic Leadership* 4, no. 2 (2013).

7. Roberts, "Leadership Coping Skills," 52–69.

8. Barry Black, *From the Hood to the Hill: A Story of Overcoming* (Nashville: Thomas Nelson, 2006).

9. S. M. Jex, *Stress and Job Performance: Theory, Research and Implications for Managerial Practices* (Thousand Oaks, CA: Sage, 1998); Roberts, "Leadership Coping Skills."

10. K. D. Killian, "Helping till [*sic*] It Hurts? A Multimethod Study of Compassion Fatigue, Burnout, and Self-Care in Clinicians Working with Trauma Survivors," *Traumatology* 14, no. 2 (2008): 32–44.

11. G. Zimmerman and W. Weber, "Care for the Caregivers: A Program for Canadian Military Chaplains after Serving in NATO and United Nations Peacekeeping Missions in the 1990s," *Military Medicine* 165, no. 9 (September 2000): 687–90.

12. Ibid.

13. Beder and Yan, "VHA Chaplains."

14. Karen Besterman-Dahan, Scott Barnett, Edward Hickling, Christine Elnitsky, Jason Lind, John Skvoretz, and Nicole Antinori, "Bearing the Burden: Deployment Stress among Army National Guard Chaplains," *Journal of Health Care Chaplaincy* 18, no. 3–4 (2012): 151–68.

15. Ibid.

16. Ibid.

17. Ibid.

18. Theodore, "Care Work."

19. Christopher Alan Lewis, Douglas W. Turton, and Leslie J. Francis, "Clergy Work-Related Psychological Health, Stress, and Burnout: An Introduction to This Special Issue of Mental Health, Religion and Culture," *Mental Health, Religion & Culture* 10, no. 1 (2007): 1–8.

20. Doolittle, "Burnout and Coping."

21. C. R. Brewin, B. Andrews, and J. D. Valentine, "Meta-Analysis of Risk Factors for Post-traumatic Stress Disorder in Trauma-Exposed Adults," *Journal of Consulting and Clinical Psychology* 68 (2000): 748–66; S. Maguen, D. Turcotte, A. L. Peterson, T. L. Dremsa, H. N. Garb, R. J. McNally, and B. T. Litz, "Description of Risk and Resilience Factors among Military Medical Personnel before Deployment to Iraq," *Military Medicine* 173 (2008): 1–9.

22. Brewin et al., "Meta-Analysis of Risk Factors."

23. Kathleen Galek, Kevin J. Flannelly, Paul B. Greene, and Taryn Kudler, "Burnout, Secondary Traumatic Stress, and Social Support," *Pastoral Psychology* 60, no. 5 (October 2011): 633–49.

24. Ibid.

25. Levy et al., "Deployment Stressors and Outcomes."

26. B. E. Taylor, A. J. Weaver, K. J. Flannelly, and D. J. Zucker, "Compassion Fatigue and Burnout among Rabbis Working as Chaplains," *Journal of Pastoral Care & Counseling* 60, nos. 1–2 (2006): 35–42.

27. Ibid.

28. C. Maslach and M. P. Leiter, "Early Predictors of Job Burnout and Engagement," *Journal of Applied Psychology* 93, no. 3 (2008): 498–512.

29. R. S. Bebe, "Predicting Burnout, Conflict Management Style, and Turnover among Clergy," *Journal of Career Assessment* 15, no. 2 (2007): 257–75.

30. Maureen Miner, "Burnout in the First Year of Ministry: Personality and Belief Style as Important Predictors," *Mental Health, Religion & Culture* 10, no. 1 (2007): 9–16.

31. Killian, "Helping till [*sic*] It Hurts?"

32. L. J. Francis, S. H. Louden, S. H., and C. J. F. Rutledge, "Burnout among Roman Catholic Parochial Clergy in England and Wales: Myth or Reality," *Review of Religious Research* 46 (2004): 5–19; Miner, "Burnout in the First Year."

33. Francis et al., "Burnout among Roman Catholic Parochial Clergy."

34. Miner, "Burnout in the First Year."

35. Ibid.

36. Ibid.

37. Besterman-Dahan et al., "Bearing the Burden."

38. Doolittle, "Burnout and Coping."

39. J. Golden, R. L. Piedmont, J. W. Ciarrocchi, and T. Roderson, "Spirituality and Burnout: An Incremental Validity Study," *Journal of Psychology and Theology* 32, no. 2 (2004): 115–25.

40. Lewis et al., "Clergy Work-Related Psychological Health."

41. Doolittle, "Burnout and Coping."

42. Francis et al., "Burnout among Roman Catholic Parochial Clergy."

43. Ibid.

44. K. J. Randall, "Burnout as a Predictor of Leaving Anglican Parish Ministry," *Review of Religious Research* 46 (2004): 20–26.

45. Levy et al., "Deployment Stressors and Outcomes."

46. Ibid.

47. Della W. Stewart, "Compassion Fatigue: What Is the Level among Army Chaplains?" *Journal of Workplace Behavioral Health* 27, no. 1 (2012): 1–11.

48. Ibid.

49. Golden et al., "Spirituality and Burnout"; Doolittle, "Burnout and Coping"; Lewis et al., "Clergy Work-Related Psychological Health."

50. Howard Gardner, *Frames of Mind: The Theory of Multiple Intelligences* (New York: Basic Books, 1993); Robert. A. Emmons, "Is Spirituality an Intelligence? Motivation, Cognition, and the Psychology of Ultimate Concern," *International Journal for the Psychology of Religion* 10, no. 1 (2000): 3–26.

51. *Spiritual Intelligence: A Special Issue of the International Journal for the Psychology of Religion* 10, no. 1 (2000).

52. L. I. Sawyer, "Seeding and Sustaining Transformative Learning, Development, and Spiritual Growth in Higher Education: A Case Study," *Dissertation Abstracts International, Section A: Humanities and Social Sciences* 65, no 12-A (2005): 4431; H. B. Mull, "Spiritual Intelligence in Psychotherapy with Grieving Clients," *Dissertation Abstracts International, Section A: Humanities and Social Sciences*, 65, no. 2-A (2004): 420; M. Delaney, "The Emergent Construct of Spiritual Intelligence: The Synergy of Science and Spirit," *Dissertation Abstracts International, Section B: The Sciences and Engineering* 3, no. 5-B (2002): 2565.

53. P. Primeaux and M. L. Pava, eds., *Spiritual Intelligence at Work: Meaning, Metaphor and Morals* (San Diego: Elsevier Science & Technology Books, 2003); C. Mc-Geachy, *Spiritual Intelligence in the Workplace* (Dublin: Veritas, 2005).

54. F. J. MacHovec, *Spiritual Intelligence, Behavioral Sciences, and the Humanities* (Lewiston, NY: Edwin Mellen Press, 2002).

55. Emmons, "Is Spirituality an Intelligence?"

56. Roberts, "Leadership Coping Skills," 52–69.

57. Ibid.

58. Romans 8:28 and Genesis 50:20.

59. Romans 8:28.

60. Jex, *Stress and Job Performance*.

61. Gary Roberts, "Servant Leader Human Resource Management: A Moral and Spiritual Perspective" (unpublished book manuscript).

11

Contemporary Challenges and Future Opportunities for U.S. Chaplains

Jason Klocek and Ron E. Hassner

In August 1898, Chaplain William D. McKinnon had occasion to be present at a heated debate between the U.S. commanders in charge of planning the impending assault on Manila. As those in attendance weighed military challenges and options, the commander of the First Philippine Expeditionary Force, Brigadier General Thomas M. Anderson, asked half-jokingly, "Why in the name of common sense don't some of you Catholics enter Manila and tell that archbishop of yours to call this whole thing off?" Unfazed, the chaplain asked for and received permission to do exactly that. McKinnon approached the Spanish lines, unaccompanied and unarmed, to negotiate the surrender of Manila. His initial attempt met with hostility: the Spanish sentries shot at the chaplain. Grazed by a bullet, he withdrew but resumed his efforts soon thereafter. On August 9, several hours before U.S. ships were to begin their bombardment of the city, he finally succeeded in meeting with the Philippine archbishop, Bernardino Nozaleda, and the Spanish governor-general of the Philippines, Captain-General Fermin Jaudenes. The chaplain's mission allowed U.S. Admiral George Dewey to plan a sham battle with his Spanish counterparts, to commence four days after McKinnon's mission, which produced an instant Spanish surrender with minimal fatalities. A contemporary journalist described McKinnon's action as "without parallel in the history of modern warfare—an act of unselfish bravery, of devotion to the sacred cause of peace, which should make his name live forever."[1]

The chaplain's courageous efforts to act as intermediary during the Spanish-American War are not, however, without historical parallel. American chaplains have acted as peacemakers as early as the War of Independence, when Chaplain Thomas Allen "threw himself between the two armies" at the Battle of Bennington (1777) because he was certain of American victory and wanted to avert unnecessary bloodshed.[2] Leander Kerr, the chaplain attached to Fort Leavenworth in the 1850s, relied on his familiarity with the language and rituals of the Kansas Missouri Indians to avert bloodshed on multiple occasions.[3] Chaplain Toussaint Mesplie successfully convinced the Umatilla Indians not to take the warpath with Chief Joseph during the Nez Perce War of 1877 and was later commissioned by President Rutherford B. Hayes to conduct peace negotiations with several Northwest tribes.[4] After McKinnon's heroic mission, U.S. Army chaplains implemented a "hearts and minds" campaign to suppress the Philippine insurrection, which included the construction of schools, supplying medicine and aid, and improving sanitary conditions.[5] In the great wars of the twentieth century, chaplains presided over the truces that permitted rival armies to carry their men back to the lines, including soldiers who fell near or within enemy positions.[6]

Indeed, a close examination of chaplain duties over the course of the last three centuries suggests that the tasks of American chaplains were never restricted to the pastoral. Often their role as morale boosters, counselors, teachers, and intermediaries overshadowed, perhaps even occluded, their spiritual function. Civil War chaplains wrote and mailed letters on behalf of soldiers; delivered news, gifts, and clothing from their families; maintained libraries; and offered literacy classes.[7] First World War chaplains ran canteens; distributed food, cigarettes, and gifts; and functioned as postmasters, librarians, athletic officers, and education officers.[8] Second World War chaplains ran errands on soldiers' behalves, led orchestras, organized boxing matches, screened movies, wrote newsletters, and organized reading and debate clubs.[9] The war in Vietnam saw chaplains in classrooms, teaching "moral leadership" and ethics courses.[10] At all times, chaplains were expected to accomplish these tasks in addition to their core functions: providing religious ministry, leading religious services, preaching to troops, and, most crucial of all, supporting individual soldiers in their hour of need.

As this volume demonstrates beautifully, U.S. chaplains today continue this tradition of assuming tasks that go well beyond the strictly pastoral. The preceding chapters chronicle this latest, and heretofore untold, period of the Western military chaplaincy. By bringing together contributions from a diverse set of experienced practitioners, the contributors to this volume offer important insight into the meaning, promises, and challenges associated with religious engagement and advisement.

In this concluding chapter, we summarize these key observations and point to challenges as well as avenues for future research. We begin by summarizing the four primary ways in which chaplains have recently contributed to stability operations and peace building: conciliation, mediation, diplomacy, and expertise. Next we outline three primary difficulties that chaplains will have to confront in the near future if they are to continue to perform these tasks: the persistent lack of clear role definition, inadequate training, and uncertainty about the future function of the chaplaincy. We conclude by proposing avenues for further research that draw from the literatures on religion and peace building, foreign policy, and state building. This affords us an opportunity to ask critical questions about the drawbacks and limitations of chaplain involvement with new tasks. We hope that this analysis will shed light on how the evolving roles and responsibilities of chaplains over the past two decades have affected and will continue to shape both the chaplaincy and the military more broadly.

WHAT WE HAVE LEARNED: CHAPLAINS IN STABILITY OPERATIONS AND PEACE BUILDING

Much of this volume chronicles the activities of chaplains who have embraced a call to move beyond their traditional religious ministries within the armed forces to engage with local communities and directly advise combatant commanders from Central Asia to the Middle East to East Africa. From these reflections, we gain insight into four primary ways that chaplains have contributed to stability operations and peace-building efforts over the past two decades, as well as the challenges impeding their more robust participation in these new activities. We discuss each in turn.

Conciliation

First, chaplains help communities in deeply divided societies overcome distrust exacerbated by years of fighting. This work involves developing dialogue between local communities, especially among leaders, that may have previously had little to no contact.

The chapter by Padre (Lt. Col.) S. K. Moore, for instance, recounts how a French military priest in Kosovo, Chaplain (LTC) Father Michel de Peyret, convinced senior Muslim and Christian leaders to convene together after months of intercommunal violence. In a similar way, Chaplain (Colonel) Mike Hoyt reports that the Iraq Inter-Religious Congress (IIRC) brought together high-ranking religious leaders in Iraq for the first time since sectarian violence escalated there in early 2006. Most impressively, this meeting actually included delegates who had been personally involved in planning or conducting violent attacks only a few months earlier.

The chapter by Chaplain (Captain) Jon Cutler serves as a further illustration of chaplains in their role as conciliators. Because he was the first rabbi encountered by many East African clergy, local communities often viewed him as an independent arbitrator on interfaith issues. Accordingly, he was able to identify substantial fault lines between Christian and Muslim groups in the region and organize activities to reduce tension and emphasize common goals, including a cleanup day in Uganda's capital that brought together youths of both religious traditions.

Because these efforts by chaplains to bridge the gap between divided segments of a population are oftentimes self-initiated, they face significant bureaucratic obstacles. Moore notes how the late arrival of the Serbian Orthodox bishop nearly unraveled the meeting in Kosovo. Hoyt details numerous setbacks in Iraq, including planning meetings that were "unpredictable in frequency, content, and especially mood." For Cutler, the challenge came more from commanding officers. While they envisioned his role as primarily attending to the pastoral needs of military personnel, he saw an opportunity for broader outreach.

In each case, however, military chaplains remained committed to and persistent in their work. As a consequence, their efforts not only strengthened ties between communities in the short-term but also developed into larger initiatives. The introductory luncheon between religious leaders in Kosovo led to subsequent gatherings. Meetings in Iraq became institutionalized in the High Council of Iraqi Religious Leaders, which continues to model effective interfaith dialogue today. The service project organized by Cutler in Uganda offered a model that was eventually emulated in neighboring Kenya.

Mediation

Second, as mediators, chaplains serve as neutral parties that help resolve disputes between local communities. For example, Cutler notes how he helped negotiate an issue concerning a water project for a mosque in Ethiopia. Here the goal is not merely to bring two sides together to reduce tensions and correct misperceptions; it is also to help both parties find win-win solutions to core disagreements.

One of the best examples in this volume of a chaplain serving as mediator is the activity of Canadian Armed Forces chaplain Imam Suleyman Demiray. As depicted by Moore, Demiray helped local Sunni and Shia leaders in Kandahar resolve a dispute that had led representatives of the latter community to withdraw from the regional Ulema Council two years prior. By drawing attention to shared anxiety over youth recruitment by extremist organizations, he was able to convince each side that their interests were better served by working together.

Successful mediation, of course, does not come quickly or easily. Cutler notes that it took several meetings with the supreme judge of the Islamic Council of Ethiopia to develop trust. Demiray carefully listened to and then conveyed the concerns of each community to the other over a period of several months. However, by being actively present to local communities and meeting members on their own terms, both chaplains created new openings for conflict resolution. In East Africa, Cutler was seen as an honest broker for negotiations; in Afghanistan, Demiray convinced Shia representatives to rejoin the council and use this forum to chart out solutions that benefited all sides.

Diplomacy

Third, as informal ambassadors, chaplains serve as a key, and often the first, point of contact between the armed forces and local communities. In this capacity, chaplains strive to improve the image of the military and to develop working relationships with local populations, particularly their leaders. This may range from disseminating information to active participation in postconflict reconstruction projects.

For example, Chaplain (Lt. Col.) Eric Keller highlights an important exchange between influential Iraqi religious leaders and U.S. Army chaplains during a 2007 conference sponsored by the Department of Defense. This meeting provided American chaplains with the opportunity to directly address the concerns of those leaders. It also allowed U.S. chaplains to teach their counterparts about the training of Muslim chaplains and the importance of having chaplains serve the needs of soldiers regardless of religious persuasion.

Chaplain (Lt. Col.) David West and Cutler also note how their efforts aimed at improving the image of both the U.S. military and government. West, for instance, discusses how chaplains assigned to U.S. Central Command coordinated with numerous governmental and nongovernmental agencies to facilitate religious-leader outreach in Afghanistan and Pakistan. Through these efforts, madrassa leaders from both countries were able to learn more, and express concerns, about the U.S. military and its postconflict reconstruction efforts. Cutler, in turn, shares how he organized a three-week conference on the U.S. military chaplaincy at Camp Lemonier to strengthen ties between Kenyan and U.S. armed forces. In a broader effort to put a positive face on the U.S. government's respect and tolerance for religion, especially Islam, he also helped coordinate a goodwill visit by an American imam to several countries in East Africa.

Chaplains also promote the militaries and governments they represent by assisting with reconstruction initiatives. Keller suggests, for example, that religious-support teams in Iraq and Afghanistan might work with village mullahs to rebuild mosques using U.S. funds and local labor. Similarly, Moore notes how Father de Peyret organized programs to rebuild cultural and religious sites after three days of rioting in Kosovo.

These good-faith efforts serve numerous purposes. Meetings between local leaders and representatives of the armed forces can increase the legitimacy of military operations by clarifying the military's intentions and correcting misperceptions. In addition, they provide an effective means for the military to assess and respond to local concerns and needs.

Reconstruction projects, in turn, attend to the physical and spiritual needs of a population with the hope of reducing tensions. They aim to undermine religious extremism by increasing the capacity and capabilities of more moderate religious leaders. And they improve the image of the armed forces, especially in deeply religious communities, by demonstrating respect and tolerance for all faith traditions.

Expertise

Fourth, and finally, as religious consultants, chaplains collect information and advise on the local cultural context. Broadly construed, this work can vary in scope from evaluating local religious needs to identifying influential elites to assessing factors that may complicate combat operations or diplomatic efforts, such as religious holidays or sacred spaces. For example, Keller notes that combatant commanders tasked chaplains in Iraq with relaying information on the religious and spiritual beliefs and practices of the local population. West further acknowledges that U.S. Central Command sought to identify the most influential religious leaders within, and without, Afghanistan and Pakistan.

Chaplain advisement on religious and cultural issues is not limited to combat zones. Former U.S. naval chaplain Dayne Nix discusses, for instance, how senior political and military leaders frequently consulted with him on their planning of, and participation in, special religious and cultural observances, including the organization of an annual Eid dinner for local Muslims in Iceland.

Compared to their other roles, assessment of the religious and cultural context of conflict and postconflict zones stands out as the task that was most controversial. At the same time, it was also one of the tasks for which chaplains were least prepared. As noted by West, critics fear violations of the chaplain's noncombatant status, since the line between religious advisement and intelligence gathering remains unclear. While several contributors seek to dispel this concern, it is an issue that remains unresolved both in this volume and within the military chaplaincy.

Additionally, chaplains may have significantly less experience in charting the religious dimensions of a conflict environment than with engaging religious leaders and communities. For the latter task, chaplains might draw from their pastoral training and experience ministering to a diverse set of faith traditions within the armed forces. The type of preparation and practice that might qualify chaplains to map the human terrain of a conflict zone, however, remains less clear. While chaplains are presumed to be subject experts on world religions, the fact remains that many are not.[11]

In sum, the contributions in this volume point to four substantial ways chaplains may contribute to stability operations and peace-building efforts. As conciliators or bridge builders, chaplains assist divided societies in overcoming distrust and reducing tensions. As moderators, they also help communities resolve long-standing disputes and disagreements. As ambassadors or diplomats, chaplains promote partnerships between the military and local communities. And as religious consultants, they collect and disseminate information to their superiors on the local religious and cultural context.

REMAINING CHALLENGES

In addition to shedding light on the above functions, contributions to this volume also point to three important challenges that currently hinder a more efficient and robust participation by chaplains in their new roles. These are the remaining confusion about the precise functions that chaplains are expected to perform, the lack of comprehensive training for such functions, and the difficulty in assessing what future challenges the chaplaincy will have to address.

Ambiguous Role Definition

First, contributors to this volume have stressed the need for further clarification of what exactly the military expects of chaplains tasked with religious engagement and advisement. As several authors point out, chaplain assignments in the aftermath of 9/11 were frequently underspecified and disconnected from larger operational objectives. More often than not, combatant commanders within a particular context provided specific details, but chaplains lacked a formal doctrine.

The chapter by Nix summarizes the utility of efforts made in recent years to address this issue as well as their shortfalls. For example, while the most recent document guiding joint operations, "Joint Publication 1-05: Religious Affairs in Joint Operations," provides a specific definition of religious advisement, its primary focus remains on outlining the responsibilities for the provision of traditional forms of religious ministry within the armed forces.[12] Furthermore, beyond this definition, JP 1-05 addresses the requirements for religious-liaison activities and advisement in only "a broad and general way." Further guidance is reserved for particular military branches.

Yet chaplains continue to receive inconsistent clarification regarding the doctrine of religious engagement. Each of the services may have its own policy and doctrine regarding the role of the chaplain as an advisor on religion and its impact on military operations, but there is no agreement across branches as to how far and in what manner that authority extends. Moreover, some branches, such as the U.S. Air Force, provide almost no additional instruction to chaplains on their new roles and duties. Thus, many chaplains are still constrained by the obscurity of their assignments.

Inadequate Training

Second, programs that train and support chaplains in their new roles need to be more systematic and wide-scale. While all the initiatives outlined in this volume are certainly commendable, they also illustrate how deeply dependent their success is on the characteristics of specific individuals. How might other chaplains develop the "skill, maturity, and professional commitment" that Hoyt, and others, point to as critical to effective religious engagement and advisement? Several contributors point to noteworthy initiatives, but these remain, in the end, rather isolated examples.

Keller, for instance, discusses how U.S. Army chaplains stateside initiated and developed short-term training programs on religious support in the aftermath of 9/11. Similarly, Nix, points to courses at the Naval War College and professional-development sessions at U.S. Central Command on the cultural and religious dynamics of conflict environments. West, in turn, highlights a particularly interesting model for supporting and complementing the activities of chaplains. By bringing together representatives from a number of governmental agencies, nongovernmental organizations, academic institutions, and the military chaplaincy, the Strategic Outreach Initiative Working Group on Afghanistan took advantage of the varied resources and expertise of its participants to provide a more accurate and helpful understanding of the role of religion in that conflict zone.

While these programs suggest the potential benefits of better connecting actors and offices related to religious-support missions, they also highlight the ad hoc fashion of current training and support for chaplains. Failure to provide more comprehensive and coordinated programming means that chaplains will continue to operate in much the same way they did in Iraq: as Keller puts it, rather than drawing on clear training and doctrine to fulfill their new roles, chaplains will be forced to rely on best practices and "word-of-mouth shared from unit to unit over time."

Uncertain Trajectories

While the primary purpose of this volume is to record the changing nature of the military chaplaincy over the last two decades, such transformations are, of course, not entirely new. As we suggested in the introduction to this chapter, the military establishment and chaplain commanders have sought in equal measure to expand or constrict the role of the chaplaincy at particular historical moments. What lessons might we draw if we resist the temptation to see religious engagement and advisement as entirely new roles for chaplains?

Given that developments in the chaplaincy appear often and regularly, one avenue for future research is to outline more systematically when and how such changes evolve. In terms of initiation, several chapters in this volume suggest at least one critical pathway: engagement in new conflict zones.

By emphasizing how a shift in chaplain duties followed military operations in societies with high levels of religiosity, this volume draws attention to the need to better understand how military planners adapt to novel environments and how these adjustments can affect organizational changes within the armed forces, especially the chaplaincy.

In addition, we challenge scholars to consider more carefully the conditions that trigger such reforms. What was it about the conflicts in Iraq and Afghanistan that spurred these changes? Why did such reforms not take on greater saliency during conflicts in the Balkans? Finally, what other pathways might trigger changes in the military chaplaincy, ranging from shifts in military doctrine and technology to changes in U.S. society?

To summarize, the contributors to this volume provide rich insight into what religious engagement and advisement look like in practice, the promise of these chaplain-led initiatives, and the remaining obstacles to their full integration into military operations. How might the military chaplaincy best build on these successes and respond to the lingering challenges? In the following sections, we stress that important lessons can be drawn from wider currents in the scholarship on religion and international relations.

LOOKING AHEAD: AVENUES FOR FUTURE RESEARCH

The central themes in this volume also relate to broader interest in the role of religion in peace building, foreign policy, and state building. Collectively the preceding chapters offer important insight into the scholarship on each of these topics as well as open avenues to exciting future research. At the same time, these literatures raise difficult questions about the limits and drawbacks of nontraditional chaplain roles.

Religion and Peace Building

The first strand of research that this volume contributes to is the literature on religious peace building. Over the past decade, analysts have chronicled an impressive array of organizations and individuals engaged in such efforts across the globe. Yet these accounts overwhelmingly focus on nonstate entities.[13] This volume, in contrast, draws attention to an important set of religious actors that operate within and on behalf of particular governments. Such an analytic move challenges scholars to consider a broader range of religious actors as well as reevaluate the "secular" characterization of Western states offered in previous studies.[14]

Moving forward, future investigation would do well to document more systematically the full range of chaplains' activities, identify patterns in their implementation, and assess their overall effectiveness. Does religious engagement concentrate on particular sectors (health, economic development, etc.), involve activities beyond those summarized in this volume, and lead to more stable postconflict environments? When and in what ways do chaplains partner with religious or secular nonstate actors? How would we best assess the impact of chaplains on conflicts? What other religious factors might shape state actions, even in seemingly secular conflicts?

In addition, more attention could be paid to the possibly unintended consequences of chaplains assuming a more active role on the battlefield and in postconflict settings. At least three consequences stand out as particularly problematic.

First, past research suggests that the influence of chaplains can often have mixed results. In terms of increasing military effectiveness, for instance, just as Chaplain (Colonel) Eric Wester's chapter suggests that chaplains can foster ethical conduct and improve the personal resilience of soldiers, their preaching has also contributed to a sense of fatalism among the ranks in past eras, such as during the American Civil War.[15] What might be the unintended consequence of religious advisement? Will military commanders become oversensitive to religious and cultural differences? Will opposing combatants adapt to take advantage of these new conditions?

Second, the physical and emotional demand of a new role for chaplains remains underspecified. While the heroic image of chaplains present amid the carnage of warfare provides a dominant theme for this volume, chaplains have been equally derided as less than "real" soldiers, given their noncombatant status. The chapter by Gary Roberts and L. Diane Hess-Hernandez nicely illustrates the occupational stress inherent in the chaplaincy, but it remains unclear how the new duties and responsibilities outlined in this volume might affect chaplains' coping and adapting abilities. This and other questions remain important lines of inquiry for evaluating the short- and long-term effects of religious engagement and advisement.

Third, further analysis could also consider the normative concerns regarding the more frequent interaction of chaplains with local populations. Who decides which religious communities to engage with and according to what criteria? To what extent do such decisions reify religious identities? Can chaplains avoid the bias of past religious engagement that all too often targets older, male representatives and overlooks young people and women? To what extent do such activities impose on postconflict societies a particular understanding of religious freedom? Should and can chaplains avoid proselytizing?

Religion and Foreign Policy

A second current of scholarship addressed in this volume relates to the growing interest among scholars and policymakers alike in the nexus of religion and foreign policy. For example, several contributors invoke Douglas Johnston's call for American foreign policy analysts to be more attentive to the religious and cultural factors in international relations.[16] Chaplains, it has been argued, are ideally situated to help with this task, since neither traditional diplomats nor politicians are necessarily comfortable dealing with such issues. Thomas Farr, the first director of the U.S. State Department's Office of International Religious Freedom, more pointedly states that "most analysts lack the vocabulary and the imagination to fashion remedies that draw on religion."[17]

Why would chaplains be particularly effective in this role? Contributions by Nix, Keller, Cutler, and West shed light on two possible reasons. First, chaplains operate in a religiously diverse and pluralistic environment on a daily basis. As a result of their education in, and sensitivity to, different faith communities, they are uniquely qualified to liaise with civilian religious leaders and adherents. For example, Moore points to the weak interaction between the Kandahar Provincial Reconstruction Team and local religious leaders prior to the arrival of Canadian Forces chaplain Imam Suleyman Demiray, who was more aware of the type of forum that would attract the participation of local imams.

Second, because chaplains demonstrate their faith openly, they may receive more legitimacy, public respect, and credibility with local communities than the average combatant or diplomat. Their religious calling, combined with their noncombatant status and their abstention from carrying arms, places them in a unique position to mediate between the military and civilians. As noted above, Hoyt's chapter offers one excellent example of how his credibility as a chaplain, along with Canon Andrew White's, helped bring together senior religious leaders within Iraqi society and push along a process fraught with frequent setbacks.

Further investigation could add to these insights by more systematically isolating the characteristics that benefit chaplains in their roles of engagement and advisement. For example, conspicuously absent from the analysis in this volume, but not other studies, is the contribution of personal charisma to a religious actors' authority.[18] To what extent does this also apply to chaplains? What other qualities might assist chaplains in their diplomatic roles?

Additional research could also shed light on the conditions that either bolster or constrain the efforts of chaplains. To what extent does the religiosity of a local population determine a chaplain's effectiveness? Will chaplains be as effective in societies with high levels of religious fractionalization as more homogenous populations? Should we expect chaplains to be equally effective liaisons with representatives of all, or only certain, types of religious traditions? What exactly does a healthy working relationship between official diplomats and chaplains look like? How would they best complement one another's activities? How, if at all, should such working relationships be formally instituted? Should we expect all chaplains to be equally adept in their diplomatic roles?

A final avenue of future study on the diplomatic role of chaplains would require scholars to take a critical stance toward the new direction of the military chaplaincy. Since the majority of contributors in this volume support the changing role of Western military chaplains, they have said little about how such increased involvement might undermine foreign policy initiatives. Will chaplains necessarily prioritize the same issues as the militaries and governments they represent? Will they feel compelled to raise moral or ethical objections to particular state actions? Might the very same personal religious commitments that drive and equip chaplains to act as intermediaries also produce biases against local religions? It is not unreasonable to suspect that the presence of men or women of the cloth on the battlefield, visibly loyal to a foreign religion and engaging in unfamiliar religious practices, might increase rather than decrease religious friction. Under what conditions might local religious practitioners place less trust in a chaplain than in a secular counterpart?

Religion and State Building

The literature on the link between religion, nationalism, and state building stands out as a third strand of research connected to this volume.[19] While not a dominant theme, several contributions touch on the potential use of religion as a source of legitimacy for government officials. Pauletta Otis, for instance, acknowledges the pervasive question of whether the chaplaincy brings the blessing of religion to war.

Since the recent study of the instrumental use of religion by political elites attends overwhelmingly to civil wars, a focus on the chaplaincy provides a helpful reminder that states, even seemingly secular ones, are not above using religion to legitimize certain activities.[20] Even though the religious-advisement role is intended to be solely that, providing an assessment rather than proscribing an official course of action, the mere involvement of religious authorities may offer a layer of justification for final decisions. Thus additional research could shed light on when and how a chaplain's presence can legitimate state actions and to what effect. Does a chaplain's endorsement increase the motivation or resolve of combatants? Under what circumstances might a more public role for religion in the military provoke a popular backlash?

In addition, the new role of chaplains may place unique challenges on the middle ground they occupy between religious and military authorities. As they become more directly involved in command decisions, chaplains could be tempted to adopt a larger role as moral advocates. How will military commanders respond to such advice? Will chaplains be free to voice criticism? Despite the moral authority they might hold elsewhere, chaplains have found past attempts to advise military commanders on tactical and operational objectives to be "difficult at best."[21] Do chaplains then run the risk of losing moral authority if they remain silent on key issues?

Finally, while this volume focuses on Western militaries, the potential for the chaplaincy to legitimate state activity extends to many other possible cases.[22] For example, to what extent will the reestablishment of military chaplaincies in post-Soviet states or new chaplaincies, such as in South Sudan, contribute to nationalist projects? To what extent might they help generate or undermine religious tolerance? What lessons might Western, military chaplains convey to these new institutions? While these questions are beyond the scope of this volume, the contributions within provide a helpful starting point for further inquiry related to the evolving role of military chaplains in the twenty-first century.

NOTES

1. Earl F. Stover, *Up from Handymen: The United States Army Chaplaincy, 1865–1920* (Honolulu: University Press of the Pacific, 2004), 121–22, citing V. Edmund McDevitt, *First California's Chaplain* (Fresno, CA: Academy Library Guild, 1956), 85–96.

2. The English responded by puncturing his hat with bullets, whereupon the chaplain joined the attack. Parker C. Thompson, *From Its European Antecedents to 1791: The United States Army Chaplaincy* (Honolulu: University Press of the Pacific, 2004), 163, citing Frank Moore, ed., *Diary of the American Revolution, from Newspapers and Original Documents*, vol. 1 (New York: Charles Scribner Sons, 1860), 482.

3. Herman A. Norton, *Struggling for Recognition: The United States Army Chaplaincy: 1791–1865* (Honolulu: University Press of the Pacific, 2004), 57.

4. Stover, *Up from Handymen*, 39–40.

5. Ibid., 124–25.

6. Duff Crerar, *Padres in No Man's Land: Canadian Chaplains and the Great War* (Montreal: McGill-Queen's University Press, 1995), 127; and Tom Johnstone and James Hagerty, *The Cross on the Sword: Catholic Chaplains in the Forces* (London: Geoffrey Chapman, 1996), 207.

7. Gardner H. Shattuck Jr., "Faith, Morale, and the Army Chaplain in the American Civil War," in *The Sword of the Lord: Military Chaplains form the First to the Twenty-First Century*, ed. Doris L. Bergen (Notre Dame: University of Notre Dame Press, 2004), 62; Randall M. Miller, Harry S. Stout, and Charles Reagan Wilson, eds., *Religion and the American Civil War* (New York: Oxford University Press, 1998), 268; and Steven E. Woodworth, *While God Is Marching On: The Religious World of Civil War Soldiers* (Lawrence: University Press of Kansas, 2001), 156.

8. Edward Madigan, *Faith Under Fire: Anglican Army Chaplains and the Great War* (New York: Palgrave Macmillan, 2011), 105–12; Stover, *Up from Handymen*, 5, 44, 47, 75, 113, 116, 166; Alan Wilkinson, *The Church of England and the First World War* (Southampton, UK: Camelot Press, 1978), 148; and Linda Parker, *The Whole Armour of God: Anglican Chaplains in the Great War* (Solihull, UK: Helion, 2009), 40.

9. Robert L. Gushwa, *The Best and Worst of Times* (Washington, DC: Office of the Army Chief of Chaplains, 1977), 23–26 and 124–27.

10. Anne Loveland, "From Morale Builders to Moral Advocates: U.S. Army Chaplains in the Second Half of the Twentieth Century," in *The Sword of the Lord: Military Chaplains from the First to the Twenty-First Century*, ed. Doris L. Bergen (Notre Dame: University of Notre Dame Press, 2004), 241–43.

11. Oftentimes chaplains gain initial knowledge of the religions and cultures where they are deployed by browsing the Internet or reading a few books. See George Adams, *Chaplains as Liaisons with Religious Leaders: Lessons from Iraq and Afghanistan*, Peaceworks no. 56 (Washington, DC: United Institute of Peace, 2006), 42.

12. U.S. Department of Defense, "Joint Publication 1-05: Religious Affairs in Joint Operations," November 20, 2009, http://www.dtic.mil/doctrine/new_pubs/jp1_05.pdf.

13. For examples, see Gerard Powers, "Religion and Peacebuilding," in *Strategies of Peace: Transforming Conflict in a Violent World*, ed. Daniel Philpott and Gerard Powers (Oxford: Oxford University Press, 2010); Thomas Banchoff, ed., *Religious Pluralism, Globalization, and World Politics* (Oxford: Oxford University Press, 2008); David Little, ed., *Peacemakers in Action: Profiles of Religion in Conflict Resolution* (Cambridge: Cambridge University Press, 2007); R. Scott Appleby, *Ambivalence of the Sacred: Religion, Violence and Reconciliation* (Lanham, MD: Rowan & Littlefield, 2000); Cynthia Sampson, "Religion and Peacebuilding," in *Peacemaking in International Conflict: Methods and Techniques*, ed. I. William Zartman and J. Lewis Rasmussen (Washington, DC: United States Institute of Peace Press, 1997), 273–316.

14. For a notable exception on the latter point, see Al Stepan, "Religion, Democracy, and the 'Twin Tolerations,'" *Journal of Democracy* 11, no. 4 (2000): 37–57.

15. Shattuck, "Faith, Morale, and the Army Chaplain," 105–24.

16. Douglas Johnston, ed., *Faith-Based Diplomacy: Trumping Realpolitik* (Oxford: Oxford University Press, 2003).

17. See Thomas Farr, "Diplomacy in an Age of Faith: Religious Freedom and National Security," *Foreign Affairs* 87, no. 2 (2008): 110–24. It is noteworthy that in its early years the State Department's Office of International Religious Freedom did have a military chaplain on loan from the Department of Defense. A former chaplain also worked there for a summer in 2011, again on loan from a military university.

18. Max Weber, "Politics as Vocation," in *From Max Weber: Essays in Sociology*, ed. and trans. H. H. Gerth and C. Wright Mills (New York: Oxford University Press, 1946), 77–128; Ron E. Hassner, *War on Sacred Grounds* (Cornell: Cornell University Press, 2009), ch. 6.

19. See Mark Jurgensmeyer, *The New Cold War? Religious Nationalism Confronts the Secular State* (Berkeley: University of California Press, 1993); Peter Van der Veer, *Religious Nationalism: Hindus and Muslims in India* (Berkeley: University of California Press, 1994); Adrian Hastings, *The Construction of Nationhood: Ethnicity, Religion and Nationalism* (Cambridge: Cambridge University Press, 1997).

20. See Timothy D. Sisk, *Between Terror and Tolerance: Religious Leaders, Conflict, and Peacemaking* (Washington, DC: Georgetown University Press, 2011); Monica Duffy Toft, "Getting Religion? The Puzzling Case of Islam and Civil War," *International Security* 31, no. 4 (2007): 97–131.

21. See Loveland, "From Morale Builders," 243.

22. On the contemporary role of chaplains in militaries around the globe, see Ron E. Hassner, ed., *Religion in the Military Worldwide* (Cambridge: Cambridge University Press, 2014).

Index

About the Contributors

Eric Patterson, PhD, is dean of the Robertson School of Government at Regent University and senior research fellow at Georgetown University's Berkley Center for Religion, Peace and World Affairs. His research and teaching focus on religion and politics, ethics and international affairs, and just war theory in the context of contemporary conflict. Prior to his arrival at Regent, Dr. Patterson served as associate director of the Berkley Center and held a visiting appointment in the department of government at Georgetown University. As part of the Berkley Center's Government Outreach program he has spoken and led seminars at the U.S. Military Academy, the U.S. Naval Academy, the Armed Forces Chaplains Center, National Defense University, the Pentagon, the Naval Postgraduate School, the Foreign Service Institute, and other government venues. He has served as a White House Fellow and spent two stints in the State Department's Bureau of Political and Military Affairs and continues to serve as an officer and commander in the Air National Guard. Dr. Patterson is author or editor of nine books, including most recently *Ending Wars Well: Order, Justice, and Conciliation in Contemporary Post-Conflict* (2012), *Ethics Beyond War's End* (2012), and *Politics in a Religious World* (2011).

Douglas L. Carver served as U.S. Army chief of chaplains until 2011 with the rank of major general. He presently serves as executive director of chaplain services for the North American Mission Board (NAMB) of the Southern Baptist Convention. Before retiring in summer 2011, the two-star general spent thirty-eight years in the U.S. Army, twenty-seven of them as army chaplain. As chief of chaplains he was responsible for some 2,900 chaplains in the active army, the Army Reserves, and the National Guard. Carver's four years as chief of chaplains came during a time when the United States was fighting dual wars in Iraq and Afghanistan. During his tenure, he ensured comprehensive and religious support to a total of 1.2 million soldiers deployed in more than eighty nations, three hundred thousand Department of Defense civilians, and seven hundred thousand military families. Carver graduated with a BA from the University of Tennessee, Knoxville, and was initially appointed as a regular army officer in the field-artillery branch of the U.S. Army. After serving on active duty for six years, he resigned his commission to enter the ministry. He was later commissioned as an army chaplain in June 1984.

Captain **Jon Cutler**, CHC, USN, earned a BA and MA from Temple University and a Master of Hebrew Letters and was ordained rabbi in 1987 from the Reconstructionist Rabbinical College (Wyncote, Pennsylvania); he also received doctor of ministry from Hebrew Union College-Jewish Institute of Religion (New York). Presently he is rabbi of a congregation in Darkaynu, in Bucks County, Pennsylvania. His military service includes service as deputy force chaplain for Command Naval Installations (2011); he also mobilized to East Africa, Combined Joint Task Force–Horn of Africa, as force chaplain and director of religious affairs (2011–2012) and to Operation Iraqi Freedom 2008, Al Anbar, Province, Iraq, as 3rd Marine Aircraft Wing chaplain (and the only Jewish chaplain) (2008–2009). On September 11, 2001, he ministered to military and civilian personal at the Pentagon in Arlington, Virginia. During Desert Storm he served with the First Marine Expeditionary Force as the only Jewish chaplain for Marines and naval personnel in Saudi Arabia and Kuwait (1991). He is author of "The Role of the Military Chaplain in the '3D' Process" in *InterAgency Journal* (2012).

Ron E. Hassner is associate professor of political science at the University of California, Berkeley, codirector of Berkeley's Religion, Politics and Globalization Program, and chair of the ISA section on Religion and International Relations. He studies the role of symbols and ideas in international security with particular attention given to the relationship between religion and conflict. He is editor of *Religion in the Military Worldwide* (2013), a collection of essays on religious practices in contemporary and professional armed forces, and author of *War on Sacred Grounds* (2009), an analysis of the causes and characteristics of disputes over sacred places around the globe and the conditions under which these conflicts can be managed.

L. Diane Hess-Hernandez holds an MA in government from the Robertson School of Government at Regent University, where she serves as assistant to the dean. A native of Illinois, she has worked in research for the University of Illinois and the textbook publisher McGraw-Hill. Her research interests include issues surrounding government regulations, law and public policy, and the impact of religious faith in these areas. She is author of two journal articles and proud mother of two sons, one of whom served in the U.S. Armed Forces.

Chaplain (Colonel-Ret.) **Micheal Hoyt** retired from thirty-five years of army service in 2011. He served at every level of command from battalion through theater army, several joint and multinational commands, and Department of Army Staff. He does consulting work on the issues of religion and its role in government policy, command decision making, and military operations. In 2012 he served as part of a U.S. delegation to Tunisia, meeting with nineteen prominent religious leaders from five North African countries to examine the role of religion in emerging governments. He is member of the board of directors of the Wounded In Action Family Foundation, dedicated to transitioning severely wounded military members from medical facilities to sustainable lifetime independence. He currently teaches leadership and character development through the JROTC program in an inner-city high school in Indianapolis.

Chaplain (Lieutenant Colonel) **Eric Keller**, USA (retired), served twenty-two years as an active duty chaplain with a wide range of troop and staff assignments, culminating in his service in the U.S. Army Chief of Chaplains' Office (2004–2008). During active duty, he acquired an MS in family studies from Kansas State University as well as a Master's of Military Arts and Science (MMAS) from U.S. Army Officer Command and General Staff College. He was ordained from the Presbyterian Church U.S.A. after completing seminary in 1984. Currently he is a PhD candidate in political science at University of Tennessee, with a focus on American politics.

Jason Klocek is doctoral candidate in the Travers Department of Political Science at the University of California, Berkeley, where he researches international security, civil wars, and religious violence. His dissertation explores how states respond to insurgent groups with religious identities and what impact this has on conflict outcomes. Additional projects examine how religious dynamics shape third-party interventions in armed conflicts and forgiveness in postconflict societies. He has also conducted fieldwork in South Sudan and Rwanda on the role of religious actors in postconflict reconstruction efforts. Klocek holds an MA in political science from Berkeley, an MA in conflict resolution from Georgetown University, and a BA in psychology from the University of Notre Dame. From 2003 to 2005 he served with the U.S. Peace Corps in Turkmenistan.

S. K. Moore served as padre in the Canadian Armed Forces (CAF) for twenty-two years. His operational tours include pre–Dayton Accord Bosnia (1993), Haiti (1997), and the Kandahar Provincial Reconstruction Team, Afghanistan, where he conducted doctoral research (2006), completing his PhD in 2008. The experience of engaging the religious leaders of greater Sarajevo left an indelible mark on his life, where he observed men of faith and leaders of communities endeavoring to lead their people during a time of intense conflict. Dr. Moore's last three years in uniform were with the Canadian Army Land Warfare Center, where he further developed his concepts. A chaplain capability, religious-leader engagement (RLE) is now policy (January 2013) with the CAF Chaplain Branch and Doctrine (July 2013) with the Canadian Army, due in large part to his efforts. RLE has been incorporated into curriculum at the United Nations Training School–Ireland in Dublin. He is currently developing a graduate diploma program in integrative peace building at Saint Paul University, Ottawa. In 2013 he published *Military Chaplains as Agents of Peace: Religious Leader Engagement in Conflict and Post-conflict Environments*.

Dayne Nix is retired U.S. Navy chaplain (rank of commander) and served in billets throughout the navy and Marine Corps, including an Individual Augment tour with CENTCOM Forward, located in Doha, Qatar, in 2004. He also served in the U.S. Marine Corps as a communications officer from 1974 to 1979. Nix received numerous military awards, including four Meritorious Service Medals. Professor Nix has taught joint maritime operations for the Naval War College since 2009, where he has served on faculty since 2004. He served at the Naval Chaplain School from 2001 to 2004 as the advanced course instructor. Dr. Nix holds a BA degree from the University of Colorado in international affairs, an MDiv from Denver Seminary, a ThM from Duke University, an MA from the Naval War College (with distinction) in national security affairs, and a PhD from Salve Regina University in humanities. Dr. Nix is author of *The Integration of Philosophy, Politics, and Conservative Islam in the Thought of Muhammad Iqbal* (2012) and "American Civil-Military Relations: Samuel P. Huntington and the Political Dimensions of Military Professionalism" (2012), as well as other articles and conference papers.

Pauletta Otis, PhD, was professor of Security Studies at the Command and Staff College, Marine Corps University, until 2013. She served as senior research fellow for religion in international affairs at the Pew Forum (Washington, D.C.) and previously taught as tenured full professor at Colorado State University–Pueblo. She held the positions of distinguished visiting professor of international security studies at the Joint Military Intelligence College, visiting scholar at the National Security Education Program, and professor of international security studies. She has served as a member of the defense Intelligence Advisory board, Defense Sciences Policy Board

Summer Study on Homeland Security, and in a senior advisory capacity for the U.S. military chaplaincy. Dr. Otis has special expertise in the study of subnational violence and combines both theoretical and operational experience and expertise. She received her PhD and MA from the graduate School of International Studies at the University of Denver, as well as an MA in anthropology from the University of Southern Colorado.

Gary Roberts is professor of government at Regent University, with over twenty years of experience in higher education in graduate government and business degree programs. His primary teaching areas are nonprofit administration, human-resource management, and public administration. Current research interests center on workplace spiritual intelligence and how Christians integrate faith into the workplace, servant-leader human-resource policy and practice, the impact of the religious-friendly workplace, and organizational policies to promote employee work-life balance. He has authored over forty journal articles, books, and book chapters on various human-resource and public-management issues. He is currently working on three books in the area of leadership, servant-leader human-resource management, and workplace spiritual intelligence. Dr. Roberts serves on the boards of several nonprofit organizations and is an active member of Vineyard Community Church.

Chaplain (Colonel) **David West** (U.S. Army, Ret.) enlisted in the South Carolina National Guard as combat engineer in 1976. He attended Officer Candidate School and was commissioned an engineer officer in 1979. After more than ten years as a regular army engineer officer, he attended Southwestern Baptist Seminary and became a chaplain in the U.S. Army Reserve. West was recalled for service in 2002 with USCENTCOM and retired from active duty in December 2010 with thirty-five years of service. West is currently pursuing a PhD in ecclesial leadership at Regent University.

Eric Wester, MDiv, ThM, serves as assistant to the presiding bishop and director, Federal Chaplaincy Ministries, for the Evangelical Lutheran Church in America. His ministry supports 230 chaplains and chaplain candidates in the military, veterans administration, and federal prisons. He retired from the army chaplain corps as a colonel. Chaplain Wester completed thirty-two years in the army chaplaincy, ending as the senior military fellow at National Defense University, Fort McNair, Washington, D.C. For four years at NDU he taught ethics, religion, and security. He currently serves as adjunct instructor at the Lutheran Theological Southern Seminary, Columbia, South Carolina, and senior instructor for the Leader Development Education for Sustained Peace (LDESP), Naval Postgraduate School, Monterey, California. Research interests include ethics, just war thinking, and the spirituality of soldiers. He has published several peer-reviewed articles addressing these topics. In 2012 his research on spirituality in combat was published by the Lejuene Leadership Institute at Marine Corps College, Quantico, Virginia, in a new book on ethics and leadership. He earned an MDiv from Trinity Lutheran Seminary (Columbus, Ohio), a Master of Theology from New Brunswick Theological Seminary (New Jersey), and a Master of Strategic Studies from the Army War College (Carlisle, Pennsylvania).